# LAS VE... ACCESS®

S0-BZL-781

- Baccarat
- Blackjack
- Craps
- Keno
- The Money Wheel
- Roulette
- Slots
- Sports Betting
- Video Poker

- Red Rock Canyon
- Hoover Dam
- Lake Mead
- Valley of Fire
- Death Valley
- The Grand Canyon
- Zion
- Bryce Canyon

PARKING 6
CAR 3C

# Orientation

Whether you first glimpse Las Vegas from an airplane window at night or approach it via highway after a dusty drive through the desert, it's a surreal panorama of flashing lights, bright neon, and exaggerated architecture—a unique shrine to the phantasmagoric extremes of the American Way.

At once decadent, debauched, and sublimely divine, Las Vegas represents different things to different people. To some, it's entirely about gambling: the hypnotic lure of the video-poker screen and the spinning of the roulette wheel, the hush and then the screams heard at the craps table, the ever-present clanging of the ever-present slots, the half moon of hopefuls at the blackjack table, all coexisting in a perpetual twilight zone where there is no day or night, only cards, dice, and, cross your fingers, three cherries. Put in a quarter. Hey, you never know; this may be your lucky day.

To others, Las Vegas is a playground, a place to indulge at the $4.99 buffets, bask in the sun, play golf, or hang out at the lounges.

Las Vegas is also home to a steadily increasing number of retirees, young families, and professionals who have found life in this city more affordable than San Francisco and lots warmer than Minneapolis. Nearly 1.1 million of them— at last count—have bought homes in this new frontier, this burgeoning desert neighborhood where an old-timer is someone who's lived here for 10 years.

Las Vegas began as an Old West whistle-stop and might have remained one if not for two significant events: the construction of **Hoover Dam** and the legalization of gambling. The Boulder Canyon Project Act of 1928 put

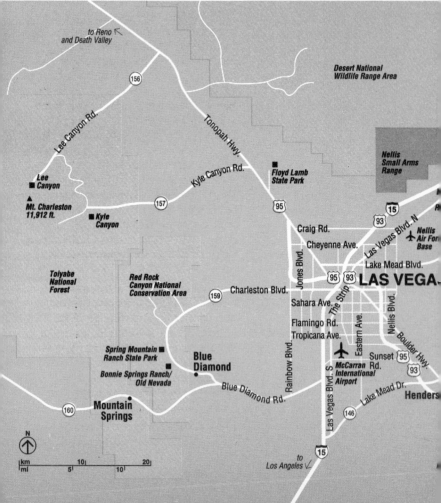

approximately 3,500 people to work for five years, nearly doubling the population of the town. In 1931, Nevada bucked the Great Depression by legalizing gambling and setting its sights on tourists. The payoff has proved bigger than any lucky gambler's jackpot; in 1996, 30 million visitors filled nearly 101,000 hotel rooms and generated more than $16 billion, including gaming revenues.

Most people begin their visit to Las Vegas on the **Strip**. Originally **Highway 91** to Los Angeles, **Las Vegas Boulevard** began its evolution into the Strip in 1941, when the builders of **El Rancho Vegas**—Las Vegas's first resort hotel—sought to avoid city taxes by moving to unincorporated land on the outskirts of town, in this case a large piece of low-cost highway property. **El Rancho** was soon joined by the **Last Frontier**, and the four-mile stretch of freeway began filling in. Next came the **Flamingo**, the **Thunderbird**, the **Desert Inn**, the **Sahara**, the **Sands**, the **Dunes**, and by 1955, the **Riviera**, a nine-story high-rise that put to rest any notion that this city would be content to retain a low-profile, Palm Springs–style landscape.

In the past 10 years, the Strip has evolved into the ultimate pedestrian thoroughfare, its sidewalks filled with gawking tourists and hawking hucksters passing out coupons and pamphlets advertising X-rated amusements. The resorts that used to sit back from the highway have either extended their casinos to the sidewalk or—in the case of **Caesars Palace**—shuttle guests in on a moving sidewalk.

In each hotel's quest to outdo the next, **Caesars Palace** began beckoning

pedestrians with a "temple" in which a holographic emperor welcomes friends, Romans, and assorted countrymen to his realm. **The Mirage** added its landmark volcano to the horizon in late 1989. Possibly the most photographed sight in the city, the volcano belches smoke and natural-gas flames every 15 minutes from 5:30PM to midnight. In 1994, **Bally's** jumped into the fray by turning its front parking lot into a garden replete with cascading waterways and a nighttime light show. Then **Treasure Island** attempted to outgun them all with an armada of full-scale pirate ships that blast cannon fire every 1.5 hours from 4 to 11:30PM in a battle staged for the amusement of passersby.

Most recent has been the crop of multibillion dollar extravaganzas duplicating favorite foreign destinations. There is **Bellagio**, an homage to Lake Como; the **Paris–Las Vegas Casino Resort**, with its Eiffel Tower designs; and **The Venetian Resort Hotel Casino**, which captures the Grand Canal with style.

The culinary scene is changing as well. And although buffets are still the most popular choice for many, it is also possible to enjoy some of the hautest of haute cuisine west of the Rockies. The sheer numbers of new restaurants—French, Italian, Mexican, and Southwestern, to name just a few—headed by such famous chefs as Emeril Lagasse, Jean-Georges Vongerichten, and Wolfgang Puck, make it hard to resist these bastions of dining elegance.

**Fremont Street** (also known as **"Glitter Gulch"**) offers a carnival midway environment in **Downtown** Las Vegas: Sidewalk solicitors in goofy hats pepper pedestrians with "can't lose" promotions as they pass under the familiar wave of "Vegas Vic," the famous neon cowboy mascot. Some of the glamour of Fremont Street has faded since the neon first started glowing here in the mid-1940s. Local residents have taken their business to suburban casinos that sprang up closer to their own neighborhoods, while tourists head to the megaresorts on the Strip. But Downtown resort owners have joined forces to fight back with the Fremont Street Experience: four blocks of Glitter Gulch are now covered by a high-tech canopy that displays a light-and-sound show.

But there is more to Vegas than casinos and gift shops. Those with a car might want to explore **East Las Vegas**, the city's older residential area, and home to attractions such as **The Liberace Museum**, which houses the opulent jewelry, costumes, and pianos collected by the late King of Glitz, and the **Mormon Temple**, the palatial landmark on

The Strip

**Sunrise Mountain** that serves as an ever-present reminder of the area's large population of members of the Church of Jesus Christ of Latter-day Saints. **West Las Vegas** is home to the **Las Vegas Art Museum** and the **Nevada State Museum and Historical Society,** as well as some of the most popular casinos in town. Also on the Westside are newer residential developments, particularly as you approach **Red Rock Canyon**, a hundred-square-mile recreation area of sweeping, rugged red sandstone formations less than 20 miles from the concrete canyons of the Strip. On the way to the engineering marvel of Hoover Dam, stop in the suburban community of **Henderson** for a visit to the **Ethel M. Chocolate Factory**, which produces—and gives free samples of—sweet treats. Or head northwest for the higher altitudes of **Mount Charleston**, proof that people who claim to have gone skiing in Las Vegas—or at least an hour away from it—weren't kidding. Or travel 35 miles northeast on **I-15** to the **Valley of Fire**, Nevada's oldest state park, where eons of erosion have carved out geological artworks in a haven of desert flora and wildlife.

So look around. Whatever your quest—good or bad, reality or fantasy—you'll probably find it here. Las Vegas may not yet have found a way to beguile everyone, but it hasn't stopped trying.

## How to Read This Guide

ACCESS® LAS VEGAS is arranged by neighborhood so you can see at a glance where you are and what is around you. The numbers next to the entries in the following chapters correspond to the numbers on the maps. The text is color-coded according to the kind of place described:

Restaurants/Clubs: Red    Hotels: Blue

Shops/ Outdoors: Green    Sights/Culture: Black

& Wheelchair accessible

### Wheelchair Accessibility

An establishment (except a restaurant) is considered wheelchair accessible when a person in a wheelchair can easily enter a building (i.e., no steps, a ramp, a wide enough door) without assistance. Restaurants are deemed wheelchair accessible only if the above applies and if the rest rooms are on the same floor as the dining area and their entrances and stalls are wide enough to accommodate a wheelchair.

### Rating the Restaurants and Hotels

The restaurant star ratings take into account the quality, service, atmosphere, and uniqueness of the restaurant. An expensive restaurant doesn't necessarily ensure an enjoyable evening; however, a small, relatively unknown spot could have good food, professional service, and a lovely atmosphere. Therefore, on a purely subjective basis, stars are used to judge the overall dining value (see the star ratings at right). Keep in mind that chefs and owners often change, which sometimes drastically affects the quality of a restaurant. The ratings in this guidebook are based on information available at press time.

The price ratings, as categorized at right, apply to restaurants and hotels. These figures describe general price-range relationships among other restaurants and hotels in the area. The restaurant price ratings are based on the average cost of an entrée for one person, excluding tax and tip. Hotel price ratings reflect the base price of a standard room for two people for one night during the peak season.

### Restaurants

| | |
|---|---|
| ★ | Good |
| ★★ | Very Good |
| ★★★ | Excellent |
| ★★★★ | An Extraordinary Experience |
| $ | The Price Is Right (less than $15) |
| $$ | Reasonable ($15-$22) |
| $$$ | Expensive ($22-$40) |
| $$$$ | Big Bucks ($40 and up) |

### Hotels

| | |
|---|---|
| $ | The Price Is Right (less than $50) |
| $$ | Reasonable ($50-$85) |
| $$$ | Expensive ($85-$125) |
| $$$$ | Big Bucks ($125 and up) |

### Map Key

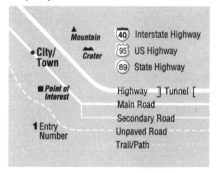

| | |
|---|---|
| ▲ Mountain | (40) Interstate Highway |
| ● City/Town | (95) US Highway |
| Crater | (89) State Highway |
| ■ Point of Interest | Highway    ] Tunnel [ |
| | Main Road |
| | Secondary Road |
| 1 Entry Number | Unpaved Road |
| | Trail/Path |

*Area code 702 unless otherwise noted.*

## Getting to Las Vegas

### Airport

#### McCarran International Airport (LAS)

Nearly 43 percent of all Las Vegas visitors and 65 percent of its convention delegates arrive via **McCarran,** the 14th busiest airport in the nation, with approximately 30.2 million passengers passing through its gates in 1998.

The airport sits on 2,820 acres off **East Tropicana Avenue,** a little over a mile east of the Strip. There are 79 gates in three terminals: 48 in the main terminal; 23 in **Concourse C,** which is serviced by a monorail; and 8 in the **Charter/International**

**Terminal,** a separate facility just north of the main terminal that handles international flights and houses all international processing operations. Ticketing, baggage claim, and transportation are found in the main terminal.

Modern and user-friendly, **McCarran** owes its size and efficiency to the local convention industry. City officials realized in the late 1950s that conventions could diversify the economy beyond gambling and made the airport a top consideration. The festive design is more like that of a shopping mall, and it boasts a wide variety of food and cocktail outlets and specialty shops—even slot machines for that first and last taste of Vegas.

Twelve commercial airlines, 10 commuter airlines, and more than 20 charters service **McCarran.**

## Airport Services

| | |
|---|---|
| Airport Emergencies | 261.5201 |
| Business Service Center | 261.5650 |
| Currency Exchange | 261.5650 |
| Customs | 388.6480, 388.3539 |
| Ground Transportation | 261.5285 |
| Immigration | 388.6024 |
| Information | 261.5211 |
| Lost and Found | 261.5134 |
| (or check with individual airlines) | |
| Parking | 261.5121 |
| Police | 261.5630 |
| Travelers' Aid | 261.5889 |

## Airlines

| | |
|---|---|
| Air Canada | 800/776.3000 |
| Alaska | 800/462.0333 |
| America West | 798.1715, 800/235.9292 |
| American | 800/433.7300 |
| Canada 3000 | 888/226.3000 |
| Canadian International | 800/665.1177 |
| Continental | 383.8291, 800/231.0856 |
| Delta | 800/221.1212 |
| Hawaiian Air | 800/367.5320 |
| Japan | 800/525.3663 |
| Midwest Express | 800/452.2022 |
| Northwest | 800/225.2525 |
| Reno Air | 800/736.6247 |
| Skywest | 800/453.9417 |
| Southwest | 800/435.9792 |
| Sun Country | 800/752.1218 |
| TWA | 739.5335, 800/221.2000 |
| United | 800/241.6522 |
| US Airways | 800/428.4322 |

## Getting to and from McCarran International Airport

### By Bus

The **Citizens Area Transit** or **CAT** (228.7433) operates buses to and from the airport departure terminal every half hour from 6AM to 1AM daily. For service to the **Downtown Transportation Center**, take the *108* or *109* ($1); to the Strip take the *302* ($1.50). Exact fare in bills or coins is required.

### By Car

The airport's main exit leads to **Swenson Street** traveling north, and the first main cross street with a traffic light is East Tropicana Avenue. A left turn on Tropicana brings you to the **San Remo, Tropicana,** MGM Grand, Excalibur, New York–New York, and **Monte Carlo** hotels. A left turn at **Las Vegas Boulevard South** (The Strip) leads to the **Luxor** and **Hacienda,** while a right turn passes most of the major hotels. For Downtown, continue on about four to five miles. To return to the airport, take **Paradise Road** south. There are both long- and short-term parking lots at the airport.

### Rental Cars

The following rental car agencies have counters at the airport, which are typically open from 5AM to 2AM. **Allstate**'s counter is open 24 hours a day.

| | |
|---|---|
| Allstate | 736.6147, 800/634.6186 |
| Avis | 261.5595, 800/331.1212 |
| Hertz | 736.4900, 800/654.3131 |

Several others are clustered along Paradise Road near the entrance to **McCarran** and offer shuttle service to the airport. Of these, only **Budget** is open 24 hours a day.

| | |
|---|---|
| Alamo | 263.3030, 800/327.9633 |
| Budget | 736.1212, 800/527.0700 |
| Rent-A-Vette | 800/372.1981 |
| Thrifty | 896.7600 |
| Value | 733.8886, 800/468.2583 |

### By Limo

Frequent visitors to Las Vegas often rely on **Bell Trans** (739.7990) limousines and buses to get from **McCarran** to their hotel. The savings can be significant compared to a taxi: **Bell** charges $3.50 from the airport to any Strip hotel and $4.75 to Downtown hotels. The trade-off is that it's usually a long ride. You share the trip with other passengers and may stop at four or five other hotels to drop them off before arriving at yours. The **Bell** booth is located inside the airport near the rental car booths.

### By Taxi

There is a taxi stand at the airport. It's approximately a 15-minute cab ride to Downtown for about $16.

## Bus Station (Long-Distance)

The **Greyhound Station** (200 S Main St, at Carson Ave, 800/231.2222) is open from 5AM each morning until 1AM the following morning. Taxis are available in front of the station.

A group of eight Las Vegas Hilton baccarat dealers pooled $80 at the beginning of the 1992 football season and planned on betting one game a week for 15 weeks, or until they lost. They won an incredible 12 games in a row, but lost the 13th—for $103,000. The odds against winning 15 straight football bets are about 33,000 to one. If they had succeeded, they would have made $1.3 million.

# Getting Around Las Vegas

It's not difficult to move around Las Vegas. The Strip is only five miles long. So walking, bicycling, public transportation, and—if you have lots of time on your hands—driving are all viable options.

## Bicycles

Though you certainly could get from place to place by bicycle if you're staying on the Strip or Downtown, most serious bicyclists prefer trips up to Mount Charleston or through the Red Rock recreation areas. There are a number of bicycle-rental outlets, including **McGhies Ski Chalet** (4503 W Sahara Ave, between Arville St and S Decatur Blvd, 252.8077; and 3310 E Flamingo Rd, between S Pecos and S Mojave Rds, 433.1120); and **Bikes USA** (1539 N Eastern Ave, at E Owens Ave, 642.2453).

## Buses

Las Vegas has an excellent bus system serving virtually every destination Downtown and on the Strip. The **Citizens Area Transit Authority** (**CAT**; 228.7433) maintains a fleet of 128 buses that carry 40 passengers each, covering 21 routes.

Bus schedules are available at the **Downtown Transportation Center** (300 N Casino Center Blvd, at Stewart Ave), the connecting point for most routes. Buses run daily from 5:30AM to 1:30AM on municipal routes and 24 hours a day on the Strip. One-way fare for adults is $1 ($1.50 on the Strip); people 65 and older, children 5 to 17, and the disabled pay 50¢. Younger children ride free. Same-day transfers from other routes are free.

## Cruises

**Lake Mead Cruises** (293.6180) offers boat trips to Hoover Dam on the *Desert Princess* from the **Lake Mead Marina**. There are two cruises a day, plus dinner cruises on Friday, Saturday, and Sunday.

## Driving

It's not necessary to rent a car if you're staying Downtown or on the Strip. Most everything you'll need or want to see is within walking distance of each other in these areas. However, if you're staying in East or West Las Vegas, you'll need a car. It can prove an ordeal to take even a short walk during the sweltering days of summer and taxis are expensive. Also, if you plan to take advantage of Vegas's proximity to the **Grand Canyon** or **Hoover Dam,** you may prefer renting a car to taking a group tour.

If you do plan to drive down the Las Vegas Strip, avoid weekend evenings, when the traffic slows to a crawl. The Strip not only lures tourists but teenagers who blast their stereos (at least until their 9PM curfew, imposed nightly on the Strip). If you're trying to get to a show on time at the other end of the Strip, use **Koval Lane** or Paradise Road to the east and **Industrial Road** to the west.

## Parking

Street parking is nonexistent on the Strip and is very difficult to find Downtown. There are public and private parking lots, and major hotels offer a choice between valet and self-parking. Valet parking is free but can mean a long wait for your car. Self-parking is sometimes easier, depending on the layout of the hotel and how recently the garage was built. The **Caesars Palace** and **Mirage** garages, for instance, are well designed and easy to navigate (although you may have trouble finding a space). At **Bally's**, parking is more problematic because the exits funnel traffic right onto the Strip or onto **Flamingo Road**. Downtown, **Fitzgeralds'** garage is downright thrilling, with turns almost as tight as a roller coaster.

## Taxis

Las Vegas is not the cheapest city in which to catch a cab across town. Because most tourists stay in the concentrated region of the Strip, which is close to the airport, it costs $2.20 to step into a cab and $1.50 for each additional mile. Waiting time is 44¢ (these rates were established by the Nevada Taxicab Authority). **Clark County** tacks on a $1.20 fee for each trip from **McCarran**.

On the positive side, Las Vegas *is* one of the *easiest* towns in which to catch a cab. On the Strip or Downtown, there's no need to call or even hail one down; they line up outside the hotels and wait. If your point of departure is not at or near a casino, you'll need to call for a dispatch. Clark County has 603 registered cabs licensed to 13 companies. The major cab companies are:

| | |
|---|---|
| Checker Cab | 873.2000 |
| Desert Cab | 376.2687, 376.2688 |
| Western Cab | 736.8000 |
| Whittlesea Blue Cab | 384.6111 |
| Yellow Cab | 873.2000 |

## Tours

There are more than 50 tour operators based in Las Vegas. The most popular is the trip to the Grand Canyon by plane or helicopter. **Scenic Airlines** (241 E Reno Ave, east of Las Vegas Blvd S, 739.1900) offers four flights daily at 7:30AM, 9:30AM, 11:30AM, and 3:30PM. **Las Vegas Helicopters** (3724 Las Vegas Blvd S, between W Tropicana Ave and W Flamingo Rd, 736.0013) offers flights that land inside the canyon on the **Hualapai Indian Reservation**. **Jeep Tours** (2810 Highland Dr, south of Presidio Ave, 796.9355) provides Jeep tours of the Grand Canyon, Red Rock Canyon, Valley of Fire, and Mount Charleston. **Grayline of Southern Nevada** (1550 Industrial Rd, at W Wyoming Ave, 384.1234) offers trips to Hoover Dam and **Laughlin,** cruises on **Lake Mead,** and river rafting, plus Grand Canyon flights.

## Trains

There are no convenient trains for travel to nearby excursions in Nevada or to the Grand Canyon.

## Walking

Walking tours of Las Vegas are not recommended, especially in summer when the temperatures soar over 100 degrees (you know what they say about "mad dogs and Englishmen"). The main section of the Strip, from the **Circus Circus** south to **Luxor,** is an interesting walk, but though it appears to be a short distance, it is actually several miles. Allow yourself two or more hours for a nice leisurely stroll, especially if you want to stop at some of the hotels along the way.

## FYI

### Accessibility for the Disabled

County law mandates that all restaurants and hotels be accessible to and provide facilities for disabled persons.

### Accommodations

Despite the fact that there are close to 110,000 hotel rooms in Las Vegas, reservations are always necessary. Especially busy times include long weekends (Fourth of July, Labor Day, and Presidents' Day), holidays, **Super Bowl,** heavyweight prizefights, and anytime there's a major convention in town, which is practically all the time. There are no bed-and-breakfasts, but there are vacation time-share facilities. For time-share information, contact **Hilton Grand Vacations** (3575 Las Vegas Blvd S, Las Vegas, NV 89109, 735.7055); **Jockey Club Resort Properties** (3700 Las Vegas Blvd S, Las Vegas, NV 89109, 798.3500); **Olympian Palms Resort Club** (3875 Cambridge St, Las Vegas, NV 89119, 732.8889); or **Polo Towers** (3745 Las Vegas Blvd S, Las Vegas, NV 89109, 261.1000).

### Climate

It seems as if Las Vegas has only two seasons: a long, hot summer and a mild winter. But don't make the same mistake as many a misinformed visitor from back East seen shivering in shorts and a T-shirt on a February evening. This is a desert town, and temperatures drop 20 degrees or more when the sun goes down.

| Average Temperatures (°F) | | |
| --- | --- | --- |
| Season | Lows | Highs |
| Winter | 33–39 | 57–63 |
| Spring | 44–60 | 69–88 |
| Summer | 69–74 | 100–106 |
| Fall | 43–66 | 67–95 |

### Dress

As Las Vegas evolved into a family and middle-class vacation destination, its dress code virtually disappeared. Dinner jackets and evening gowns are no longer necessary, although you still see people wearing them, depending on the season and occasion. T-shirts and shorts are common in the summer, even in showrooms and full-service restaurants, with the exception of gourmet dining rooms in hotels. Convention attire is a different matter, tending to be dressier.

### Drinking

The drinking age is 21. Most casinos serve cocktails 24 hours a day. Bars are open from mid-morning until the wee hours. Nevada has the second-highest alcohol-consumption rate in the US and was one of the last states to ban open containers in vehicles. Pedestrians are still allowed to carry open containers from casino to casino on Fremont Street and the Strip.

### Gambling

You must be 21 years or older to gamble in a Nevada casino, although no one checks.

### Money

The major banks in Las Vegas are **PriMerit, US Bank of Nevada,** and **Bank of America** (formerly **Valley Bank**). Most hotels and casinos are joined to an ATM network called "Casino Cash," which accepts the following cards and networks: Cirrus, Discover, The Exchange, Instant Teller, Plus, Pulse, and Star.

### Personal Safety

Las Vegas tourist zones are probably safer than the streets of New York or Los Angeles, since police concentration is heavy, and each casino maintains its own private security force. Take the usual common-sense precautions against pickpockets and purse snatchers. If you run into trouble, look for the Metro police bicycle patrol; these officers wear bright yellow shirts and black shorts and use bikes to skirt gridlocked traffic.

### Postal Service

Many hotels can handle basic postal needs, including stamps, UPS, and Federal Express. The main post office is located on **East Sunset Road** across the street from the south end of **McCarran International Airport.** The **Forum Shops at Caesars'** information desk offers postal service as well, at no extra charge.

### Prostitution

Since prostitution is illegal within Las Vegas and Clark County, it is unregulated. Prostitutes in the state's legal brothels are tested regularly for sexually transmitted diseases, including AIDS.

### Publications

The city's two daily newspapers work under a joint operating agreement, sharing business operations but maintaining separate editorial staffs. The *Las Vegas Review-Journal* is the morning newspaper and has a circulation of about 150,000 readers. The *Las Vegas Sun,* which comes out in the evening, has a circulation of about 40,000. In addition, *The New York Times, Los Angeles Times, Wall Street Journal,* and *USA Today* are sold on street racks and in hotel newsstands. Several weekly publications, such as *Showbiz, What's On,* and *Today in Las Vegas,* offer sight-seeing, restaurant, and show information and are available free of charge in hotel rooms and lobbies.

## Radio Stations

**AM:**

| 720 | KDWN | Talk Radio/Big Band/Sports |
|---|---|---|
| 840 | KXNT | News/Talk |
| 920 | KORK | Nostalgia |
| 1460 | KENO | Sports/Talk |

**FM:**

| 88.1 | KCEP | Contemporary |
|---|---|---|
| 91.5 | KUNV | University of Nevada, Las Vegas |
| 92.3 | KOMP | Album Rock |
| 95.5 | KWNR | Country |
| 96.3 | KKLZ | Classic Rock |
| 98.5 | KLUC | Contemporary |
| 102 | KFM | Country |
| 103.5 | KEDG | Alternative Rock |
| 105.5 | KOOL | Oldies |
| 105.7 | KDUQ | Traffic/Weather |

## Restaurants

For the most part, except where indicated otherwise, reservations are requested but not required. However, it is always wise to call ahead. The only constant in Las Vegas is change. Hours of operation, meals served, and prices charged may all be different. Reservations are a particularly good idea on weekends and holidays, when tables are at a premium, especially in the more expensive hotel dining rooms. Also in these establishments, you may find jackets and ties are the norm, but they are rarely required.

## Shopping

Though there are no specific shopping areas in Las Vegas, the city has an abundance of shopping centers and malls. Choose from **The Boulevard Mall, Fashion Show Mall, Forum Shops,** and **Meadows Mall.** For more details, check the index for individual listings.

## Smoking

Of all 50 states, Nevada has the highest percentage of people who smoke. Even so, smoking is prohibited by state law in most elevators and public buildings. Most hotel showrooms have banned smoking, and most casinos have large nonsmoking sections. Passengers in taxicabs may smoke.

## Street Plan

Las Vegas is divided into east and west by **Main Street** and Las Vegas Boulevard South, otherwise known as the Strip. The latter is home to most of the big hotel-casinos. It's intersected by five major east-west arterial streets, three of which carry the names of famous resorts: **Sahara, Flamingo,** and **Tropicana.** North of the Strip is Downtown, home of famous Fremont Street (also known as "Glitter

Gulch"). Two expressways form a rough "T" shape through the city: Interstate 15 runs basically parallel to the Strip, while **Highway 95** bisects it near Downtown and heads east and west.

## Taxes

Clark County has a 7 percent sales tax (food items are exempt). Hotel guests pay an 8 percent room tax (9 percent Downtown to help finance *The Fremont Street Experience*), and showgoers pay a 10 percent entertainment tax on every ticket. (The trick to the latter is discerning whether the tax is built into the advertised price or added on later. Ask when you make reservations or buy your ticket.)

## Tickets

It used to be that you could not get tickets in advance for any show in Las Vegas. You could only make a reservation on the day of the show, and even that would not guarantee you a particular location in the theater or showroom. Seating was, and still is in some venues, at the discretion of the maître d'. The management's plan was to save the best seats up until the last minute for any high rollers or other VIPs who might require them. Today there are still some shows on the reservation (i.e., no tickets) system. Or there are some that will give you a ticket, but the ticket won't specify a seat. However, more and more showrooms are switching over to a traditional ticket system. It is best to call the hotel or box office directly to find out the policy for the show you want to see. There are also recorded announcements on local events provided by **Ticketmaster** (893.3033, sales 474.4000).

## Time Zones

Las Vegas is on the eastern edge of the Pacific Standard time zone. The zone changes to Mountain Standard time on the Arizona side of Hoover Dam.

## Tipping

The hotel-casino industry is driven by "tokes" as gaming people traditionally refer to their tips. There are no concrete guidelines for tipping, but the following standards are generally accepted.

**Bellhops:** Two to five dollars, depending on whether you need service or advice.

**Bingo/Keno runners:** Not necessary for a single game (unless you win and feel like sharing the credit); a dollar from time to time if playing for an extended period.

**Cocktail waitresses:** Drinks are free if you are playing table games such as blackjack, so a dollar tip per round is still a bargain (if you hang on at the table long enough for her to return).

**Dealers:** All casinos in Las Vegas pool the tips left at the table. If your dealer acts like a robot, don't feel obligated to tip. If he or she gives good advice (within the limits of the rules), it's courteous to acknowledge the help. Many dealers enjoy having you place a side bet for them; if you win, they do, too. These can range from a dollar to half of your bet.

**Restaurants/Room service:** The standard 15 to 20 percent rule of thumb applies.

**Showroom maître d' and staff:** Most major showrooms have converted to reserved-seat ticketing systems, where no maître d' tipping is required. For rooms that still accept reservations, the unwritten code for improving seating is still in effect: Pass $5 to $10 to the maître d', and a better table usually becomes available.

If your ticket was purchased in advance, see if it says gratuity is included. If so, you are not obligated to tip. If not, tip according to the amount and quality of cocktail service provided; $2 to $10, depending on the size of your group and the service rendered.

**Taxi drivers:** One to two dollars for a direct route, more if the driver was courteous and helpful.

**Valet parking:** One dollar is standard; two dollars is proper if the service was impressively quick.

## Visitors' Information Centers

There are two visitors' information centers in Las Vegas that you can call, write, or visit. For a tourist guide to hotels, entertainment, and general information, send a self-addressed, stamped envelope with 52¢ postage to the **Las Vegas Area Chamber of Commerce** (711 E Desert Inn Rd, Las Vegas, NV 89109, 735.1616). Or you can contact the **Las Vegas Convention and Visitors Authority** (Visitor Information Center/Brochure Room, 3150 Paradise Rd, Las Vegas, NV 89109, 892.0711).

## Emergencies

| | |
|---|---|
| Ambulance/Fire/Police | 911 |
| AAA Emergency Road Service | 800/222.4357 |
| Auto Impound | 382.9261, 649.5711 |
| Auto Theft | 229.3586 |

Hospitals

| | |
|---|---|
| Boulder City Hospital | 293.4111 |
| Desert Springs Hospital | 733.8800 |
| Lake Mead Hospital Medical Center | 649.7711 |
| St. Rose Dominican Hospital | 564.2622 |
| Columbia Sunrise Hospital and Medical Center | 731.8000 |
| University Medical Center | 383.2000 |
| Valley Hospital | 388.4000 |

Pharmacies

| | |
|---|---|
| Fabulous Pharmacy | 734.6036 |
| White Cross Drugs (24 hours) | 382.1733 |
| Poison Control | 732.4989 |
| Police (nonemergency) | 795.3111 |

## Phone Book

### Visitors' Information

| | |
|---|---|
| Better Business Bureau | 735.6900, 731.9877 |
| Bell Trans (airport shuttle) | 739.7990 |
| Citizens Area Transit (bus) | 228.7433 |
| Convention and Visitors Authority | 892.0711 |
| Disabled Visitors' Information | 892.0711 |
| Greyhound Bus | 800/231.2222 |
| International Youth Hostel | 385.9955 |
| Las Vegas Strip Trolley | 382.1404 |
| Road Conditions | 486.3116 |
| Western Union | 737.7111, 800/325.6000 |
| Time and Temperature | 118 |
| US Customs | 388.6480 |
| US Passport Office | 451.3597 |
| Weather | 248.4800 |

# The Main Events

Not just a neon-lined lair for guzzling and gambling, Las Vegas proves there's more to life than green-felt tabletops. For the sports-minded, there are rodeos, golf tournaments, football championship games, and world-class boxing matches. For businesspeople, the city hosts numerous conventions, some of which—the International Food Service Executives Association (IFSEA) and Chocolate Fest, for example—are open to the public. If you're feeling philanthropic, Las Vegas is also a major venue for charity benefits, attracting (and often spearheaded by) the rich and famous who call the city home. For culture seekers, there are dance performances in winter and classical music series in summer. So take a break and sample the other Las Vegas.

## January

**Consumer Electronics Show** Techno-buffs converge on this annual event, which showcases everything that is up-and-coming in the world of electronics. Held at different venues each year, it is one of the most popular trade shows in the country. For more information, call 703/907.7600.

## February

**Las Vegas International Marathon** This 5K run attracts both world-class and recreational runners. At the end of the course, there's the **International Food Festival** with plenty of music and food for runners, their supporters, and the general public. For more information, call 876.3870

## March

**Big League Weekend** Major league baseball unfolds at **Cashman Field** with teams from both the American and National Leagues. For more information, call 386.7200.

## April

**Laughlin Rodeo Days** Join the stampede at this annual event, which features a rodeo competition along with art-and-crafts exhibitions. For more information, call 800/227.5245.

**Laughlin River Run** This **Harley-Davidson Weekend** kicks off on the shores of the **Colorado River** with a trade show, museum, poker run, bike shows, a beauty contest, and much more. For more information, call 800/357.8223.

## May

**World Series of Poker** Sponsored by **Binion's Horseshoe Casino,** high rollers compete for a million-dollar first prize at this annual event. For more information, call 382.1600.

## June

**Summer Concert Series** The annual series gets underway with many groups performing for free in local parks throughout the city. For more information, call 791.4500.

## July

**Vegas to Reno Race** The first annual off-road race from Vegas to Reno takes place on the Fourth of July with hundreds of participants driving through rural towns including **Elko, Fallon,** and **Ely.**

**Fourth of July** The annual extravaganza of fireworks and entertainment comes alive at various hotels along the **Strip.**

## August

**Helldorado Days** Dancing, exhibits, and a fun-filled three days of rodeo take over the **Thomas & Mack Center.** For more information, call 870.1221.

## September

**Las Vegas Cup Powerboat Racing** Join thousands of spectators to watch the Unlimited Hydroplane Racing Association (UHRT) and the Professional Racing Outboard Performance (PROP) compete for top prizes as they skim over the waters of **Lake Mead.**

## October

**Boulder City Art Fair** Discover up-and-coming artists at this annual fair, which showcases talent from all over the world at **Centennial Park.** For more information, call 293.4111.

**Columbus Day Parade** Italians and Italophiles celebrate their heritage in style at this annual event.

**Oktoberfest** Look for festive celebrations throughout Las Vegas at many bars, restaurants, and hotels.

**Las Vegas PGA Invitational** Noted celebrities participate in this annual competition, which takes place at the **TPC Summerlin, Las Vegas Country Club,** and **Desert Inn Golf Club.** For more information, call 242.3000.

## November

**COMDEX** With more than 200,000 attendees each year, this convention is touted as the largest of its kind for those in the know in the computer field. For more information, call 891.0711.

## December

**National Finals Rodeo** This "Super Bowl" of rodeos convenes for two weeks at the **Thomas & Mack Center.** For more information, call 895.3900.

**Las Vegas Bowl** One of the many bowl games held during college football's post season, this pits a top team from the Western Athletic Conference against a leading opponent from NCAA Division I Conference at **Sam Boyd Stadium.**

**Fremont Street Experience** Wrapping up the year in style, **Downtown** comes alive for the entire month with holiday parades, country music, and rollicking entertainment. For more information, call 678.5777.

# Downtown

Low rollers, grannies with shopping bags, and sweat-suited suburbanites parade through the central core of neon Las Vegas amid icons of kitsch, including the world's largest gold nugget (a 60-pound gem under glass); the biggest slot machine on the planet; and "Vegas Vic," a 50-foot-tall neon cowboy who stands guard over the area's 24-hour display of unapologetic tackiness. Compared with the clean and classy **Strip** (the stretch of **Las Vegas Boulevard** south of **Sahara Avenue**), honky-tonk Downtown may be found wanting. But what the city's core lacks in tastefulness, it makes up for in price. You'll find some of the most unbelievable lodging and dining bargains in a town where casino-subsidized prices already leave visitors incredulous.

Beyond the neon nucleus, however, central Las Vegas reverts to its origins—a slightly decrepit, turn-of-the-century urban core that, like scores of other decaying cities throughout the western US, was founded by a railroad company. When the train carrying its cargo of pigs rumbles through on a sweltering summer night, their aroma wafting all the way to the Strip, you can imagine the town as it was before the Downtown gulch had any glitter at all.

Las Vegas was little more than a dusty watering hole from the time the train tracks arrived in 1904, and the town was laid out a year later, until the early 1930s, when it began to perceive—and pursue—its destiny. During that period, the only real excitement took place in the brothels and bars of Downtown's red-light district, known as **Block 16.** In 1931, at the height of the Great Depression, 5,000 construction workers arrived to build **Boulder** (now **Hoover**) **Dam;** 5,000 more were turned away. They all disembarked at the Las Vegas depot, and after construction of the dam, many stayed on, doubling the population almost overnight. At the same time, gambling was legalized throughout Nevada, and the casinos that opened on **Fremont Street** enticed with roulette, alcohol, and air-conditioning. The tourists arrived right on schedule—and not only to view the dam and the new **Lake Mead** filling up behind it. Now that Downtown Las Vegas offered saloons, bordellos, and gaming, visitors were hungry to get a taste of the last slice of the Wild West.

During the 1940s the town's population doubled once again, and the massive influx of World War II personnel and their families precipitated the closing of Block 16; the War Department, prompted by the complaints of wives, didn't want to condone the sale of sex. But the Fremont Street casinos flourished from the military payroll. In the postwar boom, a rash of sleek luxury resorts began to spring up out in the desert on the newly established Las Vegas Strip. But Downtown's frontier atmosphere held fast well into the 1950s. "Vegas Vic" first graced the facade of the **Pioneer Club** in 1950; **Binion's Horseshoe Hotel and Casino** opened in 1951; and even the **Golden Nugget,** a fancy Downtown casino, clung steadfastly to its saloon ambience.

The first intimation that Downtown was on the upswing came in 1956, with the construction of the 15-story

**Fremont Hotel**, yet it was another decade until the area fully emerged into the modern era. Between 1965 and 1971, four tall and tony hotel-casinos were added to the Fremont Street skyline, ushering Downtown Las Vegas out of its historical reverie and into the last quarter of the 20th century.

Today, Downtown is a mélange of odd alliances. Remnants of the early days are jarringly juxtaposed with contemporary images. Low-roller video poker, quarter craps, and $20-a-night hotels vie with resorts packed with high-end suites with a view and gourmet restaurants.

Downtown's principal competition, of course, comes from the Strip. To better compete with the must-see megaresorts, much of Downtown resembles a pedestrian mall. The area, better known as **Glitter Gulch**, covers four blocks of Fremont Street between **Fourth** and **Main Streets** and features *The Fremont Street Experience*—a sky parade and light show. A four-block-long, 90-foot-high silver canopy constructed above this casino-lined area boasts 2.1 million lights and features a variety of video programs. The main attraction is a collection of six-minute multisensory programs on the overhead space frames.

In the meantime, Downtown hangs on to its identity as the robust, bargain basement of the city, a role that works entirely to the advantage of millions of visitors.

**1 Jackie Gaughan's Plaza Hotel-Casino** $$ With one side facing the neon playground of Glitter Gulch and the other overlooking the railroad tracks, this place embodies Downtown's dichotomy. The hotel straddles the original boundary between the railroad and the town; the railroad station adjoins the casino. A large mural graces the hallway connecting the two buildings; it depicts an illustrated map of the iron horse route linking the West Coast and eastern Utah, along with a rendering of a futuristic bullet train, proposed to zip from Los Angeles to Las Vegas in little more than an hour. The south tower addition brings the room total to more than one thousand, making this Downtown's second-largest hotel (the **Golden Nugget** takes top honors with more than 1,900 rooms and suites). Accommodations are routine and are usually available, even when the city is crowded. Amenities include swimming and tennis, and a two-block car lot that's especially convenient if you prefer ground-level parking to dizzying high-rise structures. ◆ 1 Main St (at Fremont St). 386.2110, 800/634.6575; fax 382.8281 ♿

Within Jackie Gaughan's Plaza Hotel-Casino:

**Plaza Casino** The first race and sports book (a room set aside for betting on races and sports) in a Las Vegas casino opened here in 1975. The casino also has slots and video poker aplenty, with more than 1,500 machines. Typical of Downtown, there are low blackjack minimums, and you can test your luck against craps, roulette, and keno. A bank of penny reel slots is located by the south doors. ◆ Daily 24 hours. 386.2110

**Center Stage Restaurant** ★$ The glitter has diminished at this once-popular dining room with its tinted-glass dome and tuxedoed, white-gloved wait staff. However, one thing hasn't changed: its classic views of the city. Request a front-window seat so you can face the gleaming gullet of Glitter Gulch from a second-story vantage. One of these tables is perhaps the best place in town to wine, dine, and talk a partner into doing something a little out of the ordinary—like getting married in the wedding chapel next door to the bar. The fare is typical beef and potatoes and at extremely reasonable prices. Be sure to stroll through the mezzanine and descend the curving, mirrored escalators—it's one of Las Vegas's best psychedelic experiences. ◆ Steak house ◆ Daily dinner. Reservations recommended. 386.2512

**Plaza Coffee Shop** ★$ This old-time stainless steel and bright-red eatery also features a neon jukebox. The bacon or steak and eggs platters served here are two of the town's most beloved bargain breakfasts. The atmosphere is informal, but you'll always find hearty meals at very good prices. ◆ American ◆ Daily 24 hours. 386.2110

**Omaha Lounge** This bar rocks around the clock, mostly with live country lounge acts. Though it's hit-or-miss on performance quality, the price is right. There is no cover charge or drink minimum, and it's always a lively show. The stage overlooks the casino's central gambling area. Seating is particularly prized on weekends. ◆ Free. Daily 24 hours. 386.2110

**2 Victory Hotel** $ The oldest hotel in Las Vegas, this whitewashed, Mission-style structure (pictured above) hasn't changed much since it was built in 1906. All 35 rooms are basically the same, too, but they're inexpensive and, since they surround a little courtyard, blessedly quiet. Although lovely to look at, a second-story balcony overlooking the railroad yard is off-limits to guests. There is no restaurant or casino. ◆ 307 S Main St (at Bridger Ave). 384.0260

# Golden Gate

**3 Golden Gate** $ The earliest occupant of this site was Las Vegas's first modern hotel, the **Nevada,** the picture of progress with running water and wooden walls (previously, public lodging places were made of canvas). In the lobby is a black-and-white photograph of the historic building, which was replaced in the pivotal year of 1931 (when gambling was legalized in the state) by the **Sal Sagev Hotel** (Las Vegas spelled backwards). In the mid-1950s, a group of investors from San Francisco bought the property, gave it its present name, and began making the shrimp cocktails for which the hotel's **San Francisco Deli** is renowned. The 106 rooms have been renovated and restored to their early-20th-century style. The 9,000-square-foot casino offers the usual slots and table games. ◆ 1 Fremont St (at S Main St). 385.1906, 800/426.1906

Within the Golden Gate:

**San Francisco Deli** $ In 40 years this Old West–style snack bar has served more than 28 million giant shrimp cocktails. The "giant" refers not to the size of the shrimp or the San Francisco baseball team, but to the quantity of little crustaceans in this inexpensive dish. No

lettuce, celery, or other garnishes go in the cup, though you can get crackers and lemon wedges for a nominal extra cost. The long lines are a testament to its popularity with locals and tourists alike.
◆ American ◆ Daily dinner. 385.1906

**4 Coin Castle** This slot closet will do just about anything short of kidnapping to get you inside. Ballyhooers in vests made of US currency entice you to spin the wheel out front, ply you with "Crazy Cash," and pilot you to the back of the casino, where you trade in your coupons for a "funbook" full of free food and drink offers. While you wait for the lone cocktail waitress to bring you beer, nachos, popcorn, and the like, staff with advanced degrees in marketing put you through the hard sell to pull the idiot handles. It's almost worth it, as long as you can resist the exhortations to feed, feed, feed the slots until the cocktail waitress (hopefully) returns.
◆ Daily 24 hours. 15 Fremont St (between S Casino Center Blvd and S Main St). 385.7474

**5 Vegas Vic** The neon cowboy stands 50 feet tall, puffs a hand-rolled cigarette, waves (when his elbow joint is functioning), bellows "Howdy pardner, welcome to Las Vegas" (if his voice box is working), and poses for more photos than any other sign in Las Vegas. The neon mascot for the now closed Pioneer Club—Vic's home for 44 years—still graces the facade. ◆ 25 Fremont St (between S Casino Center Blvd and S Main St)

**6 Stoney's Loan and Jewelry** The oldest hock shop in the city, and the centerpiece of Pawn Shop Plaza, publishes a little brochure that documents the unusual history of the pawnbroker as a lending institution. The pamphlet doesn't mention, however, that Nevada law permits pawnbrokers to charge a monthly six percent interest on their merchandise, which explains why most pawned goods are rarely reclaimed. If you're in the market, you can pick up used guns, cameras, furs, TVs, luggage, jewelry, and binoculars here at not unreasonable prices.
◆ Daily. 126 S First St (at Carson Ave). 384.2686

In 1905, sale of the lots of the townsite of Las Vegas attracted 3,000 people and generated $265,000. Today, some high rollers bet that much money on a single turn of the cards.

**7 Golden Nugget Hotel** $$$ Downtown's largest and classiest hotel is, and almost always has been, the showcase of Fremont Street. Rather than glaring neon, the exterior is distinguished by polished white marble and gold fixtures. The lobby is graced with etched-glass doors and leaf-glass chandeliers, and the floors, columns, and front desk are made of marble. An awe-inspiring display of—what else?—gold nuggets features two dozen of the world's largest sparklers, including a 61-pound monster found with a metal detector behind a trailer court in Wetterburn, Victoria, Australia.

When the hotel opened in 1946 it boasted Las Vegas's largest casino, brightest neon sign, and fanciest decor. But after 25 years of setting superlative standards, the luster faded. It took a visionary new management nearly two decades to restore the resort's prestige. Today the 1,907 rooms and suites are spread over two full city blocks (the most far-flung is a good 10-minute hike from the front desk) and are the most expensive accommodations Downtown, as well as the most comfortable. The beauty parlor and spa are among the finest in town, offering exquisite pampering. The pool in the central courtyard can float scores of swimmers with room to spare. ◆ 129 Fremont St (at S Casino Center Blvd). 385.7111, 800/634.3454; fax 386.8362; www.goldennugget.com ♿

Within the Golden Nugget Hotel:

**Golden Nugget Casino** Downtown's high rollers are magnetically attracted to this casino by $25 video-poker machines (9/6/$100,000, meaning a full house returns nine coins, a flush returns six, and a royal flush returns $100,000), $100 slots, and high-minimum blackjack tables sharing the baccarat pit. It's always rammin' and jammin' at the 40 additional blackjack tables, 7 craps tables, and 1,000 slot machines, all poshly appointed with white leather, crystal, and bright brass. ◆ Daily 24 hours. 385.7111

**California Pizza Kitchen** ★$ Cooked in wood-fired ovens, the gourmet pies served here are famous from Hawaii to Washington, DC. Exotic toppings include Peking duck, rosemary chicken, Caribbean-spiced pork, and goat cheese. Traditionalists can always opt for mushrooms and pepperoni. You can also partake of delicious salads, pasta, and Häagen-Dazs ice-cream sundaes. ◆ Italian ◆ Daily lunch and dinner. 385.7111

**Lillie Langtry's** ★★$$$ The decor is spectacular, with a dramatic black-and-white color scheme and bold patterning; the intimate private dining room features the **Nugget**'s signature brass and glass. The cooking is primarily classic Cantonese, with a little Szechuan spice adding a gustatory bite. Sake and plum wine complement all the dishes. ◆ Chinese ◆ Daily dinner. Reservations recommended. 385.7111

**Stefano's** ★★★$$$ The marble-tiled courtyard, trompe l'oeil ceiling, bubbling fountain, and exuberant waiters who spontaneously burst into arias set quite a stage for an exemplary Northern Italian menu. Try the veal scallopini, shrimp *fra diavolo* (sautéed in olive oil and garlic with tomatoes), cioppino, or any of the pasta dishes to see for yourself why this place has garnered a reputation for outstanding preparation, presentation, and palatability of a wide diversity of dishes. ◆ Italian ◆ Daily dinner. Reservations recommended. 385.7111

**The Buffet** ★★$ This smorgasbord is tops in steam-table cuisine, and, compared to most restaurants of this genre, is in an attractive room. The scrumptious bread pudding is home-style consolation for those temporarily down on their luck. Clever diners eat here on Sunday, when free Champagne bolsters the usual breakfast, lunch, and dinner entrées. ◆ American ◆ Daily breakfast, lunch, and dinner. 385.7111

# FOUR QUEENS

**8 Four Queens Hotel** $$ Home to the Queens Machine, the world's largest slot machine, according to the **Guinness Museum**, the "Queen of Fremont Street" is also one of the few hotels in town with 24-hour security: Guards posted by the elevator politely but firmly check for room keys; if you don't have one, a registered guest must come to the lobby to collect you. The 720 rooms are large but somewhat plain, and you can request a mini-refrigerator. Surprisingly, there's no swimming pool. A high-rise garage behind the hotel provides parking. ◆ 202 Fremont St (between S Fourth St and S Casino Center Blvd). 385.4011, 800/634.6045; fax 383.0631; www.fourqueens.com ♿

Within the Four Queens Hotel:

**Four Queens Casino** The "Queens Machine" stands 18 feet long and 9 feet high, has eight reels, and seats six un-self-conscious players.

You play one to three dollar tokens in a terminal. An employee pulls the handle, and the symbols—bars, cherries, plums, watermelons, queens—must line up consecutively from either end of the display to win. The terminal lists the payout and spits out the coins. The casino takes an innovative approach to business and continually introduces new games and gambling promotions. Multiple Action blackjack, in which players bet on three hands against the dealer's single up card, was created here and has spread quickly through Nevada. ♦ Daily 24 hours. 385.4011

**Hugo's Cellar** ★★★$$$$ For a restaurant situated right off a busy casino, the brick-and-brass ambience here achieves a remarkably secluded effect. Romance is enhanced by the fresh long-stemmed rose presented to every woman who walks through the door. The service is a big part of the pleasure, with waiters skillfully tossing salads tableside and palate-cleansing sorbet served between courses. Duck rubbed with anise and flamed in Grand Marnier is the delectable specialty, but you can't go wrong with the crab-stuffed shrimp, Indonesian lamb, filets and prime ribs, or lobster. ♦ Continental ♦ Daily dinner. Reservations required; jacket requested. 385.4011

**French Quarter** This lounge is the sole survivor of the hotel's original New Orleans theme. The music leans toward the Big Band sound. There's a two-drink minimum, but since the lounge is open to the casino, you'll be well entertained at the slots, where you can drink for free. Pick up a few pointers at the lounge's daily gambling lessons. ♦ Two-drink minimum. Daily 24 hours. 385.4011

**9 Clark County Courthouse** More than 85,000 marriage licenses are issued annually in Las Vegas, every one of them inside the big Marriage License Bureau room right off the main lobby. Over New Year's Eve and Valentine's Day weekends, more than 2,500 applications are processed, and the wait can be hours long. The rest of the year, however, the procedure is a breeze. No blood test is required, and there's no waiting period. Two people 18 or older, two IDs, and $35 are all that's asked. ♦ M-Th 8AM-midnight; F-Su 24 hours. 200 S Third St (at Carson Ave). 455.4415

**10 Office of the Civil Marriage Commissioner** If you don't want a Las Vegas wedding-chapel ceremony and prefer to let a justice of the peace do the joining, till death or divorce do you part, walk a block south of the courthouse to the civil marriage office, where a deputy commissioner will hook you up in no time flat. ♦ M-Th 8AM-midnight; F-Su 24 hours. 309 S Third St (between Lewis and Bridger Aves). No phone calls

**11 Fitzgeralds Casino/Holiday Inn** $$ Accommodations at this 655-room property feature a homey ambience of "lucky" shades of green with oak wood furnishings. Whether you're feeling the luck of the Irish or not, a 120-foot neon rainbow and 35-foot tall leprechaun beckons hopefuls into the remodeled casino. Be sure to rub a bit of the Blarney Stone (straight from County Cork) before wagering a bet. The only **McDonald's** Downtown now has solarium windows—great for sipping a soft drink and taking in the *Fremont Street Experience* show. Upstairs are **Molly's Coffee Shop and Buffet, Limericks** steak house, and **Vincenzo's** Italian cafe. ♦ 301 Fremont St (between S Fourth St and S Casino Center Blvd). 388.2400, 800/274.5825; fax 388.2181 Ᏸ

**12 Las Vegas Western Village** Subtle it's not: The neon nuggets in the pan held by the prospector who towers over the entrance of this granddaddy of Fremont gift shops flash a message Midas would understand: gold, gold, gold. Inside are all the cheesy souvenirs one expects in this den of depravity: Las Vegas back scratchers, glitter-filled paperweights, shot glasses, mugs, towels, caps, salt and pepper shakers, toothpick holders, dice clocks, personalized matchbooks, and "Are We Rich Yet?" T-shirts. The shop adds a twist to the tack and sells moccasins, miniature tepees, and even synthetic coonskin caps. ♦ Daily; Tu-Sa until 11:30PM. 323 Fremont St (at S Fourth St). 386.6933

**13 El Cortez Hotel** $ Fremont Street was but a half-paved path in 1941, when this hostelry opened way out here. Soon after the asphalt was poured, "Bugsy" Siegel and his cronies became the dominant players. The jumbo neon sign and block-long marquee appeared in the early 1950s. The casino—now arguably the oldest in the country—has had very few alterations, other than some cosmetic touches to the exterior of the original wing. Current proprietor Jackie Gaughan took over in 1981, adding the 14-story tower and expanding the gaming facilities. The tower houses 200 "mini-suites"—surprisingly roomy digs with king-size beds and couches, at reasonable rates. This is one of the best budget hotels Downtown. ♦ 600 Fremont St (at N Sixth St). 385.5200, 800/634.6703; fax 385.1433 Ᏸ

Within El Cortez Hotel:

**El Cortez Casino** Although this casino is a bit beyond Glitter Gulch proper, it's still a popular place to play and is almost always crowded with locals and regulars. The gambling house is known for a lottery-type drawing with keno-size payoffs; winning combinations correspond to your social security number (bettors fill out a form that includes their social security number; winning forms are drawn from a drum). The casino is known for introducing new games, so you might find something novel happening in the gaming rooms or around the pit in the cramped old wing. The gaming facilities in the airier wing include a poker room and a race and sports book. ♦ Daily 24 hours. 385.5200

**Roberta's** ★$$ Discover one of the greatest meal deals this side of an Eskimo cookout: a big plate of Alaskan king crab legs for a price so low that you'll get change back from a Jackson. You can also subtract some crab and add a New York steak for the same pittance. The decor is nothing to write home about, and the tables are as crowded as they are small. But neither the cramped quarters nor the out-of-the-way location discourage the crowds from queuing up for the fine and inexpensive food. ♦ Steak house ♦ Daily dinner. Reservations recommended. 386.0692

**14 Gold Spike Hotel & Casino** $ Each of the 109 medium-size rooms at this place costs no more than a minimum bet at a baccarat table. (It's a good idea to make reservations at least six months in advance.) There's a two-night minimum on weekends. The amenities are basic Vegas: a small parking lot, an archetypal snack bar, and a casino that's always bustling with natives and devoted visitors. ♦ 400 Ogden Ave (at N Fourth St). 384.8444, 800/634.6703; fax 384.8768 ₺

Within the Gold Spike Hotel & Casino:

**Gold Spike Casino** Low rollers who enter here are transported to heaven. Even on a busy Saturday night, there's usually only one $5 blackjack table; the other six host $1 and $2 games. The place is jammed with nickel slots and video poker. But the unique attraction is the array of penny video-poker machines. You can play up to one hundred pennies, and the royal flush on the max bet pays 10,000 coins ($100). The action is fierce, a veritable video-poker back-wall battle, with 13 warriors locked in combat with the machines, marked by the occasional desperate cry to the change person for more ammunition. When one challenger bows to defeat, another rushes in to pick up the cause. If you haven't been through basic training, you might want to steer clear of this foxhole. ♦ Daily 24 hours. 384.8444

**15 Sam Boyd's Fremont Hotel and Casino** $ In 1956, this 452-room, 15-story hotel was the tallest building in the state, rising a full six floors above anything on the Strip. Unusual for Downtown, this place has such amenities as elevators, showrooms, and a rooftop swimming pool. Of all the Downtown casinos, this one weathered the longest underworld involvement: Meyer Lansky's name was overheard by an FBI wiretap in the 1970s. Today, it's a typical 40-something Las Vegas hotel, a little faded but still vital thanks to its prime location in Glitter Gulch. There's a big and bold Western mural in the poker room—where aspiring cardsharps can take lessons in the mornings—and some model Conestoga wagons in the **Overland Coffee Shop.** ♦ 200 Fremont St (at N Casino Center Blvd). 385.3232, 800/634.6182; fax 385.6229

Within Sam Boyd's Fremont Hotel and Casino:

**Second Street Grill** ★★★$$$ This casual but elegant dining room is an attractive, intimate space, with dark inlaid woods, Art Deco–style fixtures, and comfortable, heavy wooden chairs. The fine fare includes such exotic and tasty Pacific Rim foods as bamboo-steamed Hawaiian snapper, grilled veal chops with soy-ginger sauce, and a crispy honey duck salad. Desserts range from a ginger crème brûlée to a macadamia nut cheesecake. ♦ Pacific Rim ♦ Daily dinner. Reservations recommended. 385.6277

**16 Binion's Horseshoe Hotel and Casino** $$ A literal wealth of Las Vegas legends are associated with this place. Of all the rough characters who ever owned a Las Vegas casino, the late Benny Binion, an urban cowboy, bootlegger, and gambler from Dallas, was the roughest. Benny made no bones about having killed people nor did he pull many punches when it came to cheaters, welshers, freeloaders, card counters, and the like. A statue of the old man astride his trusty steed stands at the corner of Ogden Avenue and First Street (overlooking what used to be Block 16). Benny Binion died in 1989 at the age of 84; his family still owns the lodging.

The older section of the hotel houses 80 rooms, all comped to high rollers, and the neighboring 25-story west wing has 300 newer and larger guest rooms. Together, they form a city block, and the two Ogden Avenue parking structures occupy another block. There's a pool and spa on top of the newer building. A hundred $10,000 bills are on display in the old wing, and though the stash is advertised as one million dollars, the old currency, out of circulation for decades, is worth far more than its face value. Go ahead—have your picture taken in front of all that beautiful money. ◆ 128 Fremont St (at N Casino Center Blvd). 382.1600, 800/237.6537; fax 384.1574 ♿

Within Binion's Horseshoe Hotel and Casino:

**Binion's Horseshoe Casino** Tables and slots pack the original casino, outfitted with dark wood and Western-style chandeliers. Eight craps tables comprise the largest dice pit in Nevada—if not the world. But the west wing—decked out in brass and glass—holds the busiest poker pit in town, and the world's biggest names in poker are its habitués. This is the joint with no house limits and where it is not uncommon to see a one-million-dollar bet placed at craps. The annual World Series of Poker—sponsored by the hotel—is held here every May; to compete for the million-dollar first prize, simply ante up $10,000. You may not win, but if you play here at least they'll feed you well; the place has a reputation for doling out some of the best meal comps in the business. ◆ Daily 24 hours. 382.1600

**Coffee Shop** $ The line forms a half hour before the 10PM serving time for the $4 New York steak dinner with all the trimmings. Be prepared to wait anywhere from 45 minutes to 1.5 hours. The steak is excellent, a loss leader for the casino. If you're still in the casino at 5:45AM, you can queue up for Benny Binion's Natural—the $2.75 ham and eggs breakfast. Be patient: Dinner and breakfast have been popular Downtown staples for years—but you only need arrive 10 minutes ahead of time for lunch. ◆ American ◆ Daily 24 hours. 382.1600

**Deli** ★$ The bagels and lox and heaping pastrami, corned beef, and brisket sandwiches served here earn the approval of experienced noshers. And of course, kosher dills are served on the side. ◆ Deli ◆ Daily breakfast, lunch, and dinner. 382.1600

**Snack Bars** $ The 24-hour snack bars in each wing of the hotel both offer the same menu. Scrambled eggs, sausage, and a biscuit set you back just one buck between 6 and 11AM. Many residents claim to have lived through lean times on the hearty ham-and-bean soup with a big piece of corn bread. The turkey sandwiches are piled high with breast meat, carved from a fresh bird roasted daily. ◆ American ◆ Daily breakfast, lunch, and dinner. 382.1600

**Binion's Ranch Steak House** ★★$$$ The ascent in the glass-enclosed elevator to this 25th-floor aerie is the best joyride Downtown. Known far and wide for its beef, which comes from the family's own Montana ranch, recommended dishes include the outstanding prime ribs and 25-ounce porterhouse. The lamb chops are also winners. Or you can just come up for a drink at the quiet bar, with its wide-angle view of the city. ◆ Steak house ◆ Daily dinner. Reservations recommended. 382.1600

**17 Sassy Sally's** Just like its sister casino (the **Coin Castle**), this Downtown slot joint will do anything to lure you inside. Some outlandish character—a woman wearing a 55-gallon Styrofoam hat and size 23 plastic cowboy boots or a guy in horse-riding gear—is bound to be stationed out front doing something outrageous to get your attention. The whole place has a strange amber glow, and the ambience can be a bit overwhelming, with flashing lights; scores of shrieking, clanging reel slots; and an army of hucksters hassling you to play. ◆ Daily 24 hours. 32 Fremont St (between N Casino Center Blvd and N Main St). 382.5777

**17 Girls of Glitter Gulch** "Vegas Vickie," a neon cowgal, sits pretty on top of the marquee at this strip club. Despite the unanimous opposition of the mayor and other city officials, as well as the majority of Downtown casino managers who are convinced that Las Vegas is now a family destination, the business remains open and is popular as ever. Although pedigree isn't usually a factor in these enterprises, this one's sort of the "Tonight Show" of jiggle joints. ◆ Cover. Daily 9AM-1AM. 26 Fremont St (between N Casino Center Blvd and N Main St). 385.4774

The cost of a hotel room in Las Vegas is determined by who's paying for it. The casino rate for preferred customers is the least expensive, although regular guests in the short off-season may get similar discounts. Packages sponsored by wholesalers, airlines, and the hotel itself offer rooms at a slightly higher rate. Then comes the corporate discount, 10 to 15 percent lower than the standard room rate. Convention rates are typically the highest.

**Restaurants/Clubs:** Red    **Hotels:** Blue
**Shops/**🍴 **Outdoors:** Green    **Sights/Culture:** Black

# All That Glitters Is Neon

Think of Las Vegas and chances are a dazzlingly bright blur of neon comes to mind. In this veritable museum of neon culture, huge glittering signs front the hotel-casinos, serving the dual role of heraldry and billboard: Above is an image, identifiable from a distance and at cruising speed; below is a marquee that announces entertainment, gambling, and dining options. The overall effect works best after darkness transforms the **Strip** and **Downtown** into a magic garden of exotic and brilliant blooms, which tint the air, dematerialize the architecture, and render the night into a frenzied crazy quilt of color.

The most concentrated and startling light show in town is the four-block stretch of **Fremont Street** downtown between **Fourth** and **Main Streets.** The stars are the neon cowboy and cowgirl: "Vegas Vic" (waving and welcoming since 1951) atop the now-closed **Pioneer Club** and "Vegas Vickie" atop the **Girls of Glitter Gulch.** The **Horseshoe** and **Fremont** hotel-casinos are fronted entirely by neon; if all the tubing were laid end to end, it would stretch more than 10 miles.

On the Strip, the **Sahara** sign is the tallest, at nearly 23 stories. The **Stardust** sign has the most animation, with 26 lighting sequences. "Lucky the Clown" at **Circus Circus** is the heaviest, at 120 tons. The **Flamingo Hilton**'s is especially stunning, with a rush of pink-petaled blooms up a single long stem, spilling out at the top in an explosion of color. And the impressive, multicolored sign at the **Rio** (emblazoned with the casino's logo and a pair of maracas) now wins the "Best of Las Vegas" poll every year.

Neon, a rare atmospheric gas, was first isolated in 1898. By the early 1900s electricity pioneers had discovered that if they filled a glass tube with neon and zapped it with high voltage, it would produce a brilliant red light. French sign maker Georges Claude installed the first neon sign, a red- and white-striped barber pole, on a Parisian barber shop in 1910. It caused such a sensation on the street that within a few years Claude Neon had become a million-dollar business. By 1930, some 300 sparkling, elegant neon creations lit up Times Square, and in the mid-1940s, considered the Golden Age of Neon, 2,000 neon-sign manufacturers employed nearly 10,000 craftspeople in America alone.

At that time, neon was highly regarded among sign makers, advertisers, architects, and artists. The flexibility of glass tubing and variety of color provided a limitless potential for conveying complex images and ideas through fluid lines, animated shapes, and abstract designs, as well as illuminating brand names, logos, and trademarks so that they appeared to spring from the flat surface of the nighttime sky. Neon transcended the mere sign to become part of the dramatic landscape of the city.

The evolution of neon as a symbol of popular American culture in the midcentury was closely related to the country's emerging passion for automobile travel and its influence on roadside architecture and advertising. Las Vegas was perfectly suited to large-scale displays of neon graphics. The flat topography, clear air, and dark desert nights lent themselves to neon's pizzazz, and Las Vegas's location on the highway to and from Los Angeles proved ideal for drawing attention to commercial establishments, especially through the windshield of a fast-moving car. But most of all, Nevada's lax sign regulations and the casinos' large advertising budgets, not to mention their intense desire to outdo each other, provided the perfect canvas for neon sign makers to practice their craft. Las Vegas attracted the cream of the industry— designers, glassblowers, electrical and structural engineers—who literally overran the town with neon, some say depreciating the effect so much by the mid-1960s that neon fell out of favor for three decades.

Today, neon is enjoying a resurgence elsewhere in the US, especially as a highlighting element for both internal and external architecture.

The technology used to fabricate neon light has changed little from the early days of the industry. Every piece of a neon sign must be produced by hand. First, the design is drawn on paper, then transferred onto an asbestos sheet. Varying lengths of glass tubing are

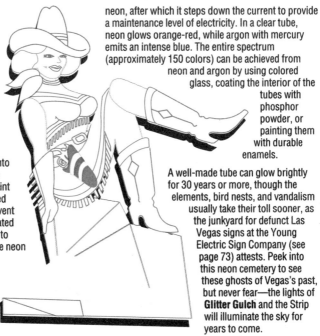

heated over Bunsen burners and bent, while soft, to correspond to the design; the glassworker blows through the tube while bending it to keep it from flattening out. Herein lies the true art of neon sign making: achieving the complexity of curves while maintaining the integrity of the glass.

Next, electrodes are melted into either end of the tube and the joints are blacked out with paint or tape. All the air is vacuumed from the tube through a tiny vent and the impurities are eliminated by shocking the tube with up to 30,000 volts. At this point, the neon (argon is sometimes used, combined with a little mercury) is injected, and then the vent is sealed. A transformer attached to the electrodes introduces 15,000 volts to fire up the

neon, after which it steps down the current to provide a maintenance level of electricity. In a clear tube, neon glows orange-red, while argon with mercury emits an intense blue. The entire spectrum (approximately 150 colors) can be achieved from neon and argon by using colored glass, coating the interior of the tubes with phosphor powder, or painting them with durable enamels.

A well-made tube can glow brightly for 30 years or more, though the elements, bird nests, and vandalism usually take their toll sooner, as the junkyard for defunct Las Vegas signs at the Young Electric Sign Company (see page 73) attests. Peek into this neon cemetery to see these ghosts of Vegas's past, but never fear—the lights of **Glitter Gulch** and the Strip will illuminate the sky for years to come.

---

**18  Las Vegas Club Hotel and Casino** $$

Topped by a 15-story tower, this place features 409 rooms boasting a Southwestern ambience of soft desert hues. The casino also lays claim to being the first theme-oriented hotel-casino studded with sports memorabilia. The centerpiece is Maury Wills's bronzed spikes from the 1962 baseball season, when he broke the stolen-bases record with 104. Among the balls, bats, and trophies, the blown-up aerial photos of stadiums provide an unusual perspective. For intimate dining, there's the **Great Moments Room** serving steaks and seafood. ♦ 18 Fremont St (between N Casino Center Blvd and N Main St). 385.1664, 800/634.6532; fax 387.6071 &

Within the Las Vegas Club Hotel and Casino:

**Las Vegas Club Casino** Dating back to the early days of legalized gambling, the casino wing of the hotel is a high-ceilinged, spacious affair, affording elbow room uncommon in Downtown. Huge signs over the pit spell out the most liberal blackjack rules in Vegas: double down on two, three, or four cards; split and resplit pairs, including aces; six cards that don't bust automatically win; surrender first two cards for half your bet. The basic strategy is a bit more advanced due to the six-card and surrender, but this is the best six-deck game

anywhere. A wing boasts a balcony and an impressive full-length wall mural of bleacher bums. ♦ Daily 24 hours. 385.1664

**19  California Hotel and Casino** $$$

Although this hotel opened in 1975 with a Southern California theme, the clientele always has hailed overwhelmingly from the Aloha State. The owners took the cue and decided to add a distinctly tropical ambience to the place, with vibrant Hawaiian prints everywhere and the **Aloha Specialties** store and restaurant upstairs. The shop sells dried fruit and nuts in bulk, while the eatery serves such traditional Hawaiian plate lunches as *saimin* (noodle soup), teriyaki chicken and rice, beef stew curry, and stir-fried vegetables. Less discerning palates go for the Spam *musubi* (rice and Spam wrapped in nori seaweed). **Dave's Bar**, also upstairs, affects a thatch-roofed, Waikiki look, and the lounge is sometimes filled with islanders jamming on ukuleles and guitars. If it wasn't for the mural of the Las Vegas banana wearing neon sunglasses, you might think you're at a luau. The Hawaiian theme carries over into the casino—a colorful room offering the basic craps, roulette, and blackjack games. The pool is on the third floor of the west wing. Altogether the hotel provides 1,000 clean, comfortable, and commodious rooms. ♦ 12 Ogden Ave (between N First and N Main Sts). 385.1222, 800/634.6255; fax 388.2670; www.vegas.com/hotels/cal &

Within the California Hotel and Casino:

# Tricks of the Trade: Nevada's Adult Entertainment Industry

No wonder visitors to Las Vegas aren't sure how much sin is legal in Sin City. Whether by design or lack of diligence, the city, county, and state governments send mixed messages—from the legality of prostitution to how close patrons can get to the topless dancers in the area's dozen or so joints.

**North Las Vegas,** for instance, allows the ladies of the palatial **Palomino Club** to dance totally nude while the clientele partakes of favorite libations within grabbing distance. On the other hand, **Clark County,** which has jurisdiction over most of the area's topless bars, has determined that alcohol and nude dancing don't mix. Consequently, clubs such as **Cheetah's** and the **Crazy Horse Too** are free to serve booze, as long as dancers keep their panties on and don't make physical contact with customers. Then there's **Henderson,** the booming suburb on the south side of Las Vegas, which requires topless dancers to wear pasties while they work. Despite rumors to the contrary, strippers who work in local topless bars generally draw the line at what they call a "table dance" (essentially a more personalized version of what they do on stage, except that it can cost customers upward of $20 a song).

For those who come to town seeking hands-on experience with the seedier side of Las Vegas, local authorities would like to make a few things clear. First, prostitution is illegal in Clark County, which contains Las Vegas and covers the southern tip of the state. It also is prohibited in four other Nevada counties: Washoe, which contains Reno; Douglas, home of Lake Tahoe; Lincoln, which outlawed prostitution by vote of the people; and Carson City, the state capital and its own county.

## Anytime of Day

That leaves the so-called "Cow Counties" (12 rural counties), where Nevada's 30 or so legal brothels have become an accepted fact of life. From the infamous **Mustang Ranch** (claiming the longest and most sordid history of the state's brothels) a few miles outside of Reno to the **Chicken Ranch** near Pahrump (about 60 miles west of Las Vegas), as many as 300 working girls ply their trade. The brothels—open 24 hours a day, seven days a week—provide a sure thing for men who can afford their services, which start at $50. Most bordellos even sell T-shirts and other souvenirs.

The Nevada Brothel Association, an industry organization that acts as a lobbying arm, boasts that the Silver State's legal prostitutes are less likely to spread sexually transmitted diseases than streetwalkers found in most resort towns, including Las Vegas. State law requires every legal prostitute to register with the state and submit to weekly exams for most sexually transmitted diseases and monthly tests for syphilis and HIV, the virus that can cause AIDS. No applicant can work in a bordello until she

has been given a clean bill of health. After more than eight years of testing, state health officials claim they have yet to find a prostitute working in one of Nevada's legal brothels infected with HIV.

Of course, none of these controls applies to the illegal prostitutes who have patrolled Las Vegas since it began as a railroad watering hole in 1905. Back then, men frequented what locals called **Block 16,** the town's original red-light district, which was bounded by **Second Street (Casino Center Boulevard), First Street,** and **Ogden** and **Stewart Avenues.** Prostitution thrived in this area until the military moved to town during World War II.

## Hot Times

The crude wooden cribs where prostitutes serviced their customers on Block 16 are a distant memory. But the oldest profession, though illegal, is still alive and well in Las Vegas. Instead of working the streets around **Downtown** and along the **Strip,** as hookers did until the early 1980s, most Las Vegas ladies of the evening have merely moved into the massive hotels. For proof, look no further than the Yellow Pages of the local phone book, where you'll find more than 80 pages of suggestive advertisements under the heading "Entertainers." Expensive full-page pitches promote businesses such as Swinging Suzy's and Satisfaction Guaranteed, each one promising to deliver the hottest male and female "dancers" and "entertainers" direct to your hotel room, 24 hours a day.

These businesses are typically fronts for pimps and prostitutes. The vice/narcotics bureau of the Las Vegas Metropolitan Police Department has conducted hundreds of undercover sting operations in an attempt to control the pesky call girl services and has yet to find one that is legitimate. However, the operators usually escape prosecution by claiming that the prostitutes were working on their own—not as their employees.

Of even greater concern to local law-enforcement authorities is the handful of "sex-tease" clubs that have surfaced in recent years. Police say these places, with names such as Black Garter and Nastys, lure lonely men with the promise of sex, force them to purchase nonalcoholic drinks for hundreds of dollars a pop, and then fail to deliver on their sexual promises.

Although local laws require such establishments to post signs stating that prostitution is illegal in Clark County, police say that the scantily clad ladies usually give their sales pitch with a wink and a suggestive smile. When the con is complete—or when the sucker comes to his senses—the would-be client is often escorted out by beefy bouncers who do their best to discourage complaints. In fact, few victims of this hustle ever report it. After all, who wants to admit that he was swindled while trying to pay for sex, much less that he struck out in Sin City?

**Pasta Pirate** ★★★$$ The design-your-own pasta dishes offered in the hotel's Italian-American eatery are huge (even the kids' plate). The fish is fresh and the surf 'n' turf combos are great to split. But the big winner here is the daily special, usually a filet mignon or top sirloin with a pair of baby lobster tails. If quantity is a major concern, you won't be disappointed; generous meals come with a house salad topped with bay shrimp, garlic bread sticks, vegetable, a side order of pasta, and a glass of wine. Don't miss the hot apple dumpling. ◆ Italian/American ◆ Daily dinner. Reservations recommended. 385.1222

**20 Main Street Station** $$ Run by the Boyd Corporation, this 400-room hotel and casino sports rich woods, antique furnishings, and a stunning stained-glass dome overlooking the main pit. Also on hand are a microbrewery and a tri-level buffet. An overpass connects the hotel-casino with the nearby **California Hotel and Casino.** ◆ 300 N Main St (at Stewart Ave). 387.1896, 800/713.8933; fax 386.4421; www.vegas.com/hotels/stardust

**21 Downtown Transportation Center** This attractive, convenient local transportation hub serves **CAT (Citizens Area Transit)** buses that traverse the valley. Inside are a ticket counter, helpful personnel, a small snack bar, and a security office. ◆ Daily 5:30AM-10PM. 300 N Casino Center Blvd (at Stewart Ave). 228.7433.

**22 Las Vegas City Hall** This 10-story semicircle of polished beige marble, designed by **Daniel, Mann, Johnson & Mendenhall** and built in 1973, stands proud and confident at the edge of Downtown. The office tower overlooks a circular courtyard that's ringed by two levels of walkways, giving the public easy access to the space. (Note: Weddings are not performed here.) ◆ M-F. 400 Stewart Ave (at N Fourth St). 229.6011

**23 Central Fire Station** A postmodern, peeled-back portico of glazed brown tile frames the entrance to the administrative offices of this station, designed in 1984 by **Harris Sharp Associates.** The garage is in the rear of the building, and the communications center for Clark County's fire services is tucked beneath a raised forecourt. It's an impressively bold statement for a civic institution. ◆ E Bonanza Rd (between Las Vegas Blvd N and N Casino Center Blvd)

**24 Las Vegas Public Library** Las Vegas's fabled architectural context—or lack thereof—is tested by this library, designed by **Antoine**

**Predock** and completed in 1990. A dynamic assemblage of such simple geometric forms as cubes, cones, and a 112-foot-tall cylinder renders the sandstone structure into an aesthete's playground (an appropriate characterization since the building also houses a children's museum). Numerous picture windows flood the rooms with natural reading light. The myriad channels and chambers promote an ongoing architectural exploration of the interior. Upstairs is the **Young People's Library,** with a circular-plan reading room and computer terminals. **Predock,** an Albuquerque-based architect, received the American Institute of Architects' Award of Excellence for this project. ◆ M-Th 9AM-9PM; F-Sa; Su noon-5PM. 833 Las Vegas Blvd N (between Bell Dr and E Washington Ave). 382.3493

Within the Las Vegas Public Library:

**Lied Discovery Children's Museum** With 130 participatory exhibits that teach children about the world around them, the rpms (reve-lations-per-minute) here thrust kids' kinetic needles right into the red zone. Some displays are just for fun, like the *Toddler Towers, Bubble Pavilion,* and musical hopscotch. Others stimulate young imaginations with activities exploring technology, natural science, and art. ◆ Admission. W-Sa; Su noon-5PM. 382.3445

**25 Old Mormon Fort** Latter-day Saint mission-aries and homesteaders attempted to colonize the Las Vegas Valley in 1855. They built a large stockade to protect their possessions and gardens against the Paiute Indians—unneces-sarily, it turned out, since the indigenous Las Vegans were a hospitable bunch. But the fortress was no match for the forces of nature, and in only a couple of years the Mormons abandoned the settlement to the desert ele-ments. The oldest historic site in southern Nevada, this prosaic little adobe shack has not only endured 140 years of modern Las Vegas history, it also survived the demolition of the rest of the stockade by the fraternal society of Elks (who owned the property) in 1963. Uncharacteristically, the city rallied to rescue the structure, and today it's the only trace of Las Vegas's prerecreation, prerailroad, even preranching past. ◆ Donation requested. Daily 8:30AM-3:30PM. 850 Las Vegas Blvd N (between E McWilliams and E Washington Aves). 486.3511

**26 Las Vegas Natural History Museum** After the kids have exhausted the **Lied,** and

before they've exhausted their parents, a visit to this modern and well-laid-out wildlife museum is a must. Large galleries of taxidermied North American predators and African ungulates, sharks, birds, and dinosaurs fascinate young and old. A hands-on room has a fossil sandbox, a dinosaur "horn" (you have to see—and blow into—it to appreciate it), and more. Combining art and nature, the halls are adorned with paintings and sculptures of fauna. ♦ Admission. Daily. 900 Las Vegas Blvd N (at E Washington Ave). 384.3466

**27 Cashman Field Center** One of three major Las Vegas convention venues, this one also has a playful side, doubling as a sports facility. The **Las Vegas Stars**—the Triple-A **Pacific Coast League** team affiliated with the **San Diego Padres**—hold their home games here from early April through Labor Day. The center was built in 1983 to blueprints by **George Tate & Associates.** Two exhibition halls provide 100,000 square feet; there's also a 1,940-seat theater. The baseball stadium seats 10,000 fans. The public is invited to peruse the exhibit halls and theater even when there are no special events. ♦ Hours vary; call ahead. Las Vegas Blvd N (between E McWilliams and E Washington Aves). 386.7100; Stars ticket information 386.7200; tickets at the box office, or call Ticketmaster 474.4000

**28 Las Vegas Academy of International Studies and Performing Arts** Elaborate detailed reliefs of flora and fauna and a frieze of heroic figures bedeck Las Vegas's only example of Art Deco architecture. A state historic landmark listed on the National Register of Historic Places, the building was designed by **Ferris & Sons** (Reno-based architects descended from the inventor of the Ferris wheel)—was constructed in 1931 and served as **Las Vegas High School** for 62 years. ♦ 315 S Seventh St (between Clark and Bridger Aves). 871.7208

French Restaurant

**29 Andre's ★★★★$$$$** This award-winning French restaurant is housed in a former residence in a historic part of the city. Owner-chef Andre Rochat is in the kitchen, but makes frequent forays into the cozy dining rooms to visit with guests. Ask to tour the extensive wine cellar that includes vintages dating back to 1830, or attend one of the spectacular Thursday night wine-maker dinners held several times a year. The menu changes with the seasons, but always features *escargots de Bourgogne* (snails in garlic butter) and various presentations of smoked salmon and *coquilles St. Jacques* (scallops in the shell), plus creative preparations of fillet of beef, veal (loin, chop, and medaillons), lamb, fresh fish, poultry, and stuffed pork tenderloin. The exquisite desserts served here are legendary. ♦ Continental ♦ Daily dinner. Reservations recommended. 401 S Sixth St (at Lewis Ave). 385.5016

**30 Mad Dogs and Englishmen ★$** Sporting a dart room and dark wood bar, this is as close to an English pub as you can hope to find in the American desert. Bartenders with rugby player physiques sport big handlebar mustaches. Wash down the Lancashire hot pot (beef stew) or shepherd's pie with a draught of Taunton cider, Bass Ale, Watney's Red Label, or Guinness Stout. ♦ English ♦ Daily 24 hours. 515 Las Vegas Blvd S (between Bonneville and Clark Aves). 382.5075

**31 Gambler's General Store** Here lies your one-stop shop for every kind of gambling gadget known. The smallest item in stock is an eight-millimeter, two-ounce die. The largest is a walk-in "money chamber" (popular for check-cashing promotions). Contestants attempt to grab fistfuls of bills swirling inside the enclosure and then push them through a narrow slot. Also here are hundreds of antique and video slots, roulette wheels, blackjack tables, bulk chips and dice, king, queen, and joker directors' chairs, watches, neckties, two big walls full of books and tapes, even a dice-inlaid toilet seat (only $279). This is indisputably the best spot in town to find an authentic souvenir of a sojourn to the gambling capital of the world. ♦ Daily. 800 S Main St (between Hoover and Garces Aves). 382.9903

**32 El Sombrero ★$** If you glance at this squat adobe cantina and think that it's been around for a while, you're right. In operation since 1951, it's the third-oldest restaurant in Las Vegas. The whole place seats only 48 people, though the reverberating, high-volume jukebox might be more suited to a stadium. This is the real thing—mounds of Mexican food at prices that are a bargain even for this town. ♦ Mexican ♦ M-Sa lunch and dinner. 807 S Main St (between Hoover and Garces Aves). 382.9234

**33 Chicago Joe's** ★$ Not all dining establishments in Las Vegas are coliseum-size; these two rooms in a tiny brick house on the fringe of Downtown have just 12 tables. Lunch, with a menu of various pastas and meatball sandwiches, is quick but not too rushed. Veal, fish, chicken, and eggplant are served at dinner, but the way to go at this joint is some straight-up, down-home macaroni and marinara, with a glass of house red. ♦ Italian ♦ M-F lunch and dinner; Sa dinner. Reservations recommended. 820 S Fourth St (between Hoover and Gass Aves). 382.5637

**34 Doña Maria's** ★★$ This Las Vegas–Mexican-food institution serves tamales as good as any you'll find north of the border; try them enchilada-style with green or red salsa. Chips, a beer, and an à la carte taco will set you back less than a minimum blackjack bet on the Strip and will fill you up until breakfast (whenever that is). ♦ Mexican ♦ Daily breakfast, lunch, and dinner.1000 E Charleston Blvd (at S 10th St). 382.6538

**35 Gambler's Book Club** If your brother-in-law's system crashes or your lucky numbers fail, consult the experts. Anything that you might need to know about every aspect of gambling is right here. The stacks are conveniently organized into categories: card and dice games, sports and the horses, probability theory, casino management, the mob, gambling economics, dealer's manuals, and more. Also sold here are videotapes and software. Be sure to pick up the giant mail-order catalog published by the store. ♦ M-Sa. 630 S 11th St (at Garces Ave). 382.7555, 800/522.1777

## Bests

### Larry Grossman
Columnist/Photojournalist/National Radio Talk Show Host, American Sports Network

Feel the Old West at **Binion's Horseshoe.** If you like to play craps, the **Horseshoe** offers 100 times odds. If you happen to be there in the late evening, take advantage of the best deal in town: a complete steak dinner for two dollars between 10PM and 5:45AM.

The **Forum Shops** at **Caesars** must be seen to be believed. The architecture transports you to old Rome. Statues move and entertain. The sky subtly and realistically fades from day to night. **Spago** and **Palm** also have restaurants in the mall.

For people with a big appetite, the buffet at the **Rio Suite Hotel** will fill your stomach with a wide variety of foods, without draining your wallet.

The lights on the **Strip** and **Downtown** at night.

**The Mirage** when the volcano erupts.

The action never stops in Las Vegas, so you won't miss anything if you take a short drive out of town to **Mount Charleston** for fresh air and blue skies. Have a drink at the lodge or enjoy lunch with a view.

A ride in the desert when the cactus flowers are blooming.

The sports books, where you can legally put your money where your mouth is.

The pool scene at any of the major hotels is people-watching at its best.

A heavyweight championship fight.

Watching the Kentucky Derby in a race book.

The **World Series of Poker.**

### Jan Laverty Jones
Mayor, City of Las Vegas

While there are many new and exciting attractions in Las Vegas, heading the list would be the *Fremont Street Experience,* located in the heart of Las Vegas's historic gaming district—**Downtown.** This $70-million, 90-foot-high canopy and electric light show covers four blocks along famous **Fremont Street** and its 2.1 million lights provide a spectacular and unforgettable sight to behold. A definite must-see!

If you plan on bringing your children to our city, you would not want to miss the **Lied Discovery Children's Museum.** This facility offers many interesting and educational attractions for children. Across the street from **Lied** is the **Las Vegas Natural History Museum,** which is yet another fascinating learning experience for children and adults alike.

Another favorite is the breathtaking, panoramic view from atop the **Stratosphere Hotel & Casino,** the gateway to Downtown. From the observation deck of this structure, you will experience an atmosphere unmatched by any other resort in our community, and if it's challenges that thrill you, be sure to take advantage of the two amusement rides at the peak of the **Stratosphere.**

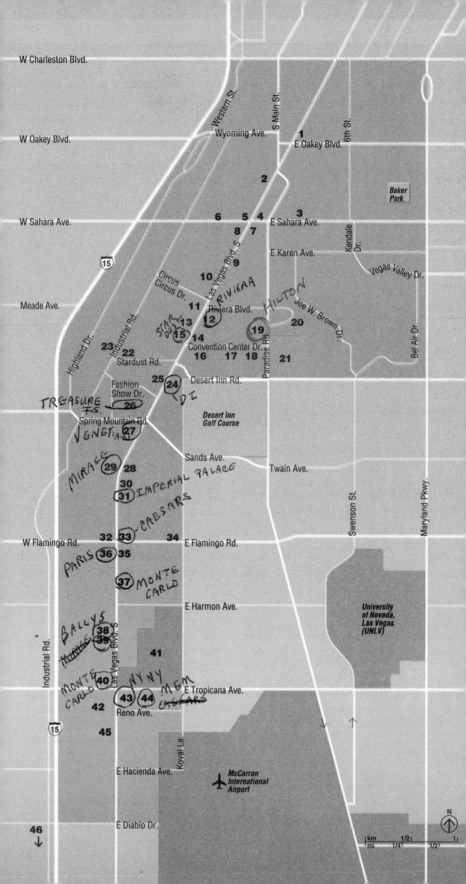

# The Strip

The Las Vegas Strip is a monument to the reworded maxim "nothing succeeds like excess." Home to some of the world's largest hotels, this four-mile corridor—centered on **Las Vegas Boulevard South** from **Sahara Avenue** to **Hacienda Avenue**—also boasts the longest and brightest stretch of neon and the most extensive gambling opportunities on any single street on the planet. Notched into a vast, monochromatic desert, shimmering through the heat and dust, the Strip defies categorization; simultaneously inviting and intimidating, it blurs the distinction between fact and fantasy.

The story of the Strip has been one of risk takers and rivalries involving entrepreneurial players from both sides of the law. In the 1940s, the Strip was a primitive gravel road (then called **Highway 91**) linking Los Angeles and Salt Lake City to Las Vegas; the town itself was little more than a collection of rooming houses and saloons surrounded by vacant, arid wasteland.

In 1941, the owner of a large chain of motels—a new type of accommodation in those days—visited Las Vegas and decided to try his luck at the casino business. Thomas Hull opened his **El Rancho Vegas** just beyond the city limits in April of that year: a 100-room resort with Spanish Mission overtones, a big parking lot, and a swimming pool strategically placed along the highway. Its instant popularity with tourists seeking comfortable, commodious lodging in the desert caught the attention of like-minded Texas movie theater mogul D.W. Griffith, who built his own 100-room motel, christened the **Last Frontier Hotel**, just a few miles down the road.

Benjamin "Bugsy" Siegel showed up a few years later, on hiatus from his East Coast gangster haunts to avoid a murder rap. After living the high life for several decades in New York, Miami, and Los Angeles, he wanted to build a suitably classy joint from which to oversee the syndicate's West Coast operations. Hollywood's interpretation of events in the film *Bugsy* to the contrary, Bugsy did not invent the Strip; he simply gave the nouveau West a certain amount of polish. The criminal's success in procuring a gambling license from the county and opening the **Flamingo** demonstrated to his partners and other interested observers the beauty of legalized gambling and the importance of personal legitimacy. Not long after Bugsy took several fatal slugs, four more mob-owned and -operated hotels opened on the Strip.

A mere decade after **El Rancho Vegas** broke ground, seven hotels populated old Highway 91. Similar in style and substance, they all faced a common dilemma: how to rise above the competition. With the advent of the cheap, highly visible neon sign, this identity crisis came to an end, and the fledgling Strip lit up the sky.

The nine-story **Riviera Hotel** opened in 1955, introducing a modern, luxurious character to the Strip. Between then and 1973, another 10 hotels were built, each one-upping the architectural ante with a bravado that had become synonymous with the city. First, the **Stardust** opened with 1,000 rooms. Then the **Tropicana** built the fanciest lobby, replete with luxurious mahogany paneling and crystal chandeliers. **Caesars Palace** went on to pioneer the theme concept, with its wholesale transplant of the Roman Empire. And in 1973, the **MGM Grand** (now **Bally's**) cracked the 2,000-room mark.

Though many of the existing hotels expanded during the 1970s and late 1980s, no new lodgings opened on the Strip during these years. Critics crowed that Las Vegas was overbuilt, the market had peaked, and no one could ever top the **MGM Grand**. They should have hedged their bets. Visitors continued to stream to the city at an accelerating pace, with attendance increasing by a million each year. Hotels are always filled to capacity. (By 1998, the annual draw reached 30.6 million; projections call for 34 million by 2001.)

In 1989, the 3,000-room **Mirage** materialized, its smoldering, six-story volcano, rain-forested lobby, and high-roller appeal sounding the first salvo in the current building boom. The **Excalibur** added 4,000 rooms in 1990, and three years later, the 5,000-room **MGM Grand Hotel/Casino** opened, which, along with two more Strip entries—**Treasure Island** and **Luxor**—gave a $2-billion boost to the local economy.

The recent era of "bigger and better" began in the mid-1990s with the $550-million **Stratosphere** and its 1,149-foot tower making it the tallest building west of the Mississippi. This was soon followed by **Monte Carlo**, the $350-million joint-venture between Mirage Resorts Inc. and Circus Circus Enterprises Inc., and the $460-million **New York–New York**, which mirrors the Manhattan skyline.

In 1998, the much-anticipated $1.6-billion **Bellagio** made the scene, followed a year later with the opening of the $950-million **Mandalay Bay Resort & Casino** and **Four Seasons Hotel Las Vegas** complex. **Hilton** entered the hotel sweepstakes with its $760-million **Paris–Las Vegas Casino Resort**, highlighted by a re-creation of the Eiffel Tower. The end-of-the-century boom continued with the opening of the $1.5-billion **Venetian Resort Hotel Casino** megaresort on the site of the old **Sands**. Scheduled to open as we went to press is a reinvented **Aladdin Las Vegas**, a $1.2-billion resort on the site of what was once the **Aladdin Hotel**.

A word to the wise: The city's scale can be deceptive. Individually, each of its amenity-packed resorts is manageable; collectively, they converge into a destination of daunting proportion. Savvy visitors explore small sections of the town at a time. But with an Egyptian pyramid next door to a Bavarian castle across the street from a mini-Manhattan down the block from a South Seas' pirate hideaway and a three-ring circus under a pink-and-white big top, the nature of the city delightfully defies conventional touristic logic and encourages all comers to indulge in its carefully cultivated fantasy.

**1 Olympic Gardens** This is the classiest burlesque show in town, a real gentlemen's—and ladies'—club (there's a private room where women can take in a show by male performers), where all the dancers are in admirably good shape. The audience is generally well dressed, well mannered, and well entertained. The drinks are noted for their fair weights and measures and are often on special. ◆ Admission. Daily 2PM-6AM. 1531 Las Vegas Blvd S (between E Oakey Blvd and Park Paseo). 385.9361

Hotel & Casino

**2 Stratosphere Tower, Hotel & Casino** $$
Opened in 1996, this $550-million property suffered some setbacks during its short life. However, in 1998 corporate mogul Carl Icahn was granted a license to operate the hotel and save it from impending bankruptcy. Icahn invested $100 million to build a new 1,000-room tower that increased room capacity to 2,500. The hotel features a massive 97,000-square-foot casino, six themed restaurants, a shopping mall, a showroom, and lounge. Although a bit off-the-beaten Strip, it boasts unsurpassed views from the 12-story observation tower, along with the **High Roller** roller coaster and **Big Shot** that rockets thrill seekers 160 feet in the air. ◆ 2000 Las Vegas Blvd S (at S Main St). 380.7777, 800/998.6937; fax 380.7732; www.stratlv.com ♿

Within Stratosphere Tower, Hotel & Casino:

**Stratosphere Casino** Here you'll find the best odds in town: Certified 98 percent or better returns on every dollar slot in the house (an unprecedented guarantee), positive video-poker machines (some have nearly a one percent player edge), single-zero roulette (which cuts the house advantage in half from all other roulette wheels in town), and 100 times odds at the craps tables (which cuts the house advantage on a bet to nearly nothing). There are few better places to play in all of Las Vegas. ♦ Daily 24 hours. 380.7777

**Stratosphere Tower** In 40 seconds, high-speed elevators whisk you up to the 12-story pod—the highest point in Las Vegas—at the 780- to 900-foot level. Floor-to-ceiling windows afford incredible views, and on a clear day you might even see the states of Arizona and California. ♦ Admission. Daily 24 hours. Level eight. 380.7777

Within Stratosphere Tower:

**Top of the World** ★★★★$$$$ If the casinos don't send you into a spin, then take in the lofty dining experience atop the **Stratosphere Tower**. The elegant restaurant affords diners panoramic views as it revolves once every hour. The menu is just as captivating: Try the chicken satay and potato-leek-garlic soup. Heartier appetites will enjoy prime filet mignon or fillet of almond-crusted salmon with mashed potatoes and baby vegetables. Desserts such as the towering chocolate "Stratosphere" are as breathtaking as the views. ♦ American ♦ Daily lunch and dinner. Reservations required. 380.7777

**Montana's** ★★$$ An Old West–style setting complete with log decor and wood floors greets guests who enjoy prime beef and fresh seafood dishes. Also on the menu are barbecued ribs, beef brisket, and honey-fried chicken. Don't forget side dishes of baked beans, country coleslaw, or the tasty house fries. ♦ Steak house ♦ Daily dinner. 382.4446

**3 Pamplemousse** ★★★★$$$ An attractive wine cellar at the entrance is the first indication of wonderful things to come at this charming, intimate French country restaurant. There's no menu—waiters recite the evening's offerings and describe their preparations and sauces. Specialties include veal medaillons with baked apples, many varieties of fresh fish, and sliced duckling imaginatively presented. Be sure to save room for dessert—profiteroles and *coupe maison* (ice cream topped with mixed fruit and whipped cream) are two outstanding choices. ♦ Continental ♦ Tu-Su dinner. Reservations recommended. 400 E Sahara Ave (at Santa Rita Dr). 733.2066 &

**4 Holy Cow! Casino** If you're in the mood, head for this popular casino and micro-brewery, under the same ownership as **Big Dog's Bar and Grill**. A 10-foot black-spotted cow with pink neon sunglasses grazes above the front door. In fact, every-thing here is colored Holstein black on white. Check out the Cow History of Moovies posters: *Amoodeus, Termoonator, Dr. Zhivacow, Cowsablanca, Ben Herd*. This microbrewery was the first (1993) to buck the mixed drink convention—the risk paid off

nicely. As you might guess, the grill serves specialty hamburgers. ♦ Daily 24 hours. 2423 Las Vegas Blvd S (between E St. Louis and E Sahara Aves). 732.2697

**5 Bonanza Gifts** The big sign out front claims that this is the "World's Largest Gift Store." Las Vegas hype notwithstanding, it might very well be. If you can't find a souvenir from among the address books, eyeglass holders, change purses, X-rated towels, T-shirts, place mats, picture books, fans, bells, bowls, mugs, shot glasses, piggy banks, plastic cups, sunglasses, earrings, shopping bags, hats, ashtrays, hot plates, party napkins, dice clocks, chips, cigarette lighters, tie tacks, and pill boxes, then you aren't really trying. ♦ Daily 8AM-midnight. 2460 Las Vegas Blvd S (at W Sahara Ave). 385.7359

**6 Golden Steer** ★★★$$$ This institution has corralled its share of famished masses since 1962. Don't let the prosaic exterior put you off; inside you'll find a typically overblown, overscaled Las Vegas eatery. The large lounge is filled with cushy high-backed chairs and has a massive wooden bar featuring one of the best-looking liquor displays in the state. The labyrinthine Western-decorated dining rooms can seat nearly 300 at one time, often feeding a thousand diners a night. The brawny brass bovine by the door does clue you in on the menu. Massive cuts of beef are the specialty, though you can also order quail, pheasant, rock partridge, frogs' legs, and Italian-style chicken and veal. ♦ Steak house ♦ Daily dinner. 308 W Sahara Ave (between Fairfield Ave and Tam Dr). 384.4470

# ♤SAHARA

**7 Sahara Hotel & Casino** $$ The sixth hotel to open on the young Strip was built in 1952 by the Del Webb Construction Company, a Phoenix-based firm that had worked on the **Flamingo Hotel** for Bugsy Siegel a few years earlier. Webb had learned a lesson or two on the previous project and garnered 20 ownership points in exchange for under-taking this one. Over the years it's gone from 200 to more than 2,000 rooms. With a recent $100-million renovation and expansion, it has been transformed into a Moroccan-themed resort and casino triple its original size. Popular with all ages is the new **Sahara Speedworld,** a virtual-reality Indy car racing game, where daredevils soar at high speed along the streets of Las Vegas. Only a two-minute cab ride away from the **Convention Center,** it's especially popular during trade shows. ♦ 2535 Las Vegas Blvd S (at E Sahara Ave). 737.2111, 800/634.6666; fax 735.5921; www.pacap.com/sahara &

Within the Sahara Hotel & Casino:

**Sahara Casino** This is Valhalla for video-poker players, with high jackpots on the progressive machines, and 1,300 such slot machines as well as 51 gaming tables were recently added. There are also several four-coin machines scattered around the casino (most machines require five coins for you to qualify for the big royal-flush jackpot; a four-coiner eliminates 20 percent of your risk). The slot club offers excellent perks, and the special gambling promotions—which change frequently—can be quite enticing; ask for the latest details. ♦ Daily 24 hours. 737.2111

**House of Lords** ★★$$$$ English decor and a classic London-style bar set the mood for this elegant gourmet restaurant. The chef's specialty here is veal, so be sure to try the succulent veal chop. Also scrumptious are the Dover sole Brittany (with lemon butter, shrimp, and capers), 26-ounce porterhouse, and rack of lamb. ♦ Continental ♦ Daily dinner. Reservations recommended. 737.2111

**Turf Club Deli** ★$ Chicken soup with matzo balls is the star of the menu at one of the most authentic kosher-style delis in a Las Vegas hotel. The mile-high cold-cut sandwiches, with names like Maven, Monte Cohen, and Abba, appear on light or Russian rye, pumpernickel, or a bagel. ♦ Deli ♦ Daily breakfast and lunch. 737.2111

**Sahara Steak House** ★★$$ The waterfalls and twinkling stars in this Moroccan-style dining room are so enchanting they might well be a stage set. The steaks and prime ribs are crowd pleasers, as are the chicken, lamb chops, and seafood specialties. Desserts won't disappoint either. ♦ Steak house ♦ Daily dinner. Reservations recommended. 737.2111 &

**8 Corner of the Strip and Sahara Avenue** Vacant for 37 years, the southwest corner of the Strip and Sahara Avenue is the former site of **El Rancho Vegas,** the first hotel-casino on the highway beyond the city limits. The resort was erected in 1941 and endured a number of mobster bosses, including Bugsy Siegel himself. In 1960, it burned to the ground in a spectacular—and suspicious—fire. A decade later **Howard Hughes** bought the lot; it was sold in 1995 to **William Bennett,** who owns the **Sahara** across the street. Believed to be one of the most valuable pieces of real estate

in the country, if not the world, its future has been widely discussed. But if Bennett has any plans for it, he's not talking.

**9 Wet'n Wild** This splashy amusement park is just the thing for kids who are bored with video arcades and the hotel pool. A dozen rides, slides, and tides include **Der Stuka,** a 75-foot near-vertical drop; **Blue Niagara,** a six-story, 300-foot-long blue water tube; a **Wave Pool** with four-foot swells; the 300-yard-long **Lazy River;** and more. ♦ Admission. Daily early Apr-Oct. 2601 Las Vegas Blvd S (between Riviera Blvd and E Sahara Ave). 737.3819, 800/565.0786

**10 Guinness World of Records Museum** The quite astounding collection displayed here features freaks of nature, quirks of fate, and extremes of physiology, behavior, topography, and human endeavor. For example, the world's heaviest man tipped the scales at a stout 1,400 pounds, while the heaviest woman weighed 840 pounds. The oldest man lived for 121 years. The most-often-married man went to the altar 28 times, a feat that undoubtedly puts a gleam into the eyes of this city's wedding chapel owners. Video loops show the highest shallow dive and 1,380,000 dominoes falling in perpetuity. There's an interesting Las Vegas exhibit, with historical black-and-white photos, tapes of local world records being set, and other trivia. ♦ Admission. Daily. 2780 Las Vegas Blvd S (between Circus Circus Dr and W Sahara Ave). 792.3766

**11 Circus Circus** $ In 1968 this circus pulled into town with just a big top and a casino geared toward high rollers; it nearly went bankrupt in the first few years. Today a resort with 3,800 of Las Vegas's gaudiest guest rooms, it caters to cautious gamesters and families, practically gives away food, and is owned by the most profitable casino corporation in the world. In fact, the family formula has been so successful that similar theme hotels and amusement parks are sprouting all over Las Vegas. But this extravaganza will not be overshadowed. The massive portico is billion-bulb brilliant. Behind it stands the pink-and-white candy-striped **Big Top,** housing the 100,000-square-foot casino and circus stage. The **Midway** features shooting games, knockdown doll games, and balloon and dart games with stuffed animals as prizes. The neon "Lucky the Clown" presides over a 50-ton marquee; his crazy expression is a perfect reflection of the bedlam within.

The world's largest permanent circus rocks 'round the clock, packed with more fun seekers at one time than an average county fair might see in a month. Trapeze and high-wire acts, dancing poodles, motorcycle daredevils, jugglers, acrobats, and the like perform on the mezzanine stage. The shows, which run continuously from 11AM to midnight every day, consistently win the "Best Free Show" award in the *Review-Journal*'s annual reader poll. Knock over the bottles, watergun races, shooting galleries, and other carnival games surround the stage. The buffet is always overrun with masticating hordes. ◆ 2880 Las Vegas Blvd S (at Circus Circus Dr). 734.0410, 800/634.3450; fax 734.2268; www.circuscircus-lasvegas.com &

Within Circus Circus:

**Circus Circus Casino** Attention tightwads! This is the joint for you. Blackjack games with two-dollar minimums abound, nickel slots are the status quo, and you can play keno all night long with a $20 bill. That is, if you can find a parking space within walking distance, an empty seat at a 21 table, or a slot machine that's not being jealously played or guarded. ◆ Daily 24 hours. 734.0410

**Steak House** ★★$$$ This is the one tranquil corner in the **Circus Circus** madhouse: a subdued dining room with a dark-wood interior that wouldn't be out of place in an English manor. A glass-walled refrigerator stores a ton or two of beef sides, which are cut into slabs and grilled on a mesquite broiler in the center of the room. Top sirloin, filet mignon, and porterhouse steaks, prime rib, surf 'n' turf, swordfish, and chicken are among the choices, all accompanied by big, fat, baked potatoes. ◆ American ◆ Daily dinner. Reservations recommended. 794.3767

Behind Circus Circus:

**Adventuredome** This five-acre, glass-enclosed amusement complex, featuring a 15-story mountain and a 90-foot waterfall, is America's largest indoor theme park. Thrill seekers will opt for a ride on the **Canyon Blaster**—the world's only indoor roller coaster—which reaches a top speed of 55 miles per hour while careening around a vertiginous double loop and double cork-screw. The park's newest action ride, the **Inverter,** swoops passengers 50 feet into the air, then makes a 180° inversion before going full circle. Also look for the **Fun House Express,** an Imax motion-simulator ride; the **Rim Runner,** a boat ride which rises 60 feet into the air before dropping down a camelback shoot; and the **Xtreme Zone,** a four-story rock-climbing wall for added adventure. ◆ Admission. M-Th, Su 10AM-6PM; F-Sa 10AM-midnight Sept-May; Daily 10AM-midnight June-Aug. 794.3939

Adjacent to Circus Circus:

 **Circusland RV Park** The resort's 35-acre campground can accommodate 421 RVs of all sizes and still has room for all the comforts of home: a disposal station, grocery store, laundry facilities, two pools, a sauna and Jacuzzi, recreation room, and playground. ◆ Reservation deposit required. 500 Circus Circus Dr (between Las Vegas Blvd S and Industrial Rd). 794.3757

**11 Slots-A-Fun** Next door to the **Big Top,** this is about as close to a downtown grind joint (one that caters to low-stakes players) as you'll find on the fancy Las Vegas Strip. A four-reel, one-dollar slot machine is so close to the street you can almost pull the handle from your car window. The minimum bet on the craps table is *raised* to two dollars for the Saturday night crowd. The blackjack tables remain a buck all week long. The snack bar also appeals to penny-pinchers, handing out free popcorn and serving shrimp or crab cocktails, waffles, hot dogs, chicken wings, pizza by the slice, tacos, and strawberry shortcake for a pittance. ◆ Daily 24 hours. 2880 Las Vegas Blvd S (between Stardust Rd and Circus Circus Dr). 734.0410 &

**12 Riviera Hotel** $$$ In 1955 this was the first high-rise on the Strip—then nine stories tall. The dubious beneficiary of several decades' worth of expansions and renovations, the hotel has an amalgamation of tacked-on towers that have turned it into a maze, and your room can be a mile from your car. But there's so much happening on site that this might not be an inconvenience after all. There are five restaurants, a good buffet, sprawling fast-food court, and choice of four shows. There's always a show-and-dinner tandem ticket—one of the most affordable nights out in town. When you're not living the lush life you can lounge at the pool, work out at the health club or on the tennis courts, shop at the upscale stores, or, if the chance presents itself, get married in the wedding chapel. ◆ 2901 Las Vegas Blvd S (at Riviera Blvd). 734.5110, 800/634.6753; fax 731.3265; www.theriviera.com &

Within the Riviera Hotel:

**Riviera Casino** At 125,000 square feet, this is still one of the largest casinos in the world. The behemoth has a wide assortment of games as well as a lively lounge featuring Monday night jazz. ◆ Daily 24 hours. 734.5110

# Low Rolling in Vegas

Las Vegas resorts are known for their opulent suites, sumptuous gourmet dining rooms, and sky's-the-limit gambling for high-rolling customers. But there's no need to spend a fortune to enjoy some of the city's most entertaining attractions.

Every true low-roller tour begins **Downtown** at **Binion's Horseshoe.** When you walk through the door, proceed directly to the **Million Dollar** display, where a house photographer will take your picture in front of $1 million in cash. The photograph is free. If you find yourself on a waiting list take a seat at the bar and order an imported beer for less than a dollar. Or if you're really hungry, the hotel features a huge $2.75 ham, steak, and eggs breakfast served 24 hours.

Another sure winner at **Binion's** is the ham-and-bean special at the snack bar. At $1.99, it will leave you with plenty of cash left over to play the machines.

Still hungry? Then try the shrimp cocktail for less than a dollar at the **Golden Gate** and take a seat in the lounge of this quaint club and listen to veteran piano players knock out your favorites for free.

To quench your thirst, try the $1.25 imported beers at the **Golden Nugget,** surely the only four-star resort on the planet with inexpensive drink specials.

You say you've had enough food already? Time your trip Downtown just right, and you'll be treated to the nightly light show under the canopy at the *Fremont Street Experience*. With two-million flashing lights, it's vintage Vegas entertainment.

Since "free" is the best price available for entertainment in Las Vegas, proceed to the **Imperial Palace** on the **Strip** and receive two free tickets to the hotel's multimillion-dollar auto collection. The hotel gives away two-million tickets a year to its popular car museum. You'll see autos owned by everyone from Elvis to Hitler—and you can't beat the price of admission.

Now cross the street, fight the crowds if necessary, and take in the nightly pirate show at **Treasure Island.** If you're traveling with a first-time visitor to Las Vegas, place a friendly wager that the pirates will prevail over the British in the mock battle. (It's a sure bet: the pirates *always* beat the British.)

One last note: When in Las Vegas, sign up for *everything*. This includes slot clubs, where players receive everything from free meals to discounts on rooms depending on how much they gamble, to those daily casino drawings for prizes ranging from show tickets to new Cadillacs. (It may sound corny, but people actually do win.) Of course, the idea is to get you and keep you inside the casino, where you are likely to pass the time by playing the machines and table games.

But if you keep your wits about you, your low-roller tour may well prove to be the highlight of your stay.

---

# *Ristorante Italiano*

**Ristorante Italiano** ★★$$$ Transport yourself to Venice simply by stepping into this Northern Italian dining room. Though it's sequestered deep in the hotel, the trattoria has windows that magically look onto the charms of *Venezia*—via murals of the Rialto, the Bridge of Sighs, and St. Mark's Square. Of course the food is also evocative of *Italia*. The *pasta e fagioli* (with beans); black-and-white fettuccine with shrimp, garlic, white wine, and sweet cream; veal chop stuffed with spinach and gorgonzola cheese served in a sweet Madeira wine sauce; and tiramisù will elicit a *"delizioso"* from all. ♦ Northern Italian ♦ Daily dinner. Reservations recommended. 794.9363

**World's Fare Buffet** ★$ A good alternative to the **Circus Circus** buffet across the street is this all-you-can-eat smorgasbord.

Fresh rotisserie-cooked chicken, pork loin, ribs, and beef roasts are featured. All the traditional buffet items are also there for the taking. Breakfast spreads include eggs, pancakes, bacon, sausage, and an assortment of rolls. ♦ American ♦ Daily breakfast, lunch, and dinner. 734.5110

**Mardi Gras Food Court** $ A convenient concentration of fast food under one roof, among the array of familiar places to grab a quick bite here are: **El Pollo Loco, Taco Rico, Wienerschnitzel, Forenza Pasta and Pizza, La Patisserie, New York Deli, Burger King, Baskin-Robbins,** and **Dunkin' Donuts.** ♦ Fast food ♦ Daily breakfast, lunch, and dinner

### Kristofer's Steak House ★★★$$$
Come here for superb aged prime cuts of steak and choose from among 32 varieties of sauce to add to the flavor. Delicious baked potatoes with cinnamon and butter and creamed spinach make fine side dishes. Best bets for desserts include the outrageous mint chocolate bonbons or the mile-high mud pie with Oreo cookie crust. ◆ Steak house ◆ Daily dinner. Reservations recommended. 794.9233

**The Riviera's Shows** The **Riviera** is the entertainment center of the Entertainment Capital. *Splash II: The Voyage of a Lifetime* whisks showgoers into the theater with a cruise-ship setting that travels across a glass-bottom bridge. Two hundred theatergoers are equipped with laser guns to provide an interactive relationship between audience, performers, musicians, and lighting effects! You can also take in top comedians at the **Riviera Comedy Club.** Dragsters do their turns on Madonna, Joan Rivers, Cher, Tina Turner, Bette Midler, and even a chorus line in *An Evening at La Cage.* And for some nearly naked bump-and-grind antics, check out *Crazy Girls.* ◆ 794.9301

**13** **Westward-Ho Hotel & Casino** $$ This sprawling complex of two- and four-story courtyard units constituting 1,000 rooms stretches all the way from the Strip to Industrial Road. The room rates are a delight to the frugal, and there's a wing of two-bedroom, one-bath apartments, each with a living room, TV, mini-bar, and refrigerator, also at a reasonable tariff. Also available are seven swimming pools, a free airport shuttle, a coffee shop, a breakfast, lunch, and dinner buffet, and a popular slot club that packs the small casino with handle-pullers and button-pushers; the 9/6 progressive video-poker machines often yield player-positive results. Split the snack bar's renowned two-pound strawberry shortcake. ◆ 2900 Las Vegas Blvd S (between Stardust Rd and Circus Circus Dr). 731.2900, 800/634.6651; www.westwardho.com ＆

**14** **Peppermill Cafe and Lounge** ★$$
Anyone familiar with the **Peppermill's** psychedelic casinos in the border burgs of Mesquite, Wendover, and Reno is in for a surprise upon entering this understated restaurant and bar. The dining room resembles a **Denny's,** but thanks to the trademark silk plants and flowers, it has the upscale air of a faux fern bar. It's an excellent asylum (so to speak) from the lunacy of the Strip, with plush carpeting, commodious velour couches, and coffee tables providing privacy and tranquillity perfect for a close encounter. Offerings include a large selection of burgers, sandwiches, steaks, seafood, and chicken; all entrées are accompanied by a fresh spinach salad or soup. The burgers are a hefty half pound, and the steak is all USDA choice. Traditional desserts include peach melba; peach, cherry, or apple deep-dish cobbler; and an incredibly creamy cheesecake. ◆ American ◆ Daily 24 hours. 2985 Las Vegas Blvd S (between Convention Center Dr and Riviera Blvd). 735.4177

**14** **Silver City** The table limits are low, and the food and drinks are very inexpensive at this casino. The mining theme, with some serious excavation action taking place above the aptly named "pit," is a nod to the seminal event of Nevada's history: the 1859 discovery of the Comstock Lode, the largest silver and gold deposits ever found in the continental US. The casino is named after the town of Silver City, which sits atop the Comstock, 15 miles east of Reno. ◆ Daily 24 hours. 3001 Las Vegas Blvd S (at Convention Center Dr). 732.4152

**15** **Stardust Resort & Casino** $$$ The largest casino in the world when it opened in 1958—baccarat made its first Nevada appearance here—this resort has had its ups, downs, and ups again over the years. In 1990, it regained much of its former glory with the addition of a 1,500-room tower. The latest renovation, a $25-million facelift expected to be completed by the beginning of the millennium, will include new exterior lighting on its 15-story-high signature sign, a remodeled porte cochere and entryway, and refurbished guestrooms. On your casino downtime, catch the Ted Lorenz production, "Enter the Night," which highlights classic Las Vegas showgirls as well as variety acts. 3000 Las Vegas Blvd S (between Stardust Rd and Circus Circus Dr). 732.6111, 800/634.6757; fax 732.6296; www.vegas.com/hotels/stardust ＆

Within the Stardust Resort & Casino:

**Ralph's Diner** $ A fun place for a bit of nostalgia, this neo-1950s diner sports black and white tiles and individual jukeboxes in the booths. Breakfast is served all day (the omelettes are four-egg affairs). Burgers and such dominate the menu, but there are also blue-plate specials and a full soda fountain with floats, sundaes, shakes, and malts. The waitresses' uniforms are apropos the period, as are their attitudes—often boogying to your table to the oldies' beat. Management's motto? "If you're not served in 5 minutes, you'll get served in 8 or 9, maybe 12." Relax! ♦ American ♦ Daily breakfast, lunch, and dinner. 732.6111

**Tony Roma's** ★★$$ Among the best rib joints in the city, this informal eatery offers slabs of pork and beef coated with a spicy barbecue sauce. The meat loaf is another great hit. Be sure to try the onion rings on the side. ♦ American ♦ Daily dinner. 732.6111

**Enter the Night** This production is Las Vegas's attempt to be avant-garde. The show is presented as a dream, or at least a waking tribute to twilight and the passions it conceals and reveals. A seamless fusion of such disparate elements as erotic and tap dancing, gymnastics and skating, laser effects and costuming, the pace is languid, and the entertainment is concentrated, enhancing the originality of this surprisingly thought-provoking performance. ♦ Admission. M, Su 8PM; W-Sa 7:30-10:30PM. 732.6111

16 **Nippon** ★★$$ With *shabu shabu* and sushi bars, a serene dining room, a solicitous staff, and excellent food, you'd think this Japanese jewel would always be crowded. But except when the nearby **Convention Center** is hosting an out-of-town entourage (when the restaurant is jammed), meals here are quiet and leisurely. The *yaki udon* (buckwheat noodles in broth) served in a big black kettle will satisfy those who haven't yet developed a taste for the seafood nibbles. ♦ Japanese ♦ M-F lunch and dinner; Sa-Su dinner. 101 Convention Center Dr (between Paradise Rd and Las Vegas Blvd S). 735.5565

17 **Piero's** ★★★$$$$ Celebrities and sports figures always find their way to this popular restaurant. For private dining, ask for seating in one of the many alcoves or dimly lit booths; if you're more of a party animal, there's also a massive bar. The service is excellent and the wine list extraordinary. Among the specialties are *zuppa di pesce* (lobster, clams, mussels, shrimp, scallops, and calamari in light fish broth with a touch of tomato), veal chop *Gran Duca D'Alba* (sautéed with mushrooms in a creamy brandy sauce), whole kosher chicken, osso buco, and such creative pastas as *linguine all'aragosta* (with fresh lobster in a light tomato sauce) and *fettuccine puttanesca* (with capers, olives, anchovies, and oregano in a tomato sauce). ♦ Italian ♦ Daily dinner. Reservations required. 355 Convention Center Dr (at Paradise Rd). 369.2305

18 **Alpine Village Inn** ★★$$ Recalling the town square of a Bavarian village, the main dining room here is replete with quaint street scenes on the walls. The waiters wear lederhosen, the waitresses are in dirndls, and the table service is primarily pewter. Entrées—Wiener schnitzel, beef fondue, sauerbraten, and steaks—are accompanied by a loaf of bread, as many tureens of chicken soup as you can eat, green beans, sauerkraut, potato pancakes, and dessert. Downstairs at the **Rathskeller,** you can enjoy a more casual menu of burgers, pizza, and sandwiches, as well as a piano sing-along. ♦ German ♦ Daily dinner. Reservations recommended. 3003 Paradise Rd (between Convention Center Dr and Riviera Blvd). 734.6888

# Hilton

19 **Las Vegas Hilton** $$$ When this hotel opened in 1969, Las Vegas had never seen a property with a 2,000-seat theater, 3,000 employees, and more than 1,500 rooms. For a while, Kirk Kerkorian, who financed the $60-million price tag out of his own pocket, stole the spotlight from Howard Hughes, who was in the middle of his own legendary spending spree. When Hilton purchased the property two years later, it became the first major hotel corporation to enter the casino business. Another 1,500 rooms were added in 1973, making it the largest resort hotel in the world, a title it held until it was eclipsed in 1990 by the **Flamingo Hilton** and then again in 1993 by the new **MGM Grand Hotel/Casino.** Today the hotel has a room count of 3,174 and primarily caters to business visitors attending the 2,500 conventions and trade shows that descend each year. It offers 250,000 square feet of meeting space, 12 restaurants, a 10-acre third-floor recreation deck (with a 385,000-gallon pool), a theater that's been playing **Andrew Lloyd Webber**'s *Starlight Express* since 1993, two shopping promenades, and a nightclub. The hotel is divided into clearly articulated sections allowing easy access to the vast meeting spaces and ballrooms by a walkway to the **Las Vegas Convention Center,** and separate entrances to the hotel and casino. ♦ 3000 Paradise Rd (between Desert Inn Rd and Karen Ave). 732.5111, 800/732.7117; fax 732.5834; www.hilton.com/hotels ⬥

Within the Las Vegas Hilton:

**Las Vegas Hilton Casino** This casino is huge: 85,000 square feet filled with thousands of slots and hundreds of table games. The race and sports room is so large it's called a super book; its walls are lined with 46 TV screens. ♦ Daily 24 hours. 732.5111

**Benihana Village** ★★★$$$ In the most exotic corner of the otherwise ordinary hotel, this popular chain restaurant inhabits a stylized Japanese village, with a trio of dining rooms and bars. The meat, fish, and vegetable dishes are prepared at the table hibachi-style in the main room; Japanese grilled seafood is served in the **Seafood Grille;** and Chinese food is offered in the excellent **Garden of the Dragon.** ♦ Asian ♦ Daily dinner. Reservations recommended. 732.5801

**Le Montrachet** ★★★★$$$$ In a sophisticated break with the quick-and-copious dining-out theory that rules Las Vegas, this place embodies the essence of French cuisine, European elegance, and artistic attention to detail. Flowers are everywhere, and the table settings are extravagant. The menu is seasonal, and everything—from the pheasant-breast mousse appetizer to such entrées as veal chops with mussel puree to the Swiss chocolate soufflé dessert—consists of only the freshest ingredients prepared with a distinctly French flair in the seasonings and sauces. There is an impressive wine list. ♦ French ♦ Daily dinner. Reservations recommended; jacket required. 732.5801

**Star Trek: The Experience** This $50-million entertainment center takes visitors on a futuristic journey that explores the 24th century through a variety of intergalatic devices. The three-part program includes: "The Exhibit," a museumlike tour of authentic *Star Trek* props, costumes, and memorabilia used in the TV and motion picture series; "The Voyage," a 22-minute simulated ride that "beams" trekkers into outer space; and "Deep Space Nine Promenade," where visitors interact with virtual reality stations, computer games—and more down-to-earth diversions including restaurants and gift shops. ♦ Daily. 732.5111

Within Star Trek: The Experience:

**Quark's Bar & Restaurant** ★★$$ Trekkies of all ages will enjoy this sci-fi-themed place replete with spacecrafts beaming down from the ceiling. Earthly starters run the gamut from chips and dip to fried calamari and foot-high stacks of crispy onion rings. House favorites include Captain Sulu's chicken salad and bayou linguine (with chicken andouille, shrimp, fresh vegetables, and Cajun sauce). If you have a sweet tooth, try the crème brûlée with raspberry sauce—a definite meltdown. ♦ American ♦ Daily lunch and dinner. 697.8725 ♿

**20 Las Vegas Convention Center** This town has been a convention destination since 1935, when 5,000 southern California Shriners converged here. As early as the mid-1940s, local boosters realized that conventions could fill hotel rooms and casinos during weekdays and low seasons, as well as help Las Vegas improve its image as a place where respectable people could hold business meetings. The Clark County Fair and Recreation Board was established in the boom year of 1955 to supervise events and encourage conventions. It took another four years for the site selection, design, financing, and construction of the convention center to be completed. The $5.3-million complex consisted of a 20,000-square-foot rotunda and a 90,000-square-foot exhibit hall. In 1959, fewer than one hundred conventions took place in Las Vegas, with a total attendance of roughly 50,000.

The current convention center, a 10-minute walk from the Strip, was most recently expanded in 1992. The 33-year-old rotunda was torn down and replaced with a fifth hall, giving the center a total of 1.3-million square feet of exhibitor space. The second-largest show facility in the country, more than 2,500 conventions and trade shows are held here each year. From the 2,500-participant American Association of Meat Processors to the 130,000 attendees of the Construction Manufacturers Association gathering, conventions pump more than $3 billion into the Las Vegas annual budget, overcrowd the town in a single bound, and inflate accommodation prices by as much as 300 percent. When you're planning a visit to Las Vegas, you should first find out how many conventioneers will be in town at the time of your trip. ♦ 3150 Paradise Rd (between Desert Inn Rd and Karen Ave). 892.0711; fax 892.2824

**21 Sun Harbor Budget Suites** $ This large and centrally located motel features 639 two-room units with kitchenettes (you'll have to supply your own plates, pots, and silverware). These mini-suites are especially popular with travelers staying a week or longer—the weekly rates further discount the already budget prices. Another plus: It's on the corner of Industrial Road, which is the only Westside shortcut to the busy Strip and interstate. ♦ 1500 Stardust Rd (at Industrial Rd). 732.1500

---

If you play perfect basic strategy for eight hours at a $1 blackjack table, your expected loss is about $1.

**22 Las Vegas Sporting House** Covering 65,000 square feet, this is an impressive athletic club. You can work out on dozens of cardiovascular and fitness machines, sign up for an aerobics class, play full-court basketball, volleyball, racquetball, squash, or tennis, run on an outdoor track with parcourse stations, swim laps in the 25-meter indoor pool, or repair to the Jacuzzi, sauna, or steam bath. ◆ Admission. Daily 24 hours. 3025 Industrial Rd (between Stardust Rd and Circus Circus Dr). 733.8999

**23 The New Frontier Hotel & Gambling Hall** $$ The name of this establishment has undergone a long evolution. The **Last Frontier** opened in 1942, the second hotel on the infant Strip and the last to embrace a Western motif. The building was razed in 1955 and replaced with the **New Frontier,** which, in the spirit of the times, had an outer-space theme; it was demolished in 1966. A year later Howard Hughes bought it and gave birth to the reincarnated hotel with its present moniker. The Elardi family took over in 1988 and opted to retain the name. In 1998, the hotel was purchased by Ruffin Gaming, who kept the name while transforming accommodations and the casino into a modern country-western motif. The ballroom was converted to **Gilley's Dance Hall, Saloon & Bar-B-Que,** with Gilley's All-Star Band playing nightly. Western dining, the famous mechanical bull, a video wall, and a merchandise store round out the activities at Gilley's. There are 1,000 guest rooms, including 500 in the modern **Atrium Suites Tower**—15 floors of reasonably priced two-room suites overlooking a picturesque lagoon and courtyard. ◆ 3120 Las Vegas Blvd S (between Fashion Show Dr and Stardust Rd). 794.8200, 800/634.6966; fax 794.8326 &

Within the New Frontier Hotel & Gambling Hall:

**Frontier Gambling Hall** This casino is a favorite haunt of old-timers, who gamble here like in the good old days—before the MBAs, CPAs, and PhDs started running the show. It sports one of the only bingo rooms on the Strip. Single-deck blackjack is the norm. ◆ Daily 24 hours. 794.8200

The worst flash flood in Las Vegas history occurred on 4 July 1975. When it was over, cars were stacked five deep in the Caesars Palace parking lot.

**Margarita's** ★$ Warm-from-the-griddle tortillas (not chips), along with guacamole, bean dip, and salsa, are brought to your table when you sit down, possibly to fuel the decision-making process of selecting an entrée from the extensive menu. Tacos, burritos, enchiladas, tostadas, fajitas, and tamales are served, and the *especiales* include *carne asada* (steak with spices), chili Colorado (chunks of beef cooked in a red-chili sauce), and *camarones* (shrimp). If you're really hungry, try one of the special-plate dinners. *Margaritas grandes* come in 45-ounce stemmed glasses (which you're free to keep). ◆ Mexican ◆ Daily breakfast, lunch, and dinner. Reservations recommended. 794.8200

## THE DESERT INN

**24 Sheraton Desert Inn** $$$$ When the original **Desert Inn** (often called the "D.I.") opened in 1950, it was the fifth hotel on the Strip and was known as "Wilbur Clark's joint." Clark started out as a busboy in San Diego restaurants and a craps dealer on gambling ships off the coast of Southern California until finally building his dream hotel-casino. With construction half finished, Clark ran out of money. He sweated for two years until Moe Dalitz, underworld boss of Kentucky and Ohio, agreed to complete the job—with Clark remaining on as the law-abiding front man. Once Dalitz demonstrated how the transition from gangster to executive could be accomplished, mobsters nationwide began migrating to Las Vegas with a vengeance.

Today, with a recent $200-million renovation, the glass-facade structure showcases a lavish Palm Beach–style lobby with vaulted ceiling, polished marble floors, and custom-designed 30-foot murals above the granite reception area. This facility, with 715 deluxe rooms (including 95 suites), concierge service, a first-run showroom, golf course, comprehensive health club, tennis courts, swimming pool with sandy beach, cabanas, and volleyball court, coupled with award-winning restaurants, is certainly among the most elegant in town.

The refurbished health spa now boasts 20 treatment rooms for a variety of massage therapy, 2,000 square feet of workout space and equipment, complimentary juice and fruit bar, sauna, and steam rooms. Locker rooms are stocked with terry robes and toiletries. ◆ 3145 Las Vegas Blvd S (between Sands Ave and E Desert Inn Rd). 733.4444, 800/634.6906; fax 733.4774; www.thedesertinn.com &

Within the Sheraton Desert Inn:

**Sheraton Desert Inn Casino** Come here to hobnob with the nabobs: a chic clientele glides through the casino, laying down stacks of blacks ($100 chips) at craps and blackjack tables with aplomb. Though the table limits are normally $5,000 per bet, if you want to go higher (and bet $10,000 or even $25,000 at a hand of cards or a roll of the dice), just ask. ♦ Daily 24 hours. 733.4444

**Portofino** ★★★$$$ Even though this restaurant is situated on the open balcony over the casino, its marble floors, black velvet booths, and lush potted foliage create an air of quiet luxury. The menu caters to most pocketbooks and all tastes, offering such affordable dishes as tortellini in vodka-spiked tomato sauce, herb-ricotta-stuffed shells, and bow tie pasta with sweet peppers and pine nuts, as well as the very expensive chateaubriand, rack of lamb with an herb-mustard crust, and lobster tail. ♦ Northern Italian ♦ Daily dinner. Reservations recommended. 733.4495

**Monte Carlo** ★★★$$$$ This is one posh and pricey restaurant—French oil paintings and gilded mirrors on the walls, crystal on the chandeliers and tables, and furniture befitting Versailles set the scene. Plan on killing half a night in these luxe surroundings from the time the appetizers (including littleneck clams, pâté, oysters Rockefeller, clams casino, and seafood crepes with lobster sauce) arrive until you polish off dessert. All is served with a dramatic continental style by suitably snooty waiters. For the main course, choose from such haute dishes as Canadian salmon with lemon-caper butter; fresh Florida stone crabs; filet mignonette sautéed with truffles and goose liver; duck in orange or cherry sauce; or Nevada quail with wild rice. ♦ French ♦ M, Th-Su dinner. Reservations recommended; jacket required. 733.4524

**25 Fashion Show Mall** If the retail anchors of this mall—**Neiman Marcus, Saks Fifth Avenue, May Company, Dillards,** and **Macy's**—don't have what you're looking for, one of the 145 boutiques surely will. **Banana Republic,** the **Gap,** and **Miller's Outpost** cover the trends; **I Love Hats** hawks you-know-what; and **Victoria's Secret** is not so secret here. Other stores to browse in are **Sharper Image, Discovery Channel, Game Keeper,** and the **Disney Store.** There's the usual preponderance of men's and women's apparel, jewelry shops, and of course a fast-food court. ♦ M-F 10AM-9PM; Sa 10AM-7PM; Su noon-6PM. 3200 Las Vegas Blvd S (at Fashion Show Dr). 369.8382 &

Within the Fashion Show Mall:

**Chin's** ★★★★$$$ Featuring modern decor designed by **Jim Cheng,** an award-winning architect, and incredibly satisfying food, this gourmet Chinese restaurant has a loyal following of locals and visitors. Hong Kong–born owner Tola Chin's imprint is on every dish. Recipes he invented, such as shredded chicken salad or crispy pudding, are often copied in other restaurants. Dim sum is offered at lunch, or you can choose from a menu that features shrimp puffs, crispy duck, lobster with mushrooms, and vegetables with meat or seafood. Special dishes are prepared on request. A piano player provides entertainment in the lounge. ♦ Chinese ♦ Daily lunch and dinner. Reservations recommended. 733.8899. Also at: Arizona Charlie's Hotel & Casino, 740 S Decatur Blvd (at Evergreen Ave). 258.5173

**Morton's of Chicago** ★★★$$$$ This branch of the Chicago-based steak house is regarded as one of the best restaurants in Las Vegas. The men's club atmosphere has been retained with a polished oak barroom, comfortable booths, and a paneled board-room for large parties. Of course steak is the raison d'être here. The extra-thick, extra-aged, extra-tender porterhouse is superb. But the broiled sea scallops wrapped in bacon, whole Maine lobster, and lemon-oregano chicken are also scrumptious. If you still have room after downing the hearty portions, the strawberries with sabayon sauce will do nicely. ♦ Steak house ♦ Daily dinner. Reservations recommended. 893.0703

**26 Treasure Island** $$$ With swaying palms atop cliffs bordering the "ocean" and a colonial Polynesian village, this $470-million, 2,900-room megaresort is a veritable South Pacific island unto itself. Starting at 11PM a lifesize British frigate sails into the bay and engages a pirate schooner in a dramatic battle, a cannonade causing impressively major damage to both ships. The crews patch up their battered craft, sail back to their respective corners, and repeat the Sisyphean performance an hour and twenty minutes later. ♦ 3300 Las Vegas Blvd S (at Spring Mountain Rd). 894.7111, 800/944.7444; fax 894.7414; www.treasureisland.com &

Within Treasure Island:

# It's a Jungle Out There

Las Vegas has often been called "a jungle," and at many of the city's top resorts that moniker is well-deserved—literally. Of course, not every animal species is represented—for that you'll have to visit the **Southern Nevada Zoological Botanical Park**—but what you will find are dolphins at **The Mirage,** flamingos at the **Tropicana.** . . . So if you're wondering if that was really an African penguin or a very short waiter waddling by, take a second look. Here's what you'll see:

**The Mirage** features Atlantic bottlenose dolphins swimming in the world's largest (2.5 million gallons) saltwater tanks. This habitat is home to four adult and three young dolphins, all rescued from the wild. Also don't miss the 20,000 gallon saltwater aquarium behind the front desk that showcases myriad tropical fish and sharks. Of course, the undisputed stars of Vegas's vast menagerie are the white tigers that appear in Siegfried & Roy's magic show. The animals live in an open-air habitat with a swimming pool, fountains, and simulated mountain terrain (colored white so they have a sense of security by blending into the background). A special slanted glass window allows visitors to view the animals round the clock.

The **Tropicana**'s "Wildlife Walk" is home to penguins, flamingos, and swans in a five-acre tropical garden pool area. Go outside and see them or ride the moving sidewalk overlooking the garden. Inside, tropical birds and reptiles are on display.

At the **Flamingo Hilton**'s lush outdoor pool area you'll find African penguins, Chilean pink flamingos, ducks, swans, and other colorful birds.

Of course, if this leaves you wanting more adventure in the animal kingdom, then head to the **Zoological Botanical Park** where Bengal tigers, African lions, monkeys, and petting zoo await. **Bonnie Springs Ranch** is a place where wildlife enthusiasts can get up close and personal with burros, horses, coyotes, deer, and bighorn sheep. There's also a petting zoo on the grounds.

---

**Buccaneer Bay** ★★★$$$ With many nooks and alcoves for intimacy, this dramatic restaurant's decor includes treasure chests, exotic cabinets, and simulated foot-thick windows overlooking **Treasure Island**'s "Bay"—complete with battleships. Not only do guests hear the guns roar, but they also feel the heat as flames break out on the ships. The theme-inspired menu covers a unique selection of seafood, beef, lamb, and desserts. Among the house specialties are Buccaneer clams (casino) and oysters topped with smoked salmon and hollandaise, lobster bisque under a puff-pastry dome, smoked salmon Napoleon (smoked salmon and herbed cream cheese between layers of fine pastry), and Pirate's Plunder for dessert—an amazing chocolate treasure chest filled with coconut rum mousse, a white chocolate treasure map, and rich dark chocolate cake.
♦ Continental ♦ Daily dinner. Reservations recommended. 894.7111

**Cirque du Soleil's Mystère** Circus Circus it ain't! This nouvelle experience is a combination of theater, dance, music, comedy, and acrobatics. The whole wild show takes place in a single ring, without animals or spoken communication, and involves the audience to an unprecedented degree. As at *Siegfried & Roy,* money can't be an object to audience members (tickets are the *third* most expensive in town); if it isn't, this is an absolute Las

Vegas must-see. (For more details, see "A Review of Revues," page 42)
♦ W-Su 7:30PM, 10:30PM. 894.7722

**27 The Venetian Resort Hotel Casino** $$$
On the site of the legendary **Sands Hotel,** this dazzling $1.5-billion megaresort pays homage to one of Italy's most exciting cities. Gracing the newly opened property is the 12-foot archangel Gabriel, overlooking **St. Mark's Square** from atop the **Campanile.** The Italian motif is captured throughout the resort's 72 acres, the public rooms, and the 3,036 suites boasting luxurious fabrics, chandeliers, and marble floors.

Just as in Venice, transportation is via a 630-foot version of the **Grand Canal.** Gondolas transport guests from the hotel to the 116,000-square-foot casino; **Madame Tussaud's Wax Museum;** and the **Grand Canal Shoppes,** which includes Warner Bros.' 55,000-square-foot venue, **Soundstage 24,** where you'll find movie-themed entertainment and retail shops, as well as strolling movie characters to provide local color. Dining is a pleasure at one of the many excellent restaurants, including Wolfgang Puck's **Postrio,** Eberhard Müller's **Lutèce,** Joachim Splichal's **Pinot Brasserie,** and Piero Selvaggio's **Valentino;** or, for those with heartier appetites, Emeril Lagasse's **Delmonico Steakhouse.** If fitness—or lack of—concerns you, visit the 65,000-square-foot **Canyon Ranch SpaClub,** a smaller version of the popular spas in Tucson and the Berkshires. At the forefront is the Wellness Center where guests can consult with a physician or nutritionist about weight loss, nutrition, or stress management. The spa also offers aerobics and relaxation classes, cardio and exercise equipment, head-to-toe body treatments, and much more. On the drawing board is the **Expo Center,** which will add another 3,000 suites—making this the largest privately owned facility of its kind in the US. ♦ 3355 Las Vegas Blvd S (between E Flamingo Rd and Sands Ave). 733.5000. 888/283.6423; fax 733.5790; www.venetian.com &

**28 Casino Royale** $$ This 150-room hotel features a 60,000-square-foot casino and a six-story, 300-car garage. Its small pit is filled with low-limit blackjack tables, along with the usual craps and roulette tables, slots, and video poker. Visitors in the know head for the upstairs lounge and snack bar when hunger strikes. Big burgers, chili dogs, Belgian waffles, shrimp cocktails, sandwiches, breakfasts, and draft beer can all be had for a song. The five window tables (plus four seats at the small counter) directly face **The Mirage,** so if it's after dark and the winds are calm, you can eat, drink, and have a ringside seat at one of the best shows in town. ♦ Daily 24 hours. 3411 Las Vegas Blvd S (between E Flamingo Rd and Sands Ave). 737.3500

**29 The Mirage** $$$$ No doubt about it. With its fire-breathing volcano, indoor rain forest, white-tiger and dolphin habitats, huge aquarium, the *Siegfried & Roy* extravaganza, high-roller casino, and overall opulence, this 3,000-room resort is the ultimate in Vegas overkill. It's also the top tourist destination in the city.

Enter these grounds, and you leave the desert far behind. A dozen waterfalls flow into a giant lagoon, ringed by hundreds of towering palm trees. A 54-foot waterfall cascades over the volcano, which punctually erupts nightly every 15 minutes (if the wind is too strong, red lights signal the volcano's temporary dormancy). The lush tropical understory grows more and more convincing as time goes by. Beyond the four bronze dolphins standing sentry at the front door, the theme continues beneath a 100-foot-high glass dome. A thick canopy of palms presides over more waterfalls and tropical foliage. After a drink in the **Lagoon Saloon,** take a peek at the 57-footlong, 20,800 gallon aquarium full of colorful ocean life behind the registration desk. Whitewashed rattan and caning lend a light accent to the rooms' bright color scheme. In addition to the restaurants cited below, three new restaurants—the **Mirage, Onda,** and **Samba Grill**—are scheduled to open at press time. Allow plenty of time to explore the seemingly unending amenities: The resort encompasses three million square feet. ♦ 3400 Las Vegas Blvd S (between W Flamingo and Spring Mountain Rds). 791.7111, 800/627.6667; fax 791.7446; www.themirage.com &

Within the Mirage Hotel:

**The Mirage Casino** The action here is rammin' and jammin', with more money passing back and forth on the craps and baccarat tables in a month than some banks, even countries, see in a year. The atrium across from the **Caribe Cafe** features $500 slot machines and $100 video poker (9/6 with a $150,000 royal jackpot on the max $500 bet). ♦ Daily 24 hours. 791.7111

# KOKOMO'S

**Kokomo's** ★★★$$$ Add a few mai tais to the tropical foliage and longhouse decor here, and you might actually believe you're in Fiji. The menu changes seasonally, and highlights might include broiled sea bass West Indies (served on a bed of wilted spinach with mustard, butter-cream sauce, and sautéed shiitake mushrooms), shrimp and scallop fettuccine, sautéed garlic shrimp, grilled swordfish, lemony herb-crusted roasted half chicken, smoked roasted pork loin, and steaks. The desserts are always sinful. ♦ American ♦ Daily lunch and dinner. Reservations recommended. 791.7111

**Moongate** ★$$$$ Passing through the restaurant's eponymous entryway, a footbridge takes you to a tranquil courtyard containing a pagoda shaded by the graceful spread of a maple tree. It's not worth the big bucks, but if shark's fin is your thing, order the soup made with shark's fin, crabmeat, and shredded chicken in a light chicken-based broth. Or try the salt-and-pepper shrimp, soothing *moo shu* plates (stir-fried vegetables and meat served with crepes), whole steamed fish, Peking duck, walnut chicken, and more. ◆ Chinese ◆ Daily dinner. Reservations recommended. 791.7111

**Mikado** ★★$$$$ The decor here is the yang to **Moongate**'s yin: square, powerful, and commanding. Bright acrylic Japanese murals grace the walls. Appetizers include sashimi, sushi, shiitake mushrooms, yakitori, and deep-fried tofu. All entrées, such as seafood tempura, vegetarian delight, and steaks, are served with a shrimp appetizer, miso soup, Mikado salad (iceberg lettuce, red cabbage, and tomatoes topped with ginger dressing), vegetables, tea, and sherbet. ◆ Japanese ◆ Daily dinner. Reservations recommended. 791.7111

**Bistro** ★★$$$$ Under a stained-glass ceiling and overlooking the casino, this is the place **The Mirage** high rollers come for classic French fare. Though the menu changes seasonally, some of its highlights include venison, lobster *en croute* (in a pastry shell) with truffles and spinach, pheasant, sirloin roquefort, rack of lamb Melba, and Lake Superior whitefish. ◆ Continental ◆ Daily dinner. Reservations required. 791.7111

**Dolphins** Imported from various marine facilities, these eight Atlantic bottlenose dolphins now call the big pools in back of the hotel home. Escorted tours are conducted in a glassed-in viewing area; the underwater scene is accented with recorded clicks, squeaks, and whistles of dolphin talk. There's a short video of the 1991 birth of Squirt, being helped to the surface by his mama for his first breath of air. At the end of the tour, you're free to wander around the pool area, have a bite at the **Dolphin Snack Bar,** or peruse the souvenirs at the **Dolphin Shop.** ◆ Admission. Tours leave every five minutes M-F 11AM-7PM; Sa-Su 9AM-7PM. 791.7111

**Tigers** These rare, royal white tigers are descendants of the felines donated to the US in 1958 by an Indian prince. Their habitat artistically reflects their heritage: white palms, a colorful tiled mural, elephant statues, and a big pool that the cats frequently dip into. A tape, produced and narrated by Siegfried and Roy (who own the tigers and use them in their illusion act), runs continuously on screens above the large glass viewing windows, and acts as a video biography of the big cats. ◆ Free. Daily 24 hours. 791.7111

**Siegfried & Roy** It's fitting that the world's preeminent illusionists stage their show at an establishment named **The Mirage.** The extraordinary sets, stunning costumes, and, of course, action-packed and theatrical illusions simply must be seen to be believed. (And even then, you never know when to trust your eyes.) When a mechanical dragon lifts Roy in its bionic claw, deposits him in a metal container 20 feet in the air, and then crushes it like a tin can, you're simply stunned. And when Siegfried is impaled by a spear, you'll have experienced "shock magic" firsthand. Note, however, that tickets are not only the most expensive in town (they're triple the price of other shows), but also the most difficult to procure. If you're not a guest at the hotel, line up at 8AM at **The Mirage** box office up to three days prior to the show of your choice, and wait, wait, wait. ◆ M-Tu, Th-Su 7:30PM, 11PM. 792.7777

# Harrah's

**30 Harrah's Hotel** $$$ With new megaresorts sprouting up all around it, **Harrah's** has spent $150 million on renovations at the company's flagship location. The Mississippi riverboat facade has been replaced by a grand contemporary entrance and an indoor-outdoor bar on the Strip sidewalk. A second-floor steak house overlooking the Strip, along with five additional new restaurants, and a 35-story hotel tower have been added, bringing the room count to 2,300. For entertainment, there's the 580-seat **Commander's Theatre,** featuring *Spellbound,* "a concert of illusion," as well as the 300-seat **Evening at the Improv** comedy club. ◆ 3475 Las Vegas Blvd S (between E Flamingo Rd and Sands Ave). 369.5000, 800/634.6765; fax 369.5008; www.harrahs.lv.com &

Within Harrah's Hotel:

**Harrah's Casino** Friendly dealers and pit bosses are the rule here, more so than at most other Strip casinos. Recent additions include 500 slot machines and 10 table games. At one group of blackjack tables known as the **"Party Pit,"** the dealers are creative jokers who clown around with the players, encouraging such silliness as clanging a bell when someone hits a natural. This conviviality, as well as the excellent cocktail service and some two-dollar minimums, always assures a crowd at the table games. Slot players will never feel left out: There's one automated opponent for every room in the hotel. ◆ Daily 24 hours. 369.5000

**31 Imperial Palace** $$$ Nevada's only casino with an Asian motif boasts 2,700 hotel rooms, a 70,000-square-foot casino, five restaurants, and two buffets. But the real entertainment here is automotive: 200 antique, classic, and special-interest cars that span a century of vehicular history are featured in a superb display. The hotel is the state's largest employer of people with disabilities and wins considerable recognition for its personnel policies. It has an abundance of facilities for physically impaired guests, including 30 rooms with roll-in showers and transfer wheelchairs, a hydraulic lift at the swimming pool, and an infrared transmitting system for sound enhancement in the showroom. ♦ 3535 Las Vegas Blvd S (between E Flamingo Rd and Sands Ave). 731.3311, 800/634.6441 outside Las Vegas; fax 735.8578; www.imperial-palace.com/vegas &

Within the Imperial Palace:

**Imperial Palace Casino** At first glance, this is a routine casino, with the usual table games in a big pit and slot and video-poker machines crowding the rest of the floor. But look around and you'll notice the confluence of Asian elegance and technological sophistication. Hissing dragon heads leap out from the carved beams overhead. The race book is unique, consisting of six levels of tiered clubhouse-style seating—with an eight-inch color monitor at each chair for close-up views of the big screens. ♦ Daily 24 hours. 731.3311, 800/351.7400 outside Las Vegas

**Embers** ★★$$$ Oysters with creamed spinach, prosciutto, and hollandaise is the specialty at this dining spot on the fourth floor. Rich, burgundy-striped walls, a recessed ceiling, and tufted booths create a comfort-able atmosphere in which to enjoy a wide range of menu items. Good choices are the pasta, chicken, and steak preparations, as well as Alaskan king crab and charbroiled salmon that's tender, juicy, and tasty. There's also a comfortable piano bar in the "courtyard" that also fronts its other restaurants, which offers a fine selection of wine by the glass. ♦ Continental ♦ W-Su dinner. Reservations recommended. 731.3311, 800/751.3400 outside Las Vegas

**Auto Collection** This 250-car collection consists of rare, famous, and infamous automobiles, trucks, tractors, motorcycles, and fire engines. The **Duesenberg Room**

houses $50-million worth of the Model J Doozies. A half-dozen presidential conveyances are in residence, including FDR's unrestored 1936 V-16 Cadillac, plus Elvis's 1976 Cadillac, and Sammy Davis Jr.'s V-8 Stutz. Al Capone's bulletproof 1930 Cadillac, and W.C. Fields's 1938 Cadillac are also on display, as are the King of Siam's 1928 Delage, an 1898 Haynes-Apperson that runs on cleaning fluid, and one of only 51 of the classic 1947 Tuckers ever manufactured. ♦ Admission (coupons for free entry are available). Daily 9:30AM-11:30PM. Fifth floor of parking structure

**Legends in Concert** In this G-rated, good-natured production, eight or so uncanny impersonators take the stage each night out of a cast of two dozen late and living luminaries: Cher, Michael, Madonna, Dolly, Kenny, Elton, Tom Jones, Buddy Holly, et al. The Elvis look-alikes are the best of the weird wannabes. But the Liberace impersonator Daryl Wagner really steals the show. Your senses are guaranteed to be thoroughly assailed by the 24 projectors flashing 1,000 slides and video on three screens, strobes, and lasers, all accompanied by a live six-piece band. Headphones are available for the hearing impaired. ♦ M-Sa 7:30PM, 10:30PM. 794.3261, 800/351.7400 outside Las Vegas

**32  Flamingo Hilton** $$$ For those who saw the movie *Bugsy,* be forewarned: Don't come here expecting to find nostalgic remnants of the past. Ben "Bugsy" Siegel's venerable rose garden, planted by the gardening gangster himself, was paved over in 1990. And his penthouse was demolished in 1993 when the original **Oregon Building** made way for the new water park. The only nod to the hotel's founder is his name, in lights, on the **Celebrity Theater.** Now a Hilton property, the five towers contain a grand total of 3,450 rooms, making it the fourth-largest hotel in town. ♦ 3555 Las Vegas Blvd S (between E Flamingo Rd and Sands Ave). 733.3111, 800/732.2111; fax 733.3528; www.hilton.com/hotels &

Within the Flamingo Hilton:

Las Vegas is the cellular phone capitol of the nation, according to Sprint Central Telephone—Nevada.

**Restaurants/Clubs:** Red      Hotels: Blue

Shops/♥ **Outdoors:** Green      **Sights/Culture:** Black

# A Review of Revues

The images assault you as soon as you step off the plane. From posters at **McCarran International Airport,** billboards along every major roadway, and postcards in gift shops along the **Strip,** leggy women in sequins, feathers, and those impossibly tall headpieces summon you like sirens.

The dancers and the variety revues they star in are synonymous with Las Vegas. Never mind that the concept originated in France (floor shows such as *Lido de Paris* were imported intact in the late 1950s to further the city's reputation as a glamorous and slightly naughty desert hot spot). While the sight of topless women parading in feathers and sequins seems less exotic now, the basic production formula remains unchanged: musical numbers interspersed with specialty acts such as jugglers, acrobats, and magicians. In the 1960s, Las Vegas was just one of several outlets for Ed Sullivan–style entertainment. Today, it's the leader of the last bastions for such extravaganzas, which harken back to the heyday of Broadway spectacles, circa Flo Ziegfeld. About 41 percent of Las Vegas visitors find time for a show, and, with the number of solo celebrity attractions dwindling, most opt for one of the big stage shows.

But with such generically exclamatory titles as *EFX* and *Jubilee!,* how can you tell them apart? Use this brief overview of the more spectacular and most enduring shows on the Strip as a guide.

The smaller rooms seat about 400 people, the larger ones more than 1,200. Most are laid out in tiers, each containing a row of booths and several long tables—a holdover from the days when most shows included an evening meal. Today, only three serve dinner regularly: the **Flamingo Hilton**'s *Great Radio City Music Hall Spectacular,* **Tropicana**'s *Folies Bergere,* and **Excalibur**'s *King Arthur's Tournament* (a medieval-themed show at which you actually munch on Cornish hen without benefit of utensils).

## Seeing Stars

Some showrooms continue to operate under the long-standing maître d' system—you call ahead to place your name on a reservations list but still stand in line (sometimes up to an hour) before curtain time. It's an unwritten custom that tipping the maître d' five dollars (or more) will improve your seating, but the hosts claim the purpose of the system is not to line their own pockets, but to allow them more flexibility in accommodating high rollers.

Today, more than half of the venues use reserved-seat ticketing, a practice familiar to the modern showgoer. Most of the celebrity rooms and some of the larger revues—including *Siegfried & Roy* and *Jubilee!*—have made the switch to tickets. Each hotel has a different policy, but most accept credit card orders by telephone as far as three months in advance or sell tickets at a box office on the premises from one to three days ahead.

Savvy patrons should ask if the advertised price includes cocktails and whether the city's entertainment and gratuity taxes are included. *Legends in Concert* is the lowest-priced show on this list; *King Arthur's Tournament* and *The Great Radio City Music Hall Spectacular* are in the midrange; and *Siegfried & Roy* commands the Strip's top dollar.

Hotels can be helpful about telling you whether their show is acceptable for children or has early performances in which the female dancers are "covered" with bras they shed for the later shows.

A final tip: If you opt to use a ticket broker (they usually sublet booths at casinos in hotels that don't have their own shows), take their recommendations with a grain of salt. They tend to promote the lower-budget revues because they often receive an "incentive" from the producers.

*Cirque du Soleil's Mystère* (Treasure Island) is understated and distinctly European in tone—a complete departure from anything previously associated with Las Vegas. The audience is seated close to a circular stage where the emphasis is on human acrobatics (no animals are used) integrated with mime and a moody New Age score. Felliniesque clowns, or *flounes,* entertain before the show and serve as stagehands for trapeze artists, foot jugglers, contortionists, and a flying man, who soars to the top of the big top and performs an aerial ballet while hanging by wrist-straps. The show is a solution to the problem of entertaining international visitors, since the only "language" spoken is the *flounes'* comic gibberish.

*Cirque du Soleil's O* (The Bellagio) takes place in an 1,800-seat theater, and like Vegas itself, it's a fantasy set in a circuslike atmosphere. The audience enjoys this water ballet of acrobats and Felliniesque clowns who entertain and mesmerize. A number of acts feature synchronized swimmers and fire-throwing aerialists who dazzle and delight to a New Age score.

*EFX* (MGM Grand Hotel/Casino) stars David Cassidy (of *Partridge Family* fame) as the Effects Master who transforms himself into four legendary characters: Merlin, the Master of Magic; P.T. Barnum, the Master of Laughter; Harry Houdini, the Master of the Spirit; and H.G. Wells, the Master of Time. This original $30-million production is staged in the 1,700-seat **Grand Theatre** and includes a cast of 70, plus high-tech effects that have to be believed to be seen.

*Enter the Night* (Stardust Resort & Casino) debuted in 1991 in an attempt to reinvent the Vegas spectacular with a Broadway aesthetic. In this $10-million production, topless female dancers in sleek and contemporary costumes abound. The original score is dynamic and engaging, performed by live musicians and leads who actually sing, rather than mouth the songs. In some numbers, the cast even interact as characters instead of simply serenading the audience. A few of the high-tech touches truly dazzle, particularly the laser number set to music reminiscent of arrangements by the Alan Parsons Project.

*Folies Bergere* (Tropicana Hotel & Casino) is the **Strip**'s longest-running show and the last of the French revues: It debuted at the **Tropicana** in 1959, and the show still has the most legitimate choreography on the Strip, with such traditional numbers as the cancan finale standing up to the test of time. Indeed, the Vegas version has outlasted its Parisian counterpart, which closed in late 1992.

The show cultivates a stylish French flavor from the opening number—a "living postcard" of the bawdy Gaelic music halls of the 1900s—to the "Grand Ladies of Paris" segment. The pièce de résistance comes when the dancers lie down on a turntable and contort into kaleidoscopic formations à la Jackie Gleason's **June Taylor Dancers**. In light of the high-tech competition from **Luxor** and the **MGM Grand Hotel/Casino**, sentimentalists might want to catch this piece of vintage Vegas before the **Tropicana** decides it's too much of an anachronism.

*The Great Radio City Music Hall Spectacular* (Flamingo Hilton), starring the **Radio City Rockettes** and Susan Anton features the world's most famous precision dance troupe. More than 10 numbers are presented, including the **Rockettes'** famous "Parade of the Wooden Soldiers," Gershwin's *Rhapsody in Blue,* and Ravel's *Bolero,* backed by an all-male drum ensemble. And Susan Anton laments in song that she's "Too Tall" to be a Rockette.

*Jubilee!* (Bally's Las Vegas) is a Las Vegas warhorse. For better or for worse, there will never be another show like it. Hydraulic lifts sink the *Titanic* right on cue on the custom-built stage, and the epic "Samson and Delilah" number brings down the house—or at least the temple—every night. This is the only enduring work of producer Donn Arden, who came to town with the opening of the **Desert Inn** and eventually staked his claim as a cross between Busby Berkeley and Cecil B. DeMille. *Jubilee!* opened in 1981, but its sexist clichés and downright hokey lyrics—"(Delilah's) got the hots for a guy named Sam/He thinks the chick is wild!"—are decades behind the times. The idea of a foxy female passenger causing the *Titanic* disaster by distracting the men in the control room seems like Mel Brooks material. Nonetheless, the spectacle still impresses all but the most callous audience.

*King Arthur's Tournament* (Excalibur Hotel/Casino/Las Vegas) came to the Strip in 1990. It's family entertainment in the oval, dirt-floor arena in the basement of the medieval-themed hotel. Knights charge one another on horseback, and the audience cheers on their favorites as they clash and joust. Merlin the Magician narrates the sketch of a plot, which barely elevates the show a level above Arthurian professional wrestling. But kids in the 8-13 range are crazy about it.

*Legends in Concert* (Imperial Palace Hotel & Casino) spawned a cottage industry in 1983—packaging celebrity impersonators into a Vegas revue. "Living Legends" such as contemporary entertainers Neil Diamond and Michael Jackson counterbalance the emphasis on such nostalgic personalities as Judy Garland and Nat King Cole. The "cast" rotates, but there's usually a Marilyn Monroe and a patriotic Elvis finale. Even those who find the concept more tasteless than tributary will have to admit the show offers fast-paced fun with a live band and no lip-syncing. It's a true variety show, respectful enough for those who take the premise seriously and wacky enough for those who appreciate its camp quotient.

*Siegfried & Roy* (The Mirage Hotel & Casino) is one of the most expensive tickets in town. It is also the show that brought the Las Vegas revue into the present when it opened in 1990. These two magicians have been repackaging the same basic repertoire of tricks on an increasingly grander scale since the 1960s. For instance, the stock illusion of "impalement" is now done on the horn of a giant mechanical dragon, a showstopping fire-breather that comes to life midway through the act.

The spectacle begins with the room itself: The stage is an immense crescent with ramps encircling part of the audience, putting them right in the middle of the action. Production designer John Napier says he's striving for a tone that combines Pink Floyd, Wagner, and Marvel Comics. Indeed, the first half of the show casts the two magicians as superheroes combatting the evil queen of a fantasy world. The recorded score is dense and operatic.

One cannot argue that the performers have single-handedly raised the standard of Las Vegas entertainment, yet it is easy to understand the minority who feel the act is too dark, cold, and pretentious. Those few will prefer the latter part of the show, during which the pace slows down sufficiently for the duo to schmooze with the crowd, chat about their careers, and let their affable, slightly goofy personalities shine through. If price is no object, this is definitely the best Las Vegas has to offer.

*Starlight Express* (Las Vegas Hilton) turned Elvis's famous showroom into a customized theater neither the King nor his minions would recognize. The $12-million production of Andrew Lloyd Webber's pop musical on roller skates features a banked dome and a stage with ramps leading into the audience. Performers donning skates portray trains in a high-tech version of "The Little Engine that Could."

The musical was not a Broadway hit on the scale of Webber's *Cats* (the Great White Way's longest running show) or *Phantom of the Opera,* and the Las Vegas effort didn't benefit by being trimmed down to 90 minutes. But the marriage of spectacle and legitimate theater is a step in the right direction for the **Strip**. Besides, *Starlight* seems more at home in Vegas's family environment than in front of a New York audience.

**Flamingo Casino** This casino not only sprawls from one end of the building to the other, but bridges a side alley. During one of the hotel's expansions, a motel and its parking lot were torn down and **O'Sheas Casino** went up in their place. Between the main joint (with the higher limits) and the smaller **O'Sheas** (with the lower), there's gambling for all budgets. ♦ Daily 24 hours. 733.3111

**Beef Barron** ★★★$$$ A rare occurrence on the modern Strip, this 250-seat room has retained the atmosphere of the Old West. A number of guns from Barron Hilton's collection, plus longhorn chandeliers and mounted deer heads decorate the walls. A crackling grill provides the sounds and smells of prime ribs being prepared much as they were 100 years ago during the famous cattle drives. The tradition of serving the cowboys as soon as they are seated is preserved here: "Texas caviar"—black-eyed peas marinated in oil and vinegar, spiced with green pepper and pimento—is presented almost immediately. Among other specialties are black bean soup with sherry, sirloins, filet mignon, porterhouse, double lamb chops, a steak and lobster combination, chicken, ribs, roasted duckling, and rack of lamb. ♦ Steak house ♦ Daily dinner. Reservations recommended. 733.3502

**Alta Villa** ★★$$ A truly Tuscan environment awaits diners here, the stone floor and ivy-covered trellis creating a rustic respite from the town's glut of glitzy restaurants. The risotto (with fish or vegetables) is superb, and the eggplant Florentine appetizer is a meal in itself. The minestrone is ladled from a 25-gallon kettle simmering in front of the exposed kitchen. Veal is the specialty; order a cutlet, or have it prepared *alla milanese* (breaded and fried). Other fare includes chicken *piccata* (sautéed in lemon and butter), salmon, calamari, pasta, and pizza. Save some room for the fruit-topped zabaglione for dessert. ♦ Italian ♦ Daily dinner. Reservations recommended. 733.3434

**The Great Radio City Music Hall Spectacular** Starring the **Radio City Rockettes** and Susan Anton, this lively show celebrates the greatest stage productions from the legendary theater's long history, including the famous "Parade of the Wooden Soldiers" from the "Christmas Spectacular." (See "A Review of Revues," page 42.) ♦ Daily 7:45PM, 10:45PM. 733.3111

**33 Caesars Palace** $$$$ Before **The Mirage** came along in 1989, this hotel-casino reigned supreme in sheer opulence and sky-high

wagering limits. But though its splashier contender has volcanoes and rain forests, former owner ITT-Sheraton invested nearly one billion dollars to meet the competition head on with major renovations and restructuring including a Roman-themed facade complete with new fountains and statues.

On the people mover, which whisks guests from the Strip to the hotel, experience a view of the $2-million holographic *World of Caesar*, where miniature Dionysian dancers and a toastmaster appear in an exquisitely rendered Roman city. Here you will also catch sight of an incongruous but impressive *Brahma Shrine,* a replica of an original statue cast in Thailand to improve the *feng shui* (vibes) of a Bangkok hotel.

The 2,456 guest rooms (in five towers, of various designs, but all with expensive furnishings and oversize baths and showers) are concealed behind lacy sunscreens that at night filter the light into a beautiful pastel-blue haze that envelops the buildings. Wandering the sculpture-strewn hallways (which include a full-size reproduction of Michelangelo's *David*) you'll encounter two casinos—the original **Forum Casino** and the newer **Olympic Casino; Cleopatra's Barge** (a lounge sitting in water); a slew of fancy shops along the **Appian Way;** the 1,200-seat **Circus Maximus** headliner room; six restaurants; a buffet and food court; the "Garden of the Gods" pool area; the 550-seat **Olympic Sports Book;** and some of the swankiest citizenry of the empire.

Also here is *Caesars Magical Empire*—a 66,000-square-foot dining and entertainment complex, where a magical kingdom awaits those who are guided through a catacomb maze.

The ongoing $900-million renovation of the hotel has resulted in the recently opened fifth tower with 1,130 deluxe rooms, each equipped with big-screen TVs, multiline phones, and Jacuzzis. A concierge lounge offering complimentary breakfast and afternoon hors d'oeuvres is located on the 28th floor. Other highlights include a 4.5-acre swimming complex and the **Café Roma** poolside restaurant. A good way to relax is at the 23,000-square-foot spa and fitness center with its fully equipped gym, rock-climbing wall, personal trainers, and body treatment facilities. ♦ 3570 Las Vegas Blvd S (at W Flamingo Rd). 731.7110, 800/634.6661; fax 731.7172; caesars.com/palace/win ♿

Within Caesars Palace:

**Caesars Palace Casinos** No longer the exclusive high-roller territory it once was, the hotel's original casino has had to lower its legendary standards slightly to compete for the middle gambling trade. At the south end of the hotel, adjacent to the **Forum Shops**, the **Olympic Casino** reflects the compromise between elegance and egalitarianism. Its interior imperial splendor—soaring ceiling, heroic marble columns and arches, and stately centurions wearing red capes, red-bristle helmets, and shiny brass shields (who hand out slot-club membership cards to the hoi polloi)—is home to humble reel slots and quarter video-poker machines. The old casino, however, is still high-roller central, and you'll rarely see higher stacks of chips on a craps or blackjack table than you will here. ♦ Daily 24 hours. 731.7110

**The Palatium** ★★$$ Named for the meeting place of the first academy of Roman chefs, this buffet consists of semicircular serving satellites around a central carving station. The food, though lavishly presented, is the usual steam-table fare: roast beef carved to order, cold cuts, salads, and desserts. ♦ Buffet ♦ Daily breakfast, lunch, and dinner. 731.7499

**Bacchanal** ★★★$$$$ Olympian meals are served under a grape arbor in this sumptuous sunken dining room around a marble-walled fountain. Enjoy a seven-course, fixed-price Roman banquet while belly dancers shimmy seductively, vestal virgins in skimpy togas pour house wine into bottomless cups, and Caesar and Cleopatra put in two appearances nightly. Dinner consists of crab cocktail, mushroom ravioli, Caesar salad, choice of entrée (chicken, duck, swordfish, salmon, filet mignon, or prime ribs), and a flaming dessert. ♦ Continental ♦ Tu-Sa dinner. Reservations required; jacket required. 731.7525

**PALACE COURT**

**Palace Court** ★★★★$$$$ The processional entrance to this superlative French restaurant is fit for Caesar: ascend a scarlet-carpeted spiral staircase with brass balustrade (or take the crystal-and-bronze elevator), then pass the view from the arched picture windows of the "Garden of the Gods" pool area and the private gambling salon and piano bar to the peach-hued foyer. The

traditional cuisine is first-rate: salmon smoked on the premises, cherrystone clams, truffled goose liver, and caviar at market price. ♦ French ♦ Daily dinner. Reservations required; jacket required. 731.7547

**La Piazza** $★★ At this fancy food court that shames its counterparts at the **Riviera Casino, Fashion Show Mall,** and **O'Sheas,** choose from American, Chinese, Italian, Japanese, Mexican, and deli fare. There's also an excellent salad bar, and an ice-cream, yogurt, and beverage station. Pull up a ringside seat to the casino; at night there's live entertainment. ♦ International ♦ Daily lunch and dinner. 731.7846

**HYAKUMI**
JAPANESE RESTAURANT & SUSHI BAR

**Hyakumi** ★★★$$$ Friendly service, spectacular specialty rolls, and an unusual assortment of sushi—yellowtail and clam—draw diners to this charming garden-style dining room. Gourmands who let the chef assemble a sushi assortment won't be disappointed. The creations are a feast for the eyes—and the palate. In addition to the raw fare, good tempura along with such selected ingredients as filet mignon, shrimp, and vegetables are prepared at the *teppan* (grill). ♦ Japanese ♦ Tu-Su dinner. Reservations recommended. 731.7110

**Terrazza**

**Terrazza** ★★★$$$ Captivating aromas greet guests who enter this flower-filled rotunda dining room. Just as warm and inviting is the seasonal Italian menu which might include halibut, pompano, lobster, osso buco, a super Caesar salad, and delectable desserts such as chocolate mousse, flan, tiramisù, and a mascarpone to die for. The service is impeccable. ♦ Italian ♦ Daily dinner. Reservations recommended. 731.7100

**Forum Shops** This recently expanded 500,000-square-foot upscale *agora* (market-place) boasts a cobblestone village with a dusk-to-dawn sky dome overhead. The *Festival Fountain* features four animatronic Roman gods (lifelike robots), laser constel-lations, dancing waters, and fiber-optic musical instruments (shows are on the hour). A 50,000-gallon aquarium showcases sharks and stingrays; it also provides a perfect backdrop for the nightly *Lost City of Atlantis Show,* which presents an explorer taking a dive and then discussing with the audience his findings in the deep.

**45**

There are art galleries such as **Galerie Lassen,** featuring landscapes and seascapes of Hawaii, and **Thomas Charles Gallery,** spotlighting such celebrity artists as Anthony Quinn and Tony Bennett. The 95-odd boutiques include **Armani, Bernini, Cazal, Davante, Gucci, Plaza Escada, Vasari, Versace,** and **Vuitton,** to name but a few of the European designers who will happily max out your credit line with a single purchase. Dine at the upscale **Palm,** with its hearty platters, or at Wolfgang Puck's popular **Spago** and his well-liked **Chinois,** the affordable **Stage Deli,** the gracious **Bertolino's,** the hectic **Planet Hollywood,** or the bargain-priced, friendly **La Salsa.** There's even a bustling branch of the **Cheesecake Factory** to try. ◆ M-F 10AM-11PM; Sa-Su 10AM-midnight. West end of Caesars Olympic Casino; exit onto north people mover back into Caesars. 893.4800

# BARBARY COAST

**34**  **Barbary Coast** $$$ Surrounded by three towering hotel-casino competitors, this tiny 200-room hotel adopted its name and decor from the San Francisco coast once frequented by pirates. Built on the site of a small motel, its rococo architecture is eye-catching, allowing the hotel to maintain the pirate tradition by stealing customers who are staying across the way at **Bally's, Caesars,** or the **Flamingo Hilton.** The mahogany and stained glass create a tony, turn-of-the-century ambience (the *Garden of Earthly Delights* on the north wall is supposedly the largest stained-glass window in the world). And in heavy-hitter tradition, the hotel's 200 rooms are mostly reserved for its steady clientele. The 30,000-square-foot casino features more than 550 slot machines, race and sports books, and the gamut of table games. There's a **McDonald's** here for tinhorns who can't go a day without a Big Mac, as well as a 24-hour Western Union office (the last resort for busted-out gamblers—or the choice of the prudent few who want to wire winnings safely home). ◆ 3595 Las Vegas Blvd S (at E Flamingo Rd). 737.7111, 800/634.6755; fax 737.6304; coastres@aol.com; www.coastcasinos.com/barbary Ᏹ

Within the Barbary Coast:

The next time people talk about "Sin City," throw this statistic at them: There are as many churches per capita in Las Vegas as in many other cities in America. Locals representing 63 religious faiths attend services in almost 500 places of worship.

**Michael's** ★★★★$$$$ One of Las Vegas's top gourmet restaurants, its lump crab cocktail, baked escargots, hearts of palm, imported French beans amandine, fresh Maine lobster (flown in daily), charbroiled ribs, Dover sole, and assorted dessert berries dipped in chocolate will please the most jaded of palates. But be forewarned: It's one of the most expensive places in town, and the menu is all à la carte. Like other Las Vegas gourmet dining venues with haute cuisine and eye-popping prices, this spot exists primarily to reward big-spending casino customers with meals on the house. For example, a dinner comp for two here might require an average blackjack bet of $100 played over an eight-hour span. By charging such exorbitant tariffs in the gourmet room, the hotel wins three ways. First, it makes the high rollers feel like they're getting their money's worth. Second, it gives the casino inflated comp expenses to deduct from the gross win. And third, it compels the paying customers to help subsidize the preferred customers. If you're paying for your meal, look around the room—you're picking up the tab for most of the other diners. ◆ French ◆ Daily dinner. Reservations required; jacket required. 737.7111

**Drai's** ★★★★$$$ This clone of noted restaurateur Victor 's now defunct West Hollywood dining room provides guests with an elegant—yet whimsical—setting of original art works, fresh plants, and plush banquettes. Menu offerings run the gamut from Maine lobster ravioli and grilled Lake Superior whitefish to osso buco and Chilean sea bass with ginger and soy sauce. Tantalizing desserts include chocolate mousse and the signature chocolate Florentine cookies. ◆ International ◆ Daily dinner. Reservations required. 737.0555

**Victorian Room** ★★$$ Perfectly capturing the ambience of a bygone era, this charming place is one of the best bets for a friendly welcome and good food. The 24-hour menu includes "Midnight Teasers" (from 11PM to 7AM), along with great breakfast, lunch, and dinner specials. Lunchtime favorites are any of the Chinese specials; dinner choices include the daily chicken, beef, and fish dishes. ◆ American ◆ Daily 24 hours. 737.7111

# maxim

**35**  **Maxim** $$ This low-key hotel-casino is just far enough off the beaten path that it has to try a little harder to compete, much to its guests' advantage. The 800 rooms in the twin 17-story towers are consistently among the least expensive and most available, even on weekends and during conventions (though the decor is a little tatty, they keep trying to improve it). There are three restaurants and three buffets. The 200-seat showroom is the perfect venue for an intimate comedy club. ♦ 160 E Flamingo Rd (between Koval La and Audrie St). 731.4300, 800/634.6987; fax 735.3252; www.maximhotel.com

**36 Bally's Las Vegas** $$$$ Even by Vegas standards, this resort is big. It was big when it opened in 1973 as the **MGM Grand,** and since then it's doubled in size. The portico could shelter a shipyard, and the casino could encompass a Super Bowl stadium.

It is also the site of the city's worst disaster— a terrible fire in 1981 closed the place for nine months. Rebuilt, fireproofed, and expanded, the hotel today features 3,000 guest rooms, a 1,400-seat headliner venue, four restaurants and a buffet, 10 lighted tennis courts, and well-appointed health clubs for men and women. Also here is the $14.5-million **Bally's Plaza,** where four 200-foot walkways move guests between the Strip and the casino. Every 20 minutes after dark, a five-minute light-sound-and-water show erupts. A milelong monorail, a joint venture with the **MGM Grand,** shuttles visitors between the properties. ♦ 3645 Las Vegas Blvd S (between E Harmon Ave and E Flamingo Rd). 739.4111, 800/634.3434; fax 739.4432; www.ballyslv.com &

Within Bally's Las Vegas:

**Bally's Casino** Size is again the object. With 50 blackjack tables, 8 craps tables, 7 roulette wheels, and 1,700 slot and video-poker machines, this gambling hall is one of the most extensive in the world. ♦ Daily 24 hours. 739.4111

**Seasons** ★★★★$$$$ The menu—as one would gather—changes four times a year to keep current with the harvest. Offerings might include fresh ahi with lotus chips, grilled boneless capon breast, roasted duckling Grand Marnier, roasted loin of venison with a pistachio-pepper crust, or *ballotine* of rabbit with roasted pine nuts. The environment is elegant with draped dining alcoves, crystal chandeliers, and gilt mirrors. ♦ French ♦ Tu-Sa dinner. Reservations recommended; jacket required. 739.4651

**Big Kitchen Buffet** ★$ Though the Great Buffet Debate is ongoing—and at times ferocious—this place is a consistent contender for the title. In one corner of the serving area is **Wong's Wok,** where a dozen Chinese dishes are prepared. The line features the customary comestibles: steak and potatoes, baked potato bar, prime rib carved to order, fresh salads, etc. To reach the room, head south inside the main entrance and take

the escalator to the buffet. The second-floor dining area is comfortable and roomy. ♦ Buffet ♦ Daily brunch and dinner. 739.4930

**Al Dente** ★★★★$$$$ Chef Michael Pergolini, formerly of Los Angeles's Il Fornaio, creates the unique Italian specialties found here. The dining room is decorated with colorful modern plastic sculptures; the cuisine is light and imaginative. Popular meals include *melanzane al formaggio di capra* (grilled eggplant); *lattughe al sapor d'uva* (mixed baby greens); *scampi alla griglia* (grilled jumbo shrimp with spinach topped with artichoke and tomato); *focaccia al formaggio* (thin pizza crust filled with mozzarella); osso buco with polenta; and *salsiccia e peperonata* (Italian sausage and peppers). Don't pass up the dessert ravioli stuffed with candied fruit, pine nuts, chocolate, and ricotta and topped with crème fraîche; or seasonal fruit tarts filled with Amaretto cream. ♦ Italian ♦ Tu-Sa dinner. Reservations recommended. 739.4656

**Sterling Brunch** ★★★★$$$$ A new standard for Las Vegas's Sunday Champagne extravaganzas is set here: The attentive waiters sport white gloves. Offerings include a sushi and sashimi bar, imaginative salads, smoked fish, and gourmet entrées that change each week. A sample menu might feature seared black tiger shrimp with peach and peanut chutney, loin of venison with fresh chanterelle mushrooms and green peppercorn sauce, and smoked marinated chicken with *pancetta* (Italian bacon) and wild rice linguine. French pastries and fresh berries are among the delectable desserts. ♦ Continental ♦ Su brunch. Reservations recommended. 739.4111

**Jubilee!** Get a glitz fix at this $12-million production of non sequitur spectacles and historical revisions that only Las Vegas could create. It's a great show, nonetheless, with larger-than-life sets, flamboyant costumes and special effects, and notably beautiful performers. In the first scene, Delilah seduces Samson, who then single-handedly destroys the temple; in Act Two, the *Titanic* sinks right through the stage. Interspersed are dance, variety acts, and a parade of exposed female torsos. ♦ M-Su 8PM; Tu-Th, Sa 8PM, 11PM. 739.4567

**36 Paris–Las Vegas Casino Resort** $$$ At a cost of $760 million, Park Place Entertainment's newest venture re-creates the city of Paris in this sprawling resort complete with a 50-story **Eiffel Tower,** the **Arc de**

**Triomphe,** and **The Louvre.** The elegant, showstopping 2,914 rooms echo the European theme with rich fabrics and marble. The casino offers 85,000 square feet of gaming tables, slot machines, and poker tables. For those who must do business, there's a 130,000-square-foot meeting and convention center. Among the eight restaurants are **La Rotisserie,** a bi-level eatery featuring meat and fish specialties; **Le Provence,** serving Italian fare with French accents; **Eiffel Tower,** a restaurant/bar—looming 100 feet above the Strip—offering gourmet French cuisine; **Le Village Buffet,** a smorgasbord of dishes from five French provinces; and **Le Cafe,** serving espresso and delicious French pastries. There are also five bars and lounges; **Le Cabaret** showroom, featuring an intimate Parisian setting; retail shops; a 20,000-square-foot health spa; and two wedding chapels. A walkway and monorail transport guests to and from the adjacent **Bally's.** ◆ 3665 Las Vegas Blvd S (between E Harmon Ave and E Flamingo Rd). 967.3836, 888/BONJOUR; www.hilton.com

**37 Bellagio** $$$$ For a city that has become more of a fantasyland with pyramid-shaped hotels and New York skylines, this $1.6-billion re-creation of a Lake Como village (complete with an 8.5-acre lake) may just outdo them all. The brainchild of mogul Steve Wynn, the 120-acre resort dazzles and delights—and with its Italian Renaissance–style decor and European refinement, it may well be the most desired oasis in the desert.

The 3,005 spacious guest rooms, decorated in rich fabrics with elegant art works and antiques, feature huge marble bathrooms with deep-soaking tubs. Other comforts include twice daily maid service and a mini-bar in every room. The resort offers an incredible 17 dining options, including branches of New York's **Le Cirque** and **Osteria del Circo** (see at right), **Jasmine** for contemporary Chinese cuisine, **Noodles** with offerings from the Orient, and an all-you-can-eat 24-hour buffet.

Along with spectacularly landscaped grounds of olive trees and Lombardy pines, there is the beautifully designed **Via Bellagio** with its parade of such swank boutiques as **Chanel, Giorgio Armani, Gucci, Hermès, Prada,** and **Tiffany & Co.** And of course the requisite 100,000-square-foot casino, as well as a theater, two wedding chapels, and a luxurious spa/fitness center offering massage and facial treatments, exercise equipment, and pools. ◆ 3600 Las Vegas Blvd S (at W Flamingo Rd). 693.7111, 888/987.6667; fax 693.8585; www.bellagiolasvegas.com ⑁

Within Bellagio:

**Bellagio Gallery of Fine Art** This exhibition overflows with Steve Wynn's $300-million private art collection, including works by Renoir, Degas, Matisse, and Monet, as well as modern masters Pablo Picasso, Jackson Pollock, Jasper Johns, and Willem de Kooning. True art aficionados should take the excellently narrated audio tour which examines—among other works—Joan Miró's *Insects*, Pablo Picasso's *Portrait of Dora Maar*, and Vincent van Gogh's compelling *Peasant Woman.* ◆ Admission. Daily. 693.7722 ⑁

# AQUA

**Aqua** ★★★$$$ Elegantly appointed with rich fabrics and terrazzo tile, this San Francisco offshoot features an excellent seafood menu created by Michael Mina. Most dishes forego the usual butter and cream, deriving their intense flavors from the reduction of vegetable or meat juices. Some fine examples include Wellington of king salmon with black truffles and Napa cabbage, Maine lobster pot pie with wild mushrooms and caramelized pearl onions, and potato-wrapped trout with a foie gras and apple stuffing. The array of ever-changing desserts look as fabulous as they taste, and the wine list is expertly matched to an excellent menu. ◆ Seafood ◆ Daily dinner. Reservations recommended. 693.7223 ⑁

BELLAGIO

**Le Cirque** ★★★★$$$$ Sirio Maccione, who created the acclaimed Le Cirque in New York, has teamed up with designer Adam Tihany to produce this exquisite dining emporium with its sleek mahogany interior, plush furnishings, and fine china and table settings. But the menu is the real star here. Choose from among such appetizers as *plateau de fruit de mer* (a tasty combination that includes oysters, clams, shrimp, and lobster) or confit of duck salad. Featured main courses are just as tantalizing: try roasted lobster in Port wine, rabbit with wild mushrooms, or wild salmon wrapped in prosciutto. Desserts are memorable, especially the irresistible "chocolate dice" filled with dense white-and-Madagascar chocolate. ◆ French ◆ Daily dinner. Reservations required; jacket required. 693.8150 ⑁

**Osteria del Circo** ★★★$$$ Brothers Mario, Marco, and Mauro Maccione, second generation of the legendary family, have re-created the same whimsical red-and-yellow circuslike atmosphere found in this restaurant's New York City counterpart. And just as in the Big Apple, you'll find such offerings as *zuppa alla frantoiana* (hearty Tuscan vegetable soup) or beef carpaccio with shaved parmesan cheese and arugula salad for starters. Any of the homemade pizzas, pastas, and perfectly prepared risottos are a delightful main course treat. Those with heartier appetites may opt for steak Florentine or one of the special seafood dishes. Don't miss the excellent crème brûlée. ◆ Northern Italian ◆ Daily lunch and dinner. Reservations recommended. 693.8150 ⑤

**Prime** ★★★$$$$ Superchef Jean-Georges Vongerichten's newest venture takes him from the canyons of New York City to the deserts of the West with this elegant re-creation of a 1930s-style chophouse complete with plush velvet drapes and gleaming marble floors. The menu is a carnivore's delight with everything from steak tartare and rack of lamb to filet mignon and prime porterhouse steaks. One factor remains constant throughout: the meals are uniquely prepared and beautifully presented. Seafood lovers will enjoy daily specials including red snapper, tuna steak, lobster, and salmon. Leave room for the sinfully rich Valrhona chocolate cake with vanilla ice cream, the pineapple-banana salad with white-pepper ice cream, or the divine crushed raspberry and almond crisp. ◆ Steak house ◆ Daily dinner. Reservations recommended; jacket required. 693.7233 ⑤

*Picasso*

**Picasso** ★★★$$$ Original Picassos—paintings, tiles, and plates—grace this Mediterranean-style dining room, where chef Julian Serrano (of San Francisco's Masa fame) takes advantage of both his Spanish heritage and French training to create some of the most innovative food in town. Be sure to try his signature foie gras chunks served with vegetable morsels bathed in a truffle sauce with just a hint of sweetness from Madeira. Other choice dishes include scallops with corn flan and saffron sauce, roasted lamb with truffles and parmesan potatoes, and veal chop with mushrooms and rosemary potatoes. For a sweet finish, select from a sumptuous variety of petits fours. There's an excellent selection of American and European wines as well. ◆ Mediterranean ◆ M-Tu, Th-Su dinner. Reservations required. 693.7223

**Cirque du Soleil's O** ★ The second production to grace this town is also a combination of theater, dance, music, and lights set in an 1,800-seat opera house. *O* conveys a story in the form of a water ballet which, at times, challenges the limits of the human body in ways beyond the imagination.

Like its sister show down the Strip, no words are spoken or animals used in this circuslike atmosphere. (For more details, see "A Review of Revues," page 42.) ◆ M-Tu, F-Su 7:30PM, 11PM. 693.7722

**38 Aladdin Las Vegas** $$$$ Located on the site of the legendary **Aladdin Hotel** is this $1.2-billion hotel-casino complex scheduled to open as we went to press. The resort boasts the 2,600-room **Aladdin Hotel & Casino; Desert Passage,** a 500,000-square-foot entertainment/retail area; and **Aladdin Music Project,** with the 7,000-seat **Aladdin Center for the Performing Arts.** ◆ Las Vegas Blvd S (between E Harmon Ave and E Flamingo Rd). No phone at press time

**39 Holiday Inn Boardwalk Casino** $$$ You'd be hard-pressed to find the boardwalk, let alone the ocean at this funky little casino and 200-room hotel. To bring back memories of its Atlantic City counterpart, black-and-white photographs (ca. 1920 and 1930) of the East Coast ocean resort town deck the halls. It's locally revered for its budget-balancing snack bar fare: fresh doughnuts baked on the premises, hearty soups, hobo stew served in a one-pound loaf of baked bread, and tiny White Castle–style burgers. The daily dinner specials are amazingly inexpensive and include a gratis glass of eminently drinkable wine. Casino-chip collectors and gambling historians will appreciate the 1967 50¢, $1, $2, and $5 gaming tokens on display at the main cage. ◆ 3750 Las Vegas Blvd S (between W Tropicana Ave and W Flamingo Rd). 735.1167, 800/635.4581; fax 739.8152; www.hiboardwalk.com

*Monte Carlo*
RESORT & CASINO

**40 Monte Carlo Resort and Casino** $$$ This $350-million Mirage Resorts–Circus Circus Enterprises venture re-creates the opulent Place du Casino in Monaco. Like its European namesake it boasts ornate fountains, marbled floors, and gaslit promenades. All 3,000-rooms and 256 suites afford a touch of elegance accented with marble and granite decor. Guests also enjoy a waterpark, six restaurants, a fully equipped spa, and tennis courts. ◆ 3770 Las Vegas Blvd S (between W Tropicana Ave and W Flamingo Rd). 730.7777, 800/311.8999; fax 739.9272; www.monte-carlo.com ⑤

Within the Monte Carlo Resort and Casino:

**Monte Carlo Casino** A pleasing combination of European elegance and American informality, this casino features 2,200 slot and video-poker machines, 100

table games, an exclusive high-limit gaming area, a high-tech race and sports book, as well as bingo, poker, and keno. Straight from the south of France is single-zero roulette, which halves the usual number of zeros, as well as the house advantage. ♦ Daily 24 hours. 730.7777

**Lance Burton Theatre** This $27-million showroom is the city's only 1,274-seat venue that's modeled after London's West End theaters. The plush interior features a New York–style lobby with murals adorning the walls, multitiered balconies, and an old-fashioned bar. Burton, the youngest American illusionist to be named a World Champion of Magic by the International Federation of Magicians, performs everything from astounding close-up sleight-of-hand to making sports cars disappear right before your eyes. ♦ Admission. M-Sa 7:30PM, 10:30PM. 730.7777

**Market City Cafe** ★★$$ A popular destination, this eatery features a menu filled with gourmet pizzas—the chicken, peanut, and barbecue sauce is terrific. Also on the bill are 65 varieties of pasta all prepared to order in an open kitchen. There's also an antipasto bar and full selection of espresso and cappuccino to round off the meal. ♦ Italian ♦ Daily dinner. 730.7777

**Monte Carlo Pub & Brewery** ★★$ This working microbrewery serves up five to six varieties that include High Roller Red (an amber ale), Silver State Stout (traditional Irish Stout), and Winner's Wheat (a sweet, unfiltered wheat ale). Also on tap are generous portions of typical pub fare such as sandwiches, salads, and burgers. Other options include sausage served with warm potato salad or penne pasta. ♦ American/Pub ♦ Daily lunch and dinner. 730.7777

**41 Smith & Wollensky** ★★★$$$ Sister to New York City's Smith & Wollensky, this western branch offers the same truly exceptional food in a noisy, cavernous dining room. Almost everything here is luscious, but the Cajun-style rib eye is a standout. The porterhouse steak is a crowd pleaser too, and such excellent desserts as Austrian strudel don't disappoint. ♦ Steak house ♦ Daily lunch and dinner. Reservations recommended. 3767 Las Vegas Blvd S (between E Tropicana and E Harmon Aves). 862.4100 ♿

**42 World of Coca-Cola** The world of soft drinks comes to life with interactive exhibits, a theater, and a folk art exhibit of soda bottles created by artists from around the world. Be sure to ride the Coke-shaped elevator with its sounds of crackling ice and vintage jingles playing in the background. There's a soda fountain and, of course, a store featuring all kinds of Coca-Cola memorabilia. ♦ Admission. Daily. 3785 Las Vegas Blvd S (between E Tropicana and E Harmon Aves). 270.5965

**43 New York–New York Hotel & Casino** $$$ Named the "Greatest City in Las Vegas," this $460-million joint venture between MGM Grand, Inc. and Primadonna Group re-creates the hustle-bustle and excitement of the Big Apple so perfectly that they named it twice. Twelve New York skyscrapers house 2,033 Art Deco–themed rooms and suites and include the **Empire State, Chrysler, Seagrams,** and **CBS** buildings; the **New York Public Library;** the **New Yorker Hotel,** and **Grand Central Station.** To complete the skyline there's a 300-

*New York–New York Casino*

foot replica of the **Brooklyn Bridge.** Greeting guests is Lady Liberty herself and for those who dare, the Manhattan Express roller coaster runs loops and dives around the perimeter of the property at a dizzying 67 miles per hour. Guests enjoy the *MADhattan* show depicting New York City's high energy during rush hour in the **MADhattan Theater,** retail shopping on Park Avenue, New York–style restaurants, and a Little Italy food court. ♦ 3790 Las Vegas Blvd S (at W Tropicana Ave). 740.6969, 800/693.6763; fax 740.6920; www.nynyhotelcasino.com &

Within New York–New York Hotel & Casino:

**New York–New York Casino** Within the 84,000-square-foot **Central Park**–themed casino are 71 gaming tables and more than 2,400 slot machines. To cash in your winning's, however, you'll have to travel to the cashier's cages located nearby in the Financial District. ♦ Daily 24 hours. 740.6969

**Coney Island Emporium** This family-style entertainment center replicates the aura of the Coney Island amusement park in the early 1900s. Located on the second floor, next to the **Manhattan Express** roller coaster, it offers fun and games for all with bumper cars, shooting galleries, and a fiber-optic fireworks show. ♦ Daily 24 hours. Second floor. 740.6969

**Gallagher's Steak House** ★★★$$$ A New York institution since 1927, this western version does not disappoint. The prime cut steaks are big and satisfying, as are the fresh seafood dishes. ♦ Steak house ♦ Daily lunch and dinner. Reservations recommended. 740.6450

**Chin Chin** ★★$$ Chinese cuisine takes an innovative turn in this cafe setting with its open kitchen. Try the shredded chicken salad and an assortment of dim sum specialties. Then follow with such entrées as country-style chicken and spinach or crispy sea bass. ♦ Cantonese ♦ Daily lunch and dinner. Reservations recommended. 740.6969

**Motown Cafe** ★★$$$ A testament to our fascination with celebrities and showbiz, this restaurant packs customers in with music mystique. It's filled with memorabilia and sounds of such legends as The Supremes, The Four Tops, The Temptations, and the more contemporary Boyz II Men. Top hits on the menu include chicken fingers with honey-mustard sauce and Buffalo wings. ♦ American ♦ Daily breakfast, lunch, and dinner. 740.6440

**Il Fornaio** ★★★$$$ The pizzas are delicious, as are the meat and pasta dishes that please the crowd. Other specialties include ravioli stuffed with lobster and ricotta, spinach linguini, or the rotisserie chicken and duck. Top off the meal with a selection from an impressive array of desserts—the sorbets are

refreshing. ♦ Italian ♦ Daily lunch and dinner. Reservations recommended. 740.6969

**44 MGM Grand Hotel/Casino** $$$ An on-going $950-million expansion has transformed this 114-acre property into "The City of Entertainment." Already considered the world's largest hotel, it boasts 5,005 spacious rooms and suites, ranging in size from 875 to a palatial 6,000 square feet in four 30-story Emerald Towers. The 200,000-square-foot casino is also dazzling. The 15,000-seat **Grand Garden** is the centerpiece of the five entertainment areas. Nestled in front of the hotel/theme park is the **Showcase,** which houses a Sega Gamework interactive center, a multiplex movie theater, and **Official All Star Cafe.** The hotel boasts 14 other restaurants, among them **The Grand Buffet at the City of Entertainment,** offering daily brunch and dinner; **Gatsby's,** featuring California/French cuisine; and **The Brown Derby,** the re-created Hollywood eatery, which serves the signature Cobb salad and a memorable grapefruit cake.

The lavish 6.6-acre pool area has five pools; a remodeled health spa featuring massage, facials, herbal wraps, and whirlpools; and excellent gym facilities with extensive cardio-vascular weight training equipment and personal trainers.

Additional facilities include a 30,000-square-foot video arcade; a youth activity center; a shopping arcade; an ice-cream parlor; and four themed casinos with 3,500 slot machines and 165 table games. In addition to featuring street scenes from Paris, New York, and Hong Kong, the hotel's 33-acre theme park offers an assortment of rides including a Mississippi riverboat, a roller coaster through darkness, a 1,600-footlong rapids ride, a flume with sheer vertical drops, bumper cars, and Skyscreamer, the world's largest sky coaster. ♦ 3799 Las Vegas Blvd S (at E Tropicana Ave). 891.1111, 800/929.1111; fax 891.1000; www.mgmgrand.com &

Within the MGM Grand Hotel/Casino:

**Emeril's New Orleans Fish House** ★★★$$$$ New Orleans's own Emeril Lagasse presents an exotic and eclectic blend of Cajun/Creole cuisine in this charming, rustic setting adorned with black-and-white photos from the bayou and a lavish floral centerpiece. The menu is delightful—and dizzying: choose from cold Maine lobster in Creole gazpacho, smoked trout wontons, duck pastrami with warm spinach and goat cheese, tuna steak with fresh foie gras, crisp-crusted Gulf pompano with bacon, double pork chop with tamarind glaze and caramelized sweet potatoes, grilled Creole-spiced rib eye, and double-cut pork chop in green-chile mole sauce. Don't leave without trying the bread pudding with whiskey sauce or the goat-cheese cheesecake. ♦ Cajun/Creole ♦ Daily lunch and dinner. Reservations recommended. 891.7374

**Coyote Cafe** ★★★★$$$ This replica of the original Santa Fe eatery is just one of Mark Miller's tremendously successful ventures scattered around the world. You have a choice of where to sit and savor the Southwestern food— in the informal **Cafe** or the elegant **Grill Room**. Imaginative soups, salads, entrées, and casseroles are highlighted on both of the delicious seasonal menus. Two of the **Cafe**'s more popular dishes are the blue-corn chicken enchilada and sizzling shrimp diablo. The **Grill Room**'s signature dishes are a little more upscale. Try the cowboy Angus rib chop or the skillet-seared Alaskan salmon in a pumpkin-seed crust served with butternut squash and lobster *jus*. ♦ Southwestern ♦ Cafe: daily breakfast, lunch, and dinner; Grill Room: daily dinner. Reservations required for Grill Room. 891.7349

**Wolfgang Puck Cafe** ★★★$$ Bright and cheerful, this popular cafe overlooking the casino is decorated with framed *Puck* magazine covers (*Puck* was a popular English humor magazine at the turn of the century) and vividly colored wall and floor tiles. Imaginative specialties prepared in the open kitchen include breakfast pizzas of focaccia with creamy scrambled eggs and cheese,

roasted prime rib hash, smoked salmon plate, and a fresh fruit plate with blueberry yogurt. For lunch and dinner, choose the roasted eggplant, tomato, and fresh mozzarella salad; vegetable spring rolls with mustard plum sauce; Barbara's fettuccine with shrimp, vegetables, and a curry sauce; Grandma Puck's linguine with chicken *bolognese;* or meat loaf with port wine sauce and garlic mashed potatoes. Among the immense variety of gourmet pizzas from the wood-burning oven are herb sausage, prosciutto with goat cheese, smoked salmon with red onions, and barbecued chicken with cilantro. ♦ American ♦ Daily breakfast, lunch, and dinner. 891.3019

**Tre Visi** ★★$$ If you just can't face another Vegas buffet, a fine alternative is this casual Italian restaurant. Early risers will enjoy fresh juices, frittatas, or smoked salmon plate. Later, the menu offers one of the city's largest choices of carpaccio (beef, salmon, or smoked mackerel), as well as pastas, pizzas, and a hearty osso buco. ♦ Italian ♦ Daily breakfast, lunch, and dinner. 739.8911

**Official All Star Cafe** ★$$ Fans of all sports in all seasons will thrill at the state-of-the-art sports experience in play here. Sports memorabilia, viewing screens, and score-boards are a hit as are the burgers, fries, and chicken wings. With sports figures Andre Agassi, Wayne Gretzky, Joe Montana, Shaquille O'Neal, Ken Griffey Jr., and Monica Seles as partners in this venture, you may never feel the need to attend a live sports event again. ♦ American ♦ Daily lunch and dinner. 795.8326

**Dragon Court** ★★★$$$ An alluring combination of purple lighting and exotic aromas are what draw diners to this oh-so-elegant dining place. From hot towels to green tea, this is the closest thing to the Orient you'll find on Las Vegas's restaurant-rich Strip. Among the favorite starters are the pot stickers, minced squab, and pork wrapped in lettuce, followed by such delicious entrées as Peking duck (sliced tableside) and steamed prawns served with a dipping sauce. ♦ Chinese ♦ Daily dinner. Reservations recommended. 891.7777 ♿

# It's an Illusion

Even at age 90, Jimmy Grippo's hands still were quicker than the eye. The house magician at **Caesars Palace,** whose sleight-of-hand entertained legions of visitors at the **Bacchanal** room and throughout the resort, was an integral part of the illusion of Old Vegas. A classic practitioner of up-close magic, Grippo is gone now.

In today's Las Vegas, with its huge showrooms, Grippo's brand of magic is impractical. Seigfried & Roy, whose shows at **The Mirage** are nightly sellouts, changed magic in Las Vegas forever with the overwhelming success of their larger-than-life acts of illusion.

Siegfried Fishbacher and Roy Horn—who have been leaving Las Vegas audiences awestruck for more than 20 years—regularly update their $30-million act at **The Mirage.** Not surprisingly, this is the hottest and most expensive ticket in town.

Lance Burton, who headlines in his own showroom at the **Monte Carlo,** represents the next generation of Las Vegas illusionists. What his act lacks in

tigers, it makes up for in dancers and over-the-top showmanship.

Of the magicians who make Las Vegas an annual stop, David Copperfield is by far the most popular. His TV specials, often filmed at **Caesars Palace,** have made him an international celebrity. It helps to be able to boast that he has made the Statue of Liberty disappear.

Penn & Teller have established themselves on the cutting edge of the profession. Their act, which plays to sell-out crowds at **Bally's,** combines black humor and grotesque images with some truly amazing feats of illusion. Their audiences scream with fright as they perform death-defying acts. The magical duo enjoys Las Vegas so much that they have built a home on the edge of the city.

Melinda Saxe, Vegas's only headlining female magician, entertains at the Downtown's **Lady Luck** and combines her undeniable sex appeal with polished sleight-of-hand. Fans have dubbed her "First Lady of Magic."

**The Rainforest Cafe** ★★$$ Thematically consistent with its name, the cafe features lifesize, robotlike animals and a 10,000-gallon double archway aquarium. This informal dining area does a credible job of preparing breakfast, lunch, and dinner specials; one standout is the rasta pasta (with grilled chicken, walnut pesto, broccoli, peppers, and spinach in an herb-garlic sauce). There are fun tropical drinks for the adults such as "Leapin' Lizards" and "Margarilla." True to its name, there's even an occasional "thunderstorm" to cool things off. ♦ American ♦ Daily breakfast, lunch, and dinner. 891.8580

**Grand Theatre** This is the scene of *EFX*, a $30-million extravaganza that stars David Cassidy as the Effects Master who portrays four historical characters. The show inaugurated the 1,700-seat theater in 1995 with a cast of 70 and utilizes cutting-edge animatronic technology to dramatic effect. (For more information, see "A Review of Revues," page 42.) ♦ Admission. M-W, F-Sa, 7:30PM and 10:30PM; Su 7:30PM. 891.7777

**Studio 54** If disco was—or is—your thing, grab a table at this nightspot which attracts a thirtysomething-and-up crowd. The music is a

throwback to New York's 1970s and the pace is frenetic. There also are 27 varieties of martinis. If you qualify (read: high roller), access to the private Clipper Club Lounge is a sure bet for excitement. ♦ M-Th 10PM-4AM; F-Sa 10PM-5AM. 891.7254

**45 Hotel San Remo** $$$ The Japanese owner of this 711-room jewel is dedicated to offering comfort and service to his guests. Those staying here need never stray far for fun. There are 50 Jacuzzi suites, a casino with blackjack, craps, keno, roulette, mini-baccarat, poker, *pai gow,* and *pai gow* poker, plus a slot club and sports book. Five restaurants on site offer a variety of gustatory experiences. **Paparazzi** offers continental dining in an intimate, romantic setting; moderately priced Italian fare is served in a relaxed, festive atmosphere at **Pasta Remo; Luigi's Place** features deli sandwiches and pizza all day; the 24-hour coffee shop offers breakfast, lunch, and an all-you-can-eat dinner buffet; and an award-winning chef creates authentic delicacies in the **Sushi Bar San Remo** every night. ♦ 115 E Tropicana Ave (between Duke Ellington Way and Las Vegas Blvd S). 739.9000, 800/522.7366; fax 736.1120; www.sanremolasvegas.com &

Gaming chips cost casinos approximately 45 cents to produce and sell for face value, making them one of the more expensive souvenirs a tourist can buy.

**46 Tropicana Hotel** $$$ Though at 300 rooms it wasn't much larger than the ranch-style lodges that preceded it, this was the last, fanciest, and most expensive of the Strip hotels to be built in the 1950s. Its $15-million price tag taxed the cash capabilities of even the richest old bootleggers. Because of the state and federal heat on organized crime figures in Nevada gambling and the growing media hysteria over Las Vegas as the vice capital of the country, another new Strip hotel didn't open for nearly a decade.

Now at 1,913 rooms, the grand dame still has a lot going for it. A quarter-mile walkway connects its two towers, with flocks of tropical birds and coral aquariums lining the path. And the five-acre pool area is a lush and cool hideaway just out of hearing range of the Strip; the famous swim-up blackjack game is played here. ♦ 3801 Las Vegas Blvd S (at E Tropicana Ave). 739.2222, 800/468.9494; fax 739.2469; www.tropicana.lv.com ਠ

Within the Tropicana Hotel:

**Tropicana Casino** The main pit here is defined by a colorful 4,000-square-foot stained-glass ceiling, making the table-game atmosphere quite dramatic. Fairly innovative with gambling promotions, the casino has introduced a progressive jackpot at roulette, blackjack, and craps (won by such feats as rolling three 11s in a row). A good place to come if you're new to gaming, the casino also offers free lessons in craps and Caribbean stud poker. There are also learning tables where dealers answer questions on how to play, and the low minimums (baccarat for $5 and blackjack for $1) make it painless. While you're in the casino, sign up for a free membership in the **Island Winners Club,** and you can earn points toward dining and the **Folies Bergere** as you play table games, slots, or video poker. Cash bonuses are also awarded to slots and video-poker players. ♦ Daily 24 hours. 739.2222

The 1.5-million-gallon dolphin habitat at The Mirage is the largest saltwater pool in the world.

The Atlantic bottlenose dolphin exhibit at The Mirage attracts more than 600,000 visitors each year, including in excess of 50,000 local school children.

**El Gaucho** ★★★$$$ Between wonderful fare at this south-of-the-border steak house and the view overlooking the **Island of Las Vegas** water park, you couldn't ask for a more enjoyable dining experience. Among the hearty specialties are oysters del Rio (oysters on the half shell baked in asiago cheese), swordfish Mazatlán (broiled swordfish with cilantro-lime sauce), and porterhouse steak. ♦ Steak house ♦ Daily dinner. Reservations recommended. 739.2376

**Play & Eat** ★★$$ This relatively recent combination casino-deli allows you to devour two-footlong hot dogs while indulging in slots or video poker. You can even order a salad or sandwich while you bet in the sports book or sip some cappuccino to keep you playing all night in the poker room. There's also a beautiful view of the hotel's lagoons, spas, waterfalls, and wildlife. ♦ Deli: Daily breakfast, lunch, and dinner until 5PM; Casino: daily 8AM-10PM. 739.2503

*Folies Bergere*

**Folies Bergere** By far the oldest show in town, this production is a throwback to a previous generation of Las Vegas extravaganzas. Turn-of-the-century Parisian song and dance, American golden oldies, cancan chorus lines, and 1950s-style dancers appeal mostly to the sentimental. Dinner is served before the early show and included in the price of admission; cocktails only are included in the price of the late show. ♦ Admission. Shows: daily 7:30PM, 10:30PM. 739.2411

**47 Excalibur Hotel/Casino/Las Vegas** $$ This 4,032-room behemoth held the title of world's largest resort hotel until the **MGM Grand Hotel/Casino** across the street overtook it by almost 1,000 chambers. The medieval detail, inside and out, renders the resort a theme park in its own right, with an overblown scale and exaggerated style. Turrets, spires, belfries, and moats usher you into the castle. The bellmen wear poofy yellow-and-black knickers, white-and-gold blouses, and purple vests (the dealers used to wear the same outfits, but mercifully, theirs have been toned down). Signs around the casino direct customers to the **Jester's Lounge, Royal Royals,** and the **Medieval Slot Fantasy.**The lower level houses the **Fantasy Faire,** a sort of Sherwood Forest of midway games, featuring the Flagon Toss, Great Racing Knights, Knock Down the Knave's Teeth, and William Tell Darts. But the main draw is **Merlin's Magic Motion Machines,** an amazing show where the theaters' benches move in sync with the wild action on the screen.

On the **Medieval Village** level are four restaurants and the megasize buffet, which seats 1,500. Singers, acrobats, magicians, jugglers, and harpists hold court at the **Court Jester's Stage. Camelot,** the third level, is where you'll find ballrooms, a beauty salon, and an excellent gourmet restaurant (also called **Camelot,** see below). For the altarbound, the **Canterbury Wedding Chapels** take brides and grooms back in time with ceremonies performed in medieval costumes. ♦ 3850 Las Vegas Blvd S (between W Russell Rd and W Tropicana Ave). 597.7777, 800/937.7777; fax 597.7009

Within the Excalibur Hotel/Casino/Las Vegas:

**Excalibur Casino** Attracting a mom-and-pop crowd, this casino offers ample opportunity to do everything from feeding nickels and quarters into machines to playing $2 blackjack. It's huge—100,000 square feet—with 80 blackjack tables, 6 craps tables, and 4 roulette tables. The table minimums are kept low: $3 blackjack, $1 craps, and quarter roulette. But mostly there are slot machines everywhere—nearly 3,000! Serious gamblers have plenty of other places to play in this town. ♦ Daily 24 hours. 597.7777; www.excalibur-casino.com

# Lance-a-Lotta Pasta

**Lance-a-lotta Pasta** ★$ If the pun on the restaurant's name doesn't deter you, you'll find plenty to eat here. The menu features antipasto, fried calamari, minestrone or the *zuppa del giorno* (soup of the day), salads, and pasta galore. Choose from six sauces or toppings while a string quartet plays in the background. ♦ Italian ♦ Daily lunch and dinner. 597.7777

# Sir Galahad's PRIME RIB HOUSE

**Sir Galahad's Prime Rib House** ★★$$ At this Olde English inn, wait staff in period costumes carve the prime ribs to order—a King Arthur's or Lady Guinevere's cut—at your table. The main course is accompanied by barley soup or salad, mashed potatoes, creamed spinach, Yorkshire pudding, and whipped-cream horseradish. At the end of the meal, you'll feel as roly-poly as Friar Tuck. If you're not up to the prime rib, opt for the less filling, but equally satisfying, breast of capon harlequin (in red wine sauce, with pearl onions and mushrooms) or the fresh catch of the "knight," and top it all off with English

trifle. ♦ English ♦ Daily dinner. Reservations recommended. 597.7777

# CAMELOT
### CASUAL FINE DINING

**Camelot** ★★★$$$ With suits of armor flanking both sides of the entry, the Round Table theme continues. Light shines through stained-glass windows in the cocktail lounge and bar, and pewter plates and swords hang from the walls of the dining room. Such appetizers as Scottish smoked salmon with grilled onion salsa or warm quail salad with balsamic vinaigrette and strips of vine-ripened tomatoes would have been ample reward for those in service to their king. Equally delicious is Queen Guinevere's soup (creamy lobster bisque with diced lobster meat). Woodland fettuccine (with smoked quail, fresh vegetables, and pesto in a creamy game sauce) and Glendale purses (fresh ravioli with veal and herbs, surrounded by a creamy porcini mushroom sauce) may not have been staples in medieval castles, but you'll be glad they're served here. Entrées include Argyle swordfish with fresh asparagus vinaigrette, Canterbury duckling (with wild rice, crispy potatoes, and port cherry sauce), and rack of lamb King James (squash-encrusted and served with potato puree). To reach nirvana, try the chocolate "decadeuce" (rich flourless chocolate cake with whipped cream) before returning to normal life. ♦ Continental ♦ Daily dinner. Reservations recommended. 597.7777

**48 Luxor Hotel & Casino** $$$ Trading on the appeal of both New Age and age-old pyramid power, this 30-story, $300-million bronze tetrahedron with 2,500 rooms and a 90,000-square-foot casino is a one-of-a-kind resort. Luxor was the original religious locus for the ancient Egyptian civilization of Thebes. A $50 million water thrill ride built inside the pyramid, replaced the "Nile River" that traversed the perimeter. "Inclinators" ascend the building at a 39° angle. Also featured are King Tut's tomb, seven restaurants, a 1,200-seat arena, and the New York City skyline. This hybrid of a historical theme and the comforts of a modern hotel are sure to lure even the most jaded visitors. ♦ 3900 Las Vegas Blvd S (between W Russell Rd and W Tropicana Ave). 262.4000, 800/288.1000; fax 262.4405; www.luxor.com ♿

# Working the Main Room

Elvis. Frank. Sammy. Dean. Liza. Wayne. Siegfried—and don't forget Roy. The Las Vegas showroom legends need only a first-name introduction, their presence looming larger than life on casino marquees visible a mile away.

Celebrity acts were part of the Las Vegas formula from the earliest days of the **Strip.** The **Flamingo Hotel**'s infamous founder, Benjamin "Bugsy" Siegel, ignored the city's Western frontier-town image when he opened his dream hotel in late 1946. He wanted to impress his Hollywood and East Coast gangster pals by building a ritzy "carpet joint" to rival the casinos in Havana. This feat required stars. Jimmy Durante and Lena Horne were the first **Flamingo** headliners.

In short order, Las Vegas was the self-proclaimed "Entertainment Capital of the World," a billing that publicity types still perpetuate. The city didn't claim more stars in residence than New York or Chicago; it was simply a novelty to have so many greats playing in this remote desert location. Hotel owners forked out ridiculous amounts to book big names, knowing the attendant media hype would lure high rollers to the gaming tables and thus make it worthwhile: Liberace set a well-publicized record when the **Riviera** paid him $50,000 per week to perform at the hotel's opening in 1955. Over the years, certain stars came to define a genre of entertainment known as the "Vegas style." Some seemed particularly attuned to the Vegas milieu; comedians Jimmy Durante, Phil Harris, and Joe E. Lewis flourished disproportionately to their popularity elsewhere. They were "down-front entertainers," as Sammy Davis Jr. put it, and they knew how to work the room, interacting with the audience and making everyone feel as if they were witnessing a unique event. As longtime *Las Vegas Review-Journal* columnist Forrest Duke defined the scene in the early 1960s: "These are primarily nightclub performers, their fans are nightclub patrons, and people who can afford to go to a nightclub usually can afford to drop some money in the casino on the way out."

By 1960, the **Sands Hotel** had a lock on the biggest names. Frank Sinatra was a heavyweight draw on his own, but the hotel capitalized on current headlines, presenting "The Summit at the Sands." The entire "Rat Pack" (Sinatra, Davis, Dean Martin, Peter Lawford, and Joey Bishop) held court in the **Sands**'s showroom for three weeks while in town filming *Ocean's Eleven* (VIPs in the audience included presidential hopeful John F. Kennedy). The town would be the Rat Pack's turf from that day on: Martin opened the **MGM Grand Hotel** (now **Bally's**) in 1973 and played there until health problems

forced him to quit in 1992. Sinatra celebrated his 77th birthday at the **Desert Inn.** When Davis died in 1990, the hotels on the Strip dimmed their lights in tribute for 10 minutes.

As the 1970s approached, Las Vegas was changing—growing bigger and more outlandish. Nightclub acts seemed like tea parties compared to the garish "feather shows" that had been getting more extravagant every year since they had first been imported from France in 1958. When the **International** (now the **Las Vegas Hilton**) opened in 1969, Barbra Streisand christened the **Showroom.** But she returned to her movie career, and management was desperate for a bigger star than the usual to fill the 1,500-seat theater—then the city's largest. Coincidentally, rock singer Elvis Presley was seeking a new direction for his career. It was the perfect marriage.

In the eyes of young people caught up in the 1960s revolution, Elvis had degenerated from the dangerous rebel of the 1950s to B-movie square. Instead of trying to establish himself with a new generation, Presley chose to reconnect with his following from the 1950s by donning a sequined jumpsuit, beefing up his rock combo with a full orchestra, and choreographing a few karate moves (which he "borrowed" from Tom Jones) into his act. The rest is showbiz history. More than 25 million people saw The King play 837 dates at the **Hilton** through 1976, and hotel officials claim there was never an empty seat. Indeed, it's reputed that fire inspectors were bribed to look the other way while an extra 500 fans were stuffed in for each show. In return, the hotel had no qualms about giving its top star the 5,000-square-foot apartment on the 30th floor: the **Elvis Suite.**

Meanwhile, the **Hilton** had another star who wasn't shy about upping his level of tastelessness to match the city's garish persona: Wladziu Valentino Liberace—known by his surname to the public and as "Lee" to his friends. He was a natural; back in 1952, Liberace made waves by trading in his black tux for a gold lamé smoking jacket. By the 1970s, Vegas had become synonymous with kitsch, and Liberace was welcomed into the fold, fueling the image with his floor-length furs, rhinestone jackets, and a harness rigging that allowed him to "fly" across the stage. The flamboyant pianist, who died in 1987, left behind costumes and custom-made pianos that are enshrined in the museum that bears his name (see page 77).

This first wave of headliners hit the Strip with some degree of star power already in place, but a story of the rags-to-riches variety also happened in Las Vegas during this period. Siegfried (Fischbacher) and Roy (Horn) first came to the **Tropicana Hotel**'s *Folies Bergere* as a specialty magic act in 1966, then secured a longer spot in the **Stardust Hotel**'s *Lido de Paris*. (The two had met several years earlier on a German cruise ship. Siegfried was the ship's magician; Roy, a homesick cabin boy who volunteered his pet cheetah for the act as an excuse to smuggle it on board.) They discovered that simply exchanging the traditional rabbit for a more exotic animal made the illusions more dramatic and added an aura of danger.

The duo hooked up with Irvin Feld, who had turned the **Ringling Brothers and Barnum & Bailey Circus** from a dying tradition into a million-dollar enterprise. First Feld signed them up for two **NBC**-TV specials in 1979. Then, having won their trust, he pitched a brilliantly simple plan: The Strip had stars, and it had production shows. Why not have both in one? *Beyond Belief* opened at the **Frontier Hotel** in late 1981 and made stars of Siegfried and Roy, who played an estimated 3,500 performances through 1987.

By then the team had a new gimmick—rare white tigers—and a deal to go to **The Mirage,** where their act raised the standards of showroom spectacle from near-naked women, circus trappings, and hyperactive musical numbers to a symphonic score and tasteful Broadway production values assimilated from the director of *Les Misérables* and the production designer of *Cats*.

A self-made product of the Vegas star machine, Wayne Newton was only 15 and needed a work permit to perform in the **Fremont Hotel** when he came from Phoenix with his brother Jerry in 1957. Newton might have been trapped in the lounge caste system forever had it not been for a booking on "The Jackie Gleason Show," which led to a meeting with Bobby Darin, who supervised the recording of Newton's 1961 breakthrough hit "Danke Schoen." Throughout the next 10 years, there were other chart-toppers for Wayne, but his bankability came from the reputation he built for having *the* must-see show on the Strip, performing 40 weeks a year at the **Sands, Desert Inn,** and **Frontier.**

When Elvis died in 1977, Vegas needed a star to fill the void. Newton was happy to take over not just the **Hilton** showroom, but to expand on the King's musical arrangements and his performance style as well. Elvis never landed on stage in a flying saucer, but Newton did, to the strains of "Thus Spake Zarathustra," zipping off his space suit to reveal a natty tuxedo jumpsuit. Leading his 36-piece orchestra through a distilled history of American music—from "Shenandoah" to "Bridge Over Troubled Water"—Newton makes each show seems like the

performance of his lifetime. Nearly every song is extended with an extra reprise, just in case the audience feels like giving him a standing ovation. And by the time he's played a plethora of instruments in one tune and implored the ushers to "lock the doors because this crowd is so hot tonight," they have dutifully given him several.

Today, the stars that helped build the town are now a niche market, and headline acts are but a shadow of the standard established during the glory days of the 1960s and 1970s. As the city zeroes in on families, showroom entertainment is becoming an endangered species. The downswing really began more than a decade ago, when hotel owners failed to groom a new generation of performers to take over from the aging perennials; simultaneously, rock 'n' roll's youthful audience turned away from the lounge lizards who made the city famous. The economics of the music business changed as well. Performers with clout can make much more money playing a one-night gig in a sports arena than from an extended run in a 1,200-seat showroom. The majority of Las Vegas visitors may still be over 40, but they prefer such classic rockers as Eric Clapton over crooners like Engelbert Humperdinck.

By 1993, only three celebrity rooms were still operating: **Bally's, Caesars Palace,** and the **Desert Inn.** Today, **Caesars** does not book an act every weekend, and the **Desert Inn**'s status as the last refuge for veteran Vegas mainstays such as Sinatra and Liza Minelli has been lost. But the **MGM Grand Hotel/Casino**—with its 650-seat room—took the **Desert Inn**'s place and kept the count at three, until March 1994, when the **Hard Rock Hotel and Casino** opened, and gave Vegas **The Joint,** a 1,400-seat headliner room.

With the turn of the century, the newest wave of blockbuster hotels will undoubtedly provide equally impressive celebrity rooms and guest stars. At press time, **Mandalay Bay**'s 12,000-seat **Events Center** had scheduled Luciano Pavarotti in concert and Oscar De La Hoya in the ring. Its **House of Blues** lineup included Neil Young, The Blues Brothers, Michael Bolton, and Bob Dylan.

While it may be harder to find the stars on certain weekends, they're not likely to totally disappear. Everyone from Noel Coward to Cheech & Chong has played Vegas, and the modern-day Strip still has a reserve of dependable headliners. Pop illusionist David Copperfield is so successful in Las Vegas he built a mansion here. And the city has embraced the country music boom, reaching out to stars such as Willie Nelson, Reba MacEntire, and George Strait. A showroom full of cowboy hats might seem odd at first, but it does take things full circle to the town's frontier origins.

Within Luxor Hotel & Casino:

**Isis** ★★★★$$$ This romantic 95-seat gourmet restaurant is set off by soft blue lights, larger-than-life Egyptian statues, and harp music. According to the embossed menus decorated with stone carvings, Isis was the ancient goddess of fertility. The appetites of guests are renewed with imaginative choices, from appetizer treasures of the sphinx to exotic desserts of the pharaohs. Among dramatically presented entrées are New York sirloin with green peppercorn sauce; lobster tail and seafood mousse in a pastry crust, topped with a white zinfandel sauce; and salmon fillet with spinach and pine nuts in papillote with lobster sauce. ♦ Continental ♦ Daily dinner. Reservations recommended. 262.4773

# Sacred Sea Room

**Sacred Sea Room** ★★★$$$ Hieroglyphic murals and tiled mosaics set the mood for this casual eatery where fresh fish is the main order of the day. Choose from a menu of lobster, scallops, Dover sole, and salmon. Other offerings include perfectly prepared New York steak, veal chop, and a variety of chicken dishes. ♦ American ♦ Daily dinner. Reservations recommended. 262.4772 ⅃

**Luxor Steak House** ★★★$$$ One of the best steak houses in Las Vegas also sports the most sophisticated decor, with dark cherry wood paneling and black trim. Start your meal with steak tartare or a Caesar salad; then try the New York cut, which is kissed with a hint of mesquite. The assortment of accompaniments —potatoes, steamed broccoli, and creamed spinach—are excellent, too. The wine list is extraordinary and the desserts are just as fine. ♦ Steak house ♦ Daily dinner. Reservations required. 262.4778 ⅃

**Ra Club** Black-and-gold Egyptian decor, fire-breathing bartenders, and a futuristic light-and-sound system set a spectacular scene at one of the city's hottest clubs. Unusual for a disco, it also sports a Japanese restaurant and lively sushi bar. ♦ Cover. W-Sa 10PM-6AM. 262.5900

### MANDALAY BAY
Resort & Casino · Las Vegas

**49 Mandalay Bay Resort & Casino** $$$ Sumptuous is the word to describe this newly opened $950-million resort. Beyond the complex's distinctive V-shaped, reflective gold facade, echoes of the Far East are expressed in lush foliage, tiny pagodas, and temples over a 60-acre expanse. The 3,300 rooms and suites are equally lavish, boasting sweeping views of the mountains or the Strip and featuring king- and queen-size beds, multi-line phones, and soaking baths. Recreational facilities and pure creature comforts abound: sand-and-surf beach, tennis courts, a health and fitness center, and more. After a day at the 135,000-square-foot casino—with its 122 gaming tables, 2,400 slot machines, and private salon for high rollers—opt for a splash in the pool located at the 11-acre surf beach or a massage at the 30,000-square-foot spa (there is a fee for using the spa and the health and fitness center). Guests have a choice of refueling at more than a dozen restaurants. The 43rd floor hosts a membership-only **House of Blues Foundation Room,** where celebrities can enjoy privacy while listening to music. There's also a 1,700-seat theater and a 12,000-seat events center. This resort is an upscale property owned by Mandalay Resorts. ♦ 3950 Las Vegas Blvd S (between W Russell Rd and W Tropicana Ave). 632.7777, 877/632.7000; fax 632.7190; www.mandalaybay-lasvegas.com ⅃

Within the Mandalay Bay Resort & Casino:

**Aureole** ★★★★$$$$ Renowned chef Charlie Palmer, who created the classic dishes for his New York restaurant, brings them to Las Vegas, while Adam Tihany designed the surroundings that highlight them. This $11-million project includes a four-story wine tower that houses wines ranging in price from $50 to $3,500 (choose from the 28-page-long wine list) and two dining rooms. Step down a chrome-railed staircase to the main dining area where Tihany's signature "mad hatter" wall lamps with tilted shades provide lighting and atmosphere. High-tech chrome furnishings are softened by plaid fabrics and butterscotch-colored leather chairs. A cascading waterfall separates this dining area from the Swan Court, where floor-to-ceiling windows provide a spectacular view of swans swimming in the man-made lake. The dining rooms have identical menus, but prix-fixe dinners are served in Swan Court, while the menu in the main room is à la carte. House chefs Joe and Megan Romano produce unique appetizers such as sea scallops sandwiched in crisp potato crusts, sautéed foie gras with roasted apple compote, and oak-smoked salmon with toasted corn. A sampling of entrées might include pepper-seared tuna wrapped in green-onion risotto, pan-roasted lobster with caramelized fennel, or tagliatelle with wild mushrooms and marinated artichokes. End this elegant repast with the sensational Meyer lemon tarte, espresso-chocolate pot du crème, crème brûlée, or fresh sorbets. ♦ Continental ♦ Daily dinner. Reservations required. 632.7425 &

**China Grill** ★★$$$ Computerized graphics of clouds, shooting stars, or other designs (which can be changed to suit the clientele) illuminate the domed ceiling of this high-tech eatery designed by Jeffrey Beers International. The glassed-in exhibition kitchen serves as an additional visual focal point. A sister of the highly-touted New York and Miami Beach establishments, this restaurant seems to please the crowds. Some of the culinary offerings, however, are more successful than others. For appetizers, try the saki-cured salmon rolls, the broccoli rabe dumplings, or beef filet satay. Main courses to opt for include Shanghai lobster with ginger, curry, and crispy spinach; sizzling whole fish in Chinese black-bean and red-chili sauce; or Japanese panko-crusted veal. Desserts are a must, especially if you're a chocolate lover: Try the warm fudge-walnut tart, Ivory Sensation (a white chocolate mousse with wild cherry sauce), Chocolate Seduction (an assortment of chocolates), or a rich banana split. ♦ Asian/Continental ♦ Daily dinner. Reservations recommended. 632.7404 &

**Trattoria del Lupo** ★★★$$$ The collaborative efforts of world-famous chef Wolfgang Puck and talented designer Adam Tihany have, once again, paid off. The comfortable decor of the Tuscan-themed trattoria—cobblestone floors, hanging cheeses and pastramis, and communal tables—complements the heart-and-soul-warming cuisine. Start with thick, Tuscan-style tomato soup or any of the homemade soups. Follow with designer pizzas such as artichoke and provolone, portabello mushrooms and goat cheese, or eggplant, shallot, fontina, and thyme. The baked spaghetti tart, rotisserie chicken, lamb chops, or grilled calamari with arugula, fennel, and lemon are also popular choices. Any of the desserts—dark chocolate apricot cake with toasted almond ice cream, chocolate hazelnut truffle torte, warm pear pie topped with vanilla ice cream, or even a light fruit sorbet—will provide a satisfying ending. ♦ Italian ♦ Daily lunch and dinner. Reservations recommended. 740.5522 &

**●9 Four Seasons Hotel Las Vegas** $$$$ This ultra-exclusive 424-room hideaway exudes elegance synonymous with all Four Seasons properties. The spacious 338 deluxe guest rooms and 86 suites offer spectacular views and are luxuriously appointed with private mini-bars, marble baths, two phones, and computer/fax hookups. Concierge, 24-hour room service, and a business center are just a few steps away. On the ground floor, two restaurants, the club bar, and lobby lounge fill guests' needs for sustenance. Conference rooms, a full-service spa, 8,000 square-foot pool area with two pools and cabanas, jogging trail, and access to additional facilities at the adjoining Mandalay Bay Resort & Casino complete the picture. ♦ 3960 Las Vegas Blvd S (between W Russell Rd and W Tropicana Ave). 632.5000, 877/632.5000; fax 632.5195; www.fourseasons.com &

Within the Four Seasons Hotel:

**First Floor Grill** ★★★★$$$$ Fresh flowers adorn this elegant, contemporary room decorated in rich shades of yellow and purple and offset with mahogany touches. The service is impeccable and the food is excellent. In fact, the appetizer of white bean and arugula soup couldn't be more perfect. Main course features include blackened *ahi*, fresh Dover sole, and grilled halibut, as well as delicious steak and chop selections. For dessert try the bourbon vanilla crème brûlée, caramelized lemon tart with orange ice, peach and bitter almond frangipane tart, or double espresso tiramisù with cappuccino-chocolate sabayon. The setting is formal and luxurious, ideal for romance and celebration. ♦ Continental ♦ Dinner Tu-Su. Reservations required. 632.5000 &

**Verandah Cafe** ★★★$$$ This Mediterranean-style eatery with white stucco walls features an intimate terrace laced with lemon and olive trees. Among the satisfying entrées offered here are grilled salmon paillard with spring vegetables, peppered *ahi*, garlicky tiger prawns, Colorado rack of lamb with cherry tomatoes and garlic chips, and osso buco with polenta. Delicious chocolate cake with raspberry coulis will satisfy any sweet lover. Open from 6AM till midnight, the restaurant offers a lighter lunch menu of sandwiches, salads, pizza, and pot stickers. ♦ Continental ♦ Daily breakfast, lunch, and dinner. 632.5000 &

"I first came to Las Vegas in November 1968 to open at the Flamingo Hotel for the brilliant singer-composer Charles Aznavour. I was so naive about the city that when I heard 'desert,' I arrived in mid-November with a wardrobe consisting only of shorts, bathing suits, and cotton dresses. I remember shivering and running back and forth each evening to the stage entrance where the stage manager waited with a hot cup of coffee."

                             **Joan Rivers**

# West Las Vegas

For more than 30 years beginning in 1905, the railroad reigned supreme in Las Vegas wielding, authority over civic affairs as if this were a company town. In fact, trains were so crucial to the city's development that they held a firm grip on the community for several decades *before* the first cars actually pulled into the station. Starting in 1871, when the first stretch of track was laid southwest from Salt Lake City in the direction of Los Angeles, and up to the turn of the century, the ranchers and cowboys of the **Las Vegas Valley**, along with everyone else familiar with the lay of the southern Nevada desert, were anxiously awaiting the imminent arrival of the iron horse.

Helen Stewart was one of those who was banking on the railroad. Her husband, Archibald Stewart, had foreclosed on the 640-acre **Las Vegas Ranch** in 1881 after its owner, original valley homesteader O.D. Gass, failed to repay a loan. Shortly thereafter, a neighboring ranch hand shot and killed Stewart, who was defending Helen's honor against gossip that she was morally fast and loose. The widow assumed control of the ranch and managed it so effectively that by the early 1900s she'd amassed an additional 1,160 acres and most of the valley's water rights. During those 20 years, she speculated that the railroad would eventually roll through. Sure enough, in 1902, the San Pedro, Los Angeles, and Salt Lake Railroad offered Helen $55,000 for most of her property (little more than $33 an acre, a paltry sum even then). It was the only offer she received, and she readily agreed to the deal.

In 1903 Helen hired J.T. McWilliams to survey the boundaries of the property she planned to sell. During the course of his scrutiny, McWilliams determined that 80 acres west of the ranch were untitled, and he promptly claimed them for himself. He then mapped out a town plan and began selling lots to the first arrivals, people who were either seeking jobs with the railroad or land investors looking to make a profit once the depot opened for business. Though neither McWilliams nor the widow Stewart got wealthy from their speculation, a town was named after McWilliams.

**McWilliamsville**, popularly known as **Ragtown** (either for its canvas dwellings or wash-strewn clotheslines), sat just west of the train tracks. It grew quickly, and after a year was a burgeoning boomtown with a population of more than a thousand. But the fledgling city was doomed when the railroad conglomerate plotted its own company town to the east. When this "official" Las Vegas was established in 1905, Ragtown's access to running water was deliberately curtailed by the railroad to hasten its demise. Within six months, McWilliamsville was nearly abandoned.

But a small shantytown remained, inhabited by squatters; cut off from Las Vegas by the railroad tracks, it was gradually ghettoized. Over the next 60 years, as the city grew up around it, McWilliams's original town site came to be designated as the **Westside.** Even today, it's still considered the wrong side of the tracks.

In the last 25 years, Las Vegas has spread west, northwest, and southwest in its quest to conquer the entire valley. The Westside is only a tiny pocket of what is now called West Las Vegas. Vacant desert a decade ago, patchy subdivisions and skeletal commercial strips a mere five years ago, today West Las Vegas is a grid of residences and retail centers, a triumph of suburbia. Embryonic planned communities continue to encroach on the sheer limestone and sandstone escarpment of the Spring Mountains, which erupt from the edge of the Las Vegas Valley.

The swelling new subdivisions, however, are merely an advance guard, comparable to what Ragtown was to **Downtown** in its day. Though they contain thousands of condos and row houses, they're dwarfed by the scale of the crowning real estate achievement of western Las Vegas: **Summerlin,** a 22,000-acre planned community.

A drive through West Las Vegas answers the oft-posed question "People actually live in Las Vegas?" Close to one million do. A territorial breed, West Las Vegans venture onto the Strip and into Downtown infrequently, rarely even going to the east side of the city. They shop at the corner supermarket and the **Meadows Mall,** eat at the many neighborhood restaurants, and play in off-Strip casinos, such as **Arizona Charlie's, Gold Coast, Palace Station, Rio, Fiesta, Texas Station,** and **Santa Fe,** all of which are among the most popular and profitable in town.

Other than the casinos, parks, and museums, the **Southern Nevada Zoological Botanical Park,** the **YESCO** neon sign company, and the largest dance floor in town at the **Gold Coast Hotel,** the primary reason to explore West Las Vegas is for the good local restaurants, bars, and shops. Even if you don't make a special trip here, certainly stop on the way to **Red Rock Canyon**—the heart of the **Spring Mountains.** The lofty and rugged Springs, southern Nevada's preeminent pinnacles, are perhaps the only barrier that can halt as inexorable a manifest destiny as that of Las Vegas.

**1 Santa Fe Hotel and Casino** $$ Far from the Strip, with Mount Charleston as a backdrop, this place offers 200 rooms decorated in soothing Southwestern style. Amenities include three restaurants; a 24-hour coffee shop; the **Lone Mountain Buffet;** a fully equipped casino with sports and race book, over 1,700 slot machines, keno, and bingo; a state-of-the art 60-lane bowling center; and the public ice-skating rink (see "Child's Play," page 93) where Olympic champions often practice when in town. ♦ 4949 N Rancho Dr (between Lone Mountain Rd and Gragson Hwy). 658.4900, 800/872.6823, fax 658.4919; www.santafecasino.com &

Within the Santa Fe Hotel and Casino:

**Ti Amo** ★★★$$ An airy courtyard setting and open kitchen make this an appealing place to relax and watch your dinner being prepared. Favorites on the innovative menu include pineapple pizza (with oven-dried pineapple and sun-dried cherries) and *française* trio (crab leg, veal, and chicken in a light wine sauce). Among the pasta specialties are *cappellini pomodoro* (thin pasta with basil and tomato sauce) and tortellini pesto. On Saturday and Sunday, there's an all-you-can-eat jazz and Champagne brunch. ♦ Italian ♦ M-F lunch and dinner; Sa dinner; Su brunch and dinner. Reservations recommended. 658.4900 &

**Suzette's** ★★★★$$$$ A perfect special occasion spot, this elegant restaurant seats only 50 guests. The formal French provincial decor is enhanced by sparkling crystal chandeliers, which are hung from a trompe l'oeil blue-sky ceiling. White-gloved waiters in formal attire serve such classic French presentations as *capon à la Suzette* (stuffed with wild mushrooms and spinach), tournedos of beef with truffles, scampi flambéed in a brandy cream sauce, and salmon poached in a Champagne sauce with smoked scallions. The extensive wine list includes Château Latour and Mondavi Opus One. ♦ French ♦ Tu-Sa dinner. Reservations recommended. 658.4900

**Kodiak Lodge** ★★★$$ Resembling a rustic hunting lodge, this charming room features rockscapes, redwood decor, and a 13-foot hand-carved bear at its entrance. Thick steaks and chops are prepared over a mesquite grill in the open kitchen. Seafood from the Pacific Northwest, including salmon, swordfish, and rainbow trout, is also featured. Chicken, pork loin, prime ribs, and baby back ribs are prepared to perfection on a rotisserie. Try the "shell and shore"—smoked scallop brochette and beef kabob. ♦ Steak house ♦ Daily dinner. Reservations recommended. 658.4900

**2 Fiesta Hotel and Casino** $$ This 100-room hotel has become a favorite with locals and a place that curious visitors—those willing to leave the Strip and Downtown areas—are sure to enjoy. Its adobe decor is festive, and its large casino has been dubbed by locals as "Royal Flush Capital of the World." Guests also enjoy one of the top buffets in town as well as the **Old San Francisco Steakhouse** and **Gardunos** Mexican restaurant. ♦ 2400 N Rancho Dr (between W Lake Mead Blvd and W Carey Ave). 631.7000, 800/731.7333; fax 631.6588 &

Within the Fiesta Hotel and Casino:

**Fiesta Casino** Video poker reigns supreme here. The casino claims more royal flushes per machine than anywhere else in Las Vegas—good payout schedules and a steady, loyal clientele combine for nonstop video-poker action. For the novice there are instructions given by a video-poker pro. And for those on the run, there's even the drive-up race and sports book window. ♦ Daily 24 hours. 631.7000

**Festival Buffet** ★★★$ What makes this buffet such a success is the huge open-fire pit where sides of beef and whole chickens are barbecued to perfection. Also on order are pork and beef ribs and smoked sausage. Don't forget the other stations, including stir-fry, Mongolian grill, fish-and-chips, and, of course, sweet treats and desserts. ♦ Barbecue ♦ Daily breakfast, lunch, and dinner. 631.7000

**3 Texas Station Gambling Hall & Casino** $$ Recently opened by the owners of **Palace Station**, this 200-room property shares the spotlight with **The Fiesta** across the street. Amenities include four restaurants; an excellent buffet; three lively lounges, including the **Armadillo Honky Tonk;** and a multiplex movie theater. ♦ 2101 N Rancho Dr (between Coran La and W Lake Mead Blvd). 631.1000, 800/654.8888; fax 631.1010; www.stationcasinos.com &

Within the Texas Station Hotel and Casino:

**Texas Casino** This casino may lure you with its winning Texas-style decor of wagon wheels, antique guns, and a recent $51-million expansion to its casino, but if it's video poker you're looking for head across the way to **The Fiesta.** For its part, though, this gaming room does have more tables than most along with bingo, a poker room, and a large race and sports book. ♦ Daily 24 hours. 631.1000

**Feast Around The World Buffet** ★★★$ An extremely popular destination, this place is actually five restaurants in one. Feast from a menu of Italian, Mexican, Chinese, Texas barbecue, and classic American specialties. There are traditional pastas in every shape and size, fajitas, enchiladas, plus a special Texas-style chili station offering vegetarian as well as "hot," "hotter," and "hottest" varieties. There also are great salad and dessert bars. ♦ Eclectic ♦ Daily breakfast, lunch, and dinner. 631.1000

**4 Southern Nevada Zoological Botanical Park** Located on 2.5 acres, this park exhibits a variety of endangered cats as well as chimpanzees, eagles, ostriches, emus, talking parrots, flamingos, as well as a large collection of venomous reptiles native to the Nevada. There are many educational exhibits by the **Las Vegas Gem Club** featuring rocks, minerals, gems, fossils, and ancient artifacts. The botanical displays are just as interesting with endangered cycads and rare bamboos topping the list. ♦ Admission. Daily. 1775 N Rancho Dr (between Sunset Dr and Melody La). 648.5955

**5 Siegfried & Roy House** Tucked away behind a high white fence and a gate guarded by lions (the statuary type), this mission-style mansion topped by a gilt dome sprawls over half a city block. The luxuriant landscape provides a suitably exotic hideaway for the two German-born magicians who shoot tigers from a cannon—and then bring them home for a dip in the pool. Siegfried & Roy are now at the top of their game: Their $57.5-million deal with **The Mirage** is, according to Guinness, one of the largest live entertainment contracts ever signed. They sell out the 1,500 most expensive seats in Las Vegas every night. (Tickets to their show are double the price of the second-most expensive one in town.) This is your opportunity to gawk at a Hollywood-type home in Las Vegas, but remember, it's private property. ♦ 4200 Vegas Dr (at Valley Dr)

**6 Lorenzi Park** David Lorenzi's Twin Lakes Resort, a ritzy hideaway for locals, stood on this site in the 1920s. The five-acre pond is still a popular place for small boating, duck feeding, and lazing on sunny afternoons, although the once-famous bandstand is now gone. In various far-flung corners of the park are the **Nevada State Museum and Historical Society,** a 20-year-old rose garden, numerous tennis courts, soccer and baseball fields, a playground, and picnic tables. Wide-open grassy areas are abundant in the center of the park and are ideal for Frisbee tossing. ◆ 3300 W Washington Ave (between N Rancho and Twin Lakes Drs). 229.6358

Within Lorenzi Park:

**Nevada State Museum and Historical Society** The exhibits at this state-run museum give visitors a surprisingly in-depth overview of the history, anthropology, and archaeology of the region. One room is devoted to natural history, where the various environmental zones of southern Nevada are presented in compelling dioramas of bighorn sheep, cougars, and a variety of snakes, cholla and cactus, and insects. Another section focuses on the historical events that shaped the state, from the era of the Pueblo and Paiute Indians through the ranching, railroad, and mining days to modern times (a particularly poignant exhibit covers the nearby Nevada Test Site and its atmospheric and underground nuclear explosions; the photos of soldiers purposely exposed to shock waves and fallout are quite graphic). A third gallery hosts changing historic and photographic exhibits. In the lobby, a gift shop sells books, cards, jewelry, and souvenirs. History buffs can consult the on-site research center for help in answering questions. ◆ Admission. Daily. 700 Twin Lakes Dr (between Avalon and W Washington Aves). 486.5205

**7 Meadows Mall** Four major department stores anchor this sprawling, two-level enclosed shopping center. Besides the usual jewelry, apparel, home furnishings, book, and toy stores, there's a merry-go-round in the mall—a great diversion for the kids. ◆ M-F 10AM-9PM; Sa-Su. 4300 Meadows La (between S Valley View and S Decatur Blvds). 878.4849

**8 Summerlin** Smitten with Las Vegas, billionaire Howard Hughes began investing in the city in the early 1950s. One deal involved purchasing 25,000 acres of desert from the Southern Pacific Railroad for $62,500. Hughes then engineered a trade for an extremely valuable 22,000-acre tract between the town and the Spring Mountains, using reasons of "national security" (in the guise of his defense contracts with the Pentagon) to steamroll the objections of locals, who were shocked that the federal government would

make such a blatantly bad exchange. For the next three decades, the 39-square-mile parcel was known as Husite.

Today, a 36-square-mile master-planned community is being developed on the property by the Howard Hughes Corporation; it is named Summerlin, after Howard's grandmother. Its slight elevation affords beautiful views of the valley, which looks especially spectacular when the sun sets over the mountains, providing a natural light show to rival the neon of Downtown. Currently, 30,000 full-time residents live in the first village. There are both public and private schools, houses of worship, lighted ball fields, shopping centers and business parks. Two professional golf courses are located in Summerlin: the **Tournament Players Club at Summerlin,** which hosts the annual Las Vegas Invitational, and the **Tournament Players Club at The Canyons,** where the Las Vegas Senior Classic is held each year. When completed (approximately 2020), the community is expected to be nearly as large as Las Vegas was in the 1980s. ◆ www.summerlin.com

In Summerlin:

THE RESORT AT SUMMERLIN

**Resort at Summerlin** $$$$ Located in the desert, this $300-million megaresort offers spectacular views of gardens and the Red Rock Canyon. Guests enjoy the relaxing surroundings featuring lush landscaping, waterfalls, and soothing accommodations within its 54 acres. Anchoring the resort are the **Regent Grand Spa** with 287 rooms and suites, and the **Regent Grand Palms** offering 253 rooms and suites—all tastefully furnished with Southwestern-style accents. Guests also enjoy other top-flight pleasures at the resort: a total of nine restaurants, including **Parvan,** touting a New American menu; a 50,000-square-foot casino; an art gallery; and marketplace.

The 40,000-square-foot **Aquae Sulis** spa and health club highlights individual exercise/diet programs, as well as a variety of hydrotherapy treatments, loofah scrubs, body wraps, aromatherapy facials and massage. State-of-the art cardiovascular and weight training equipment is also available. ◆ 221 N Rampart Blvd (between Canyon Run Dr and Summerlin Pkwy). 869.7777, 877/869.8777; www.resortatsummerlin.com &

**9 West Charleston Library** Bookies of a different sort will appreciate this 1993 work of the local architectural firm **Welles-Pugsley.** The interior is spacious and comfortable, with ample windows conducive to curling up with a classic. A high, vaulted ceiling runs down the main axis of the library, directing visitors to the reference and circulation desks. Within the 40,000-square-foot building are 160,000 volumes, a 280-seat lecture hall, conference rooms, an art gallery, a health-science library, and a young people's library complete with the **High-Flying Theater,** where storytelling programs are held. The landscaping is an artful example of Xeriscaping, which employs drought-resistant plants. ◆ M-Th 9AM-9PM; F-Sa; Su noon-5PM. 6301 W Charleston Blvd (at Verdinal Dr). 878.3682

**10 Arizona Charlie's Hotel & Casino** $$ The Southwestern flair of this 289-room neighborhood hotel-casino attracts a local patronage; it's usually jammed with video-poker players, paycheck cashers, and West Las Vegans out for a few drinks in the popular lounge. It also has a well-deserved reputation as a hot spot for video poker; look for the quarter video-poker machines that pay a thousand dollars for four aces as well as a royal flush and give you 2.5 percent edge over the house. ◆ Daily 24 hours. 740 S Decatur Blvd (at Evergreen Ave). 258.5200, 800/342.2695; www.azcharlies.com ♿

Within Arizona Charlie's Hotel & Casino:

**Chin's** ★★★★$$$ This intimate 64-seat jewel is decorated with framed antique Asian embroideries and portraits of royalty from the Qing and Tang dynasties. A stream of water (which symbolizes money and luck, according to Chinese tradition) flows through the restaurant; there are even miniature bridges across it. A pagoda in the center of the cozy room encloses the traditional round table for 10, and Chinese lanterns hung overhead create a romantic glow.

The menu duplicates that of Tola Chin's other popular, eponymous eatery on the Strip. Appetizers include *moo shu* pork (shredded pork and vegetables rolled in pancakes), steamed scallops on the half shell, and hot-and-sour and *war won ton* soups. Among the best main dishes are wok-cooked vegetables with chicken, seafood, or beef; lobster with mushrooms; spicy chicken; crispy duck; and sweet-and-sour pork. For dessert, choose the lychees and cherries jubilee, flamed at tableside. ◆ Chinese ◆ Tu-Su dinner. Reservations recommended. 258.5173. Also at: Fashion Show Mall, 3200 Las Vegas Blvd S (at Fashion Show Dr). 733.8899

**11 Aristocrat** ★★★$$$$ One of a handful of independent gourmet restaurants, this cozy hideaway with English touches reflects its British owner's heritage. It's a favorite among well-heeled locals, who come to partake of such house specialties as mussels vinaigrette, osso buco, beef Wellington, and chicken Oscar (chicken topped with crabmeat, asparagus, and béarnaise sauce). ◆ Continental ◆ M-F lunch and dinner; Sa-Su dinner. Reservations recommended. 850 S Rancho Dr (between W Charleston Blvd and Palomino La). 870.1977

# Book Magician
### Donato's Fine Books

**12 Book Magician** This haunt continues to be a favorite among lovers of used books—most of which are the 50¢ paperback variety. Stocking thousands of titles in every conceivable category, they have paperbacks, hardcovers, leatherbound volumes, and first editions and author-signed copies. It's as well organized and neat as a library (except for the children's section, which is supposed to be untidy). Best of all, a big sign on the door proclaims "Ice Cream Welcome," encouraging cone-carrying customers from the next-door **Baskin-Robbins** to come in and look while they lick. ◆ Daily. 2202 W Charleston Blvd (between S Tonopah and S Rancho Drs). 384.5838

**13 Palace Station Hotel** $$ A tiny bingo parlor opened here in the late 1970s. Since then, it's grown into one of the premier off-Strip hotels. The 12-story tower was built in 1991, and the well-maintained rooms have firm beds and comfortable chairs; they also have good views of the city. Including the older garden rooms, which are low-rise, motel style, there are 1,030 rooms. The lounge has entertainment nightly, and a free shuttle bus runs every hour to and from the Strip. ◆ 2411 W Sahara Ave (between S Rancho and Teddy Drs). 367.2411, 800/634.3101; fax 367.6138; www.stationcasinos.com ♿

Within the Palace Station Hotel:

**Palace Station Casino** The hotel sports a railroad motif, and the main casino pit offers a brief lesson in Nevada's railway heritage: Depot-type awnings advertise the **Union Pacific, Las Vegas & Tonopah; Tonopah & Tidewater;** and **Virginia & Truckee** lines. The 550-seat bingo room is one of the busiest around, and the 200-seat race and sports book has 42 TV screens. ◆ Daily 24 hours. 367.2411

---

"I came to Las Vegas in a $28,000 Cadillac and left in a $280,000 Greyhound bus."

Milton Berle

# Easy Come, Easy Go: Marriage and Divorce in Nevada

Never mind poker, baccarat, or blackjack. Each year, thousands of Las Vegas visitors choose to play the ultimate game of chance: matrimony. Approximately 85,000 marriage licenses are issued annually in **Clark County**—which includes Las Vegas and the southern tip of Nevada—alone. And while they probably don't realize it, this legion of lovers is supporting a business that's been inextricably tied to Nevada's gaming tradition for more than 60 years.

Las Vegas's wedding industry owes its existence largely to a 1931 state statute (it was passed at the same time as legislation that legalized gambling) that liberalized the state's marriage and divorce laws. Couples were now able to obtain a divorce after a mere six weeks' residency in the state. Reno-area resorts, sensing a financial gold mine, nationally touted the locale as the ideal place where the soon-to-be-separated could spend their time (and money) in comfort and style, while fulfilling the letter of the law.

In Las Vegas, some token efforts were made to follow suit. But—call it romantic, or just call it a stroke of opportunistic marketing savvy—southern Nevada entrepreneurs decided to focus on the other side of the connubial coin. They made a name for themselves by capitalizing on the lenient law's waiver of a blood test and waiting period for prospective newlyweds. In short order, wedding chapels sprouted up all over the **Las Vegas Valley,** and the city rapidly established a reputation as the place for quick, hassle-free nuptials.

That image has been enhanced over the years by the eclectic roster of celebrities who have decided to tie the knot in Las Vegas. Among the notables to have walked down the aisle here are: Mickey Rooney, Judy Garland, Joan Collins, Michael Jordan, Bruce Willis and Demi Moore, Richard Gere and Cindy Crawford, and Dennis Rodman and Carmen Electra (there's no insurance provided against splitting up). Las Vegas weddings also appeal to ordinary folk who are looking to keep the affair low-key.

If you're scheduling your own nuptials, book far in advance to get married on a Saturday or holiday (particularly Valentine's Day and New Year's Day). The typical ceremony takes anywhere from a few minutes to a half hour— the quicker to get back to the tables. In keeping with the relaxed attitude of the ordinance, those presiding tend to be amenable sorts who aren't pushy about inserting religious references into vows for couples who don't want them. Some vows are by-the-book traditional, while others resemble the results of a high school creative writing project.

In addition to being convenient, a wedding is one of the city's best bargains, costing as little as $25 (not including the license, which currently runs $35). A donation to the officiant—usually $25 to $50— is customary. For an additional fee, most facilities can also provide such extras as music, flowers, photo and videotape services, and even tuxedos.

---

**The Broiler** ★★$$$ An amazing meal deal is the main draw here. From Sunday through Thursday, the Alaskan king crab leg dinner is half price. The fat, footlong legs are cooked to steaming perfection and piled high on the plate. The food is not only first-rate, it's also reliable. Other dishes include hearty steaks, trout, orange roughy, scallops, shrimp tempura, and the catch of the day. Also look for a good selection of steaks and prime ribs on the menu. ♦ Seafood ♦ Daily lunch and dinner. Reservations recommended for dinner. 367.2411 &

**Guadalajara Bar and Grille** ★$ Stop first at the bar outside the restaurant, grab a 16-ounce margarita, and get change back from a dollar. Then sit down at a booth inside and savor the excellent burritos, *chile verde, tipico del mar* (seafood platter), the Humunga Chunga (a one-and-a-half-pound chimichanga), or *chimijitas* (grilled marinated steak with onions, green peppers, guacamole, and sour cream, wrapped in a tortilla and deep-fried). ♦ Mexican ♦ Daily lunch and dinner. Reservations recommended for dinner. 367.2411

**Feast Buffet** ★$ The feast proffered here is worthy of its moniker and good reputation. Short-order cooks prepare eggs, waffles, burgers, grilled chicken, steaks, and fish, and slice huge slabs of lamb, beef, and pork before your eyes. Salads and desserts are plentiful. ♦ Buffet ♦ Daily breakfast, lunch, and dinner. 367.2411

**14 Cafe Michelle West** ★★★$$$ A strip shopping center on one of the busiest drags in Las Vegas hosts this replica of East Las Vegas's popular **Cafe Michelle.** Lush landscaping creates a secluded, even bucolic, setting. A footbridge spans two ponds with spurting Roman fountains and leads to two courtyards that are ideal for alfresco dining. The front patio is shielded from the parking lot by thick, high shrubbery; the sheltered side piazza is shaded by ivy-covered trellises. Inside, choose between two very chic dining rooms. The menu is just as diverse as at its East Side cousin, and the Monique and Normandie crepes are just as good. ♦ Continental ♦ Daily lunch and dinner. Reservations recommended for four or more. 2800 W Sahara Ave (between Paseo del Prado and Richfield Blvd). 873.5400 ⑤

**14 Coffee Pub** ★★$$ This charming, friendly gathering spot featuring patio dining is popular with local movers and shakers. The menu includes imaginative salads, sandwiches, pastries, espresso, cappuccino, and *caffè latte*. ♦ American ♦ Daily breakfast and lunch. 2800 W Sahara Ave (between Paseo del Prado and Richfield Blvd). 367.1913

**14 In-N-Out Burger** ★$ An institution in Southern California for more than 50 years, this Las Vegas location, opened in 1992, was the chain's first venture outside the Golden State and has since spawned half a dozen more. Management claims no restaurant in the entire chain has ever owned a freezer. The french fries are peeled, cut, and fried to order, and the lemonade is freshly squeezed. The Double-Double is the specialty: two quarter-pound burgers and two slices of cheese. If you're hankering for a real cholesterol fest, order a Three-by-Three or a Four-by-Four, even though those options aren't on the menu. The building is so white and brightly lighted that it's impossible to miss; just look for the dozen or so cars lined up at the drive-through window. ♦ Burgers ♦ Daily lunch and dinner. 2900 W Sahara Ave (between Paseo del Prado and Richfield Blvd). No phone. Also at numerous locations throughout the city

**15 The Venetian Ristorante** ★★★$$$ Bearing a trompe l'oeil mural worthy of early Disney (or late **Circus Circus**), this restaurant has been a local landmark for four decades. The painter's touch continues inside, with a *Mona Lisa* replica and cityscapes of Venice adorning the walls. The menu is a work of art as well, with pages of pasta, veal, chicken,

seafood, and wine selections. The pork neck bones marinated and simmered in a vinegar, caper, and wine sauce are humble but succulent. From 4 to 6PM, a less pricey early-bird menu features bruschetta (toasted garlic bread) with roasted peppers, basil, and parmesan; Caesar salad; pizzas; and the famous Venetian greens on a bed of pasta. ♦ Italian ♦ Daily 24 hours. 3713 W Sahara Ave (between Valley View Blvd and Las Verdes St). 876.4190 ⑤

**16 Saigon Restaurant** ★★$ This intimate 12-table restaurant is the best place in Las Vegas for Vietnamese food. Anyone who tastes the imperial rolls will never accept mere egg rolls again. Other light eats are the Vietnamese pizza appetizer, sour soups, or spicy lemon-beef salad. Fifteen *pho* (noodle) dishes and a couple of clay-pot (hearty soup) selections are available. The Vietnamese version of beef fondue and several other authentic entrées are cooked right at the table. Ask for the special coconut-curry sauce to spice things up. ♦ Vietnamese ♦ Daily lunch and dinner. 4251 W Sahara Ave (between Las Verdes and Arville Sts). 362.9978

**17 Philip's Supper House** ★★$$$$ Between the Strip's **Golden Steer** and this place, upward of 2,000 steak dinners can be served on Sahara Avenue on a busy night. This rambling building is divided into a number of small dining rooms; those looking for tête-à-tête tables can reserve one of several *very* private booths. Going beyond beef, there's blackened or crab-stuffed scampi, sand dabs (small fish from the West Coast served sautéed or fried), halibut *picanti* (with hot chilies), and daily fresh fish specials. Veal, chicken, and lamb chops round out the menu. All meals come with soup or salad, potato or vegetable, and hot, fresh-baked bread. A mannequin sits at the player piano in the bar, and a sign makes the management's sentiments on unruly children perfectly clear. ♦ American/Italian ♦ Daily dinner. Reservations recommended. 4545 W Sahara Ave (between Arville St and S Decatur Blvd). 873.5222 ⑤

***Mayflower***

Cuisinier

**18 Mayflower Cuisinier ★★★$$$** Hong Kong–born chef-owner Ming See Woo and her daughter Theresa offer their well-heeled clientele (many of whom are Chinese) a unique fusion of Asian and French cuisines. Fashioning their menu after the likes of LA superchefs Wolfgang Puck and Tommy Tang, the mother-daughter team's cross-cultural recipes include roasted duck salad with plum vinaigrette, grilled tenderloin of beef with Mongolian sauce, shrimp in pineapple-apricot sauce with scallion noodles, and the ginger chicken ravioli with scallion-Szechuan sauce. The decor is sleek and modern, with Asian etchings on the walls. There's a mezzanine that seats about 30 and a patio for alfresco dining; it's heated in the winter and cooled in the summer. ♦ Asian/French ♦ M-F lunch and dinner; Sa dinner. Reservations recommended. 4750 W Sahara Ave (between Arville St and S Decatur Blvd). 870.8432

*Cafe Nicolle*

**18 Cafe Nicolle ★★★$$$** Featuring an eclectic menu of Greek, American, and Italian cuisine, this place serves spinach pie side by side with osso buco and Atlantic salmon cakes. You can also choose from a variety of pastas, egg and crepe dishes, salads (the garlicky Caesar is very popular), and seafood or chicken preparations. The outdoor patio is comfortable for alfresco dining year-round. It's heated in the winter and—more important in the desert—cooled with an overhead misting system in the summer. After dinner, move to the lounge to hear the singer–piano player perform a set combining rock, jazz, and contemporary music. Scrumptious desserts—apricot crepes, tiramisù, or *tartufos* (ice-cream balls covered with chocolate, white chocolate, or macadamia nuts)—are served here, as are cappuccino, espresso, and *caffè latte*. ♦ Continental ♦ M-F lunch and dinner; Sa dinner. Reservations recommended for dinner. 4760 W Sahara Ave (between Arville St and S Decatur Blvd). 870.7675

**19 North Beach Cafe ★★★$$** At this casual bistro, named for an Italian neighborhood in San Francisco, you can almost feel the breeze off the bay. The walls are decorated with customers' tablecloth crayon drawings and Impressionist paintings. Though owner Osvaldo Montano was born in Spain and grew up in Argentina, his father was born in Italy, as was the family of his wife and co-owner, Judy. The cuisine is mainly Northern Italian, reminiscent of the foods of Genoa, where seafood cooked in a light tomato sauce is prevalent. Among the specialties are *linguine pesto alla Genovese* (with extra virgin olive oil, fresh basil, garlic, and parmesan cheese), *agnolotti alla crema* (pasta with cream sauce) or *rigatoni pomodoro* (with basil and tomato sauce), *linguine pescatore* (pasta with shellfish) with red or white sauce, and *chicken piccata* (with capers, white wine, and lemon). ♦ Northern Italian ♦ M-Sa lunch and dinner; Su dinner. Reservations recommended. 2605 S Decatur Blvd (between Eldora St and W Sahara Ave). 247.9530 ♿

***Shalimar***

**19 Shalimar Fine Indian Cuisine ★★$$** A culinary-savvy clientele of Indian nationals and vegetarians raves about this place. Start with a vegetable or lamb *samosa* (deep-fried pastry) or the chicken *biryani* (basmati rice cooked with mildly spiced boneless chicken), then order some bread (seasoned to complement your menu choice) baked in the tandoori oven. The curries are spiced to your preference: mild, medium, hot, or incendiary. Veggie plates include eggplant stew, potato and cauliflower curry, and *chana masala* (chickpeas cooked in the traditional Punjabi style). ♦ Indian ♦ M-F lunch and dinner; Sa-Su dinner. 2605 S Decatur Blvd (between Eldora St and W Sahara Ave). 252.8320 ♿

**20 Big Dog's Cafe & Casino ★★$$** The 15-foot-tall mural of a brandy-toting Saint Bernard on the facade is a sign of things to come inside. All manner of doggie decor fills the bar: Dogs play pool and poker, pups have a picnic, hounds howl at the moon. Posters of poodles, puppies, and pugs cover the walls. The restaurant serves American, Mexican, and Italian food. Of course, there's a row of video-poker machines. On your way out, pick up a

T-shirt with the slogan "If you can't run with the big dogs, then just stay on the porch." ◆ American/Mexican/Italian ◆ Daily 24 hours. 6390 W Sahara Ave (between Verdinal and S Torrey Pines Drs). 876.3647

**21 Ferraro's Cafe** ★★★$$$ The combined aromas of bread baking and sauces simmering enhance the Old World atmosphere in this traditional Southern Italian restaurant with white walls, columns, and recessed lighting. The most popular appetizer is the *ripieno di carciofo* (artichoke stuffed with bread crumbs, fresh garlic, romano cheese, and black olives in a light wine sauce). Owner Gino Ferraro, who doubles as chef and assists his wife Rosalba in the dining room, creates imaginative pasta and seafood dishes. Osso buco is Gino's specialty, and Rosalba makes the tiramisù. There's dancing and live entertainment nightly ◆ Italian ◆ Daily dinner. Reservations recommended. 5900 W Flamingo Rd (between Lindell Rd and Red Rock St). 364.5300

**22 Traveling Books & Maps** Whether you're bound for foreign soil, looking for local info, or are an enthusiastic armchair traveler, you'll find a good selection of all kinds of guides here. Maps and atlases, a few travel accessories, globes, "Wearing the World" windbreakers, and language aids are also stocked. There's an extensive section on the Southwest, including, of course, guides and maps to Las Vegas and its environs. ◆ M-Sa. 4001 S Decatur Blvd (between W Flamingo Rd and Supai Dr). 871.8082

**23 Bamboo Garden** ★★$$ Still considered the city's sleeper restaurant, this eatery's unique and imaginative menu is known only to the most informed West Las Vegans. The cream of seafood soup is thick with crab, shrimp, and scallops. A fiery sesame sauce douses deep-fried Hunan eggplant. Other favorites include clams *dou chi* (sautéed in a hot black-bean sauce with ginger, scallions, and sherry) and *kung pao* frogs' legs served with red peppers and peanuts. The room is very comfortable, although the decor is a bit sparse—all the flourishes are found in the food. Because it's hidden away in a common corner shopping center, the restaurant is rarely crowded. The service is superb. ◆ Chinese ◆ M-Sa lunch and dinner; Su dinner. 4850 W Flamingo Rd (at S Decatur Blvd). 871.3262

**24 Terrible Herbst's Detail Plus** In the freewheeling 1930s, Old Man Herbst was such a ferocious competitor in the Midwestern oil business that he earned the nickname "Terrible." His company later moved to Las Vegas and now has a couple of dozen gasoline stations, car washes, and detail centers around town. This one will give your auto a total interior-exterior scrubbing, which includes everything from shampooing the carpets to cleaning out the heater vents and fender wells, plus a hand wash and wax. The name is something of an in-joke among residents, with a meaning more or less synonymous with a hangover or headache. (You might hear someone say, "I was at **Big Dog's** till the wee hours yesterday and I have a Terrible Herbst" or "If you don't stop bugging me, you're gonna give me a Terrible Herbst.") ◆ Daily. 4310 W Flamingo Rd (between Wynn Rd and Arville St). 876.9105

**25 Gold Coast Hotel** $$ If ever a hotel-casino tried to be all things to all people, this one did. Besides the 750 reasonably priced rooms, there are two lounges showcasing live entertainment nightly. Happy hoofers fill the largest dance floor in Las Vegas, and two movie theaters screen first-run flicks. The second floor hosts a 72-lane bowling alley and a cavernous bingo hall. A big buffet, coffee shop, and snack bar serve tons of food daily. There's also a steak house, a Mediterranean restaurant, an ice-cream parlor, a liquor store, a gift shop, a slot-club redemption center (members play slots with a type of credit card and accrue points that they cash in for prizes), two movie theaters, and a travel agency. Drive on over—thousands of cars can park here. You could stay in this hotel for weeks and never run out of things to do. Parents enjoy the complimentary child-care program. ◆ 4000 W Flamingo Rd (between S Valley View Blvd and Wynn Rd). 367.7111, 800/331.5334; fax 367.8575; www.goldcoastcasino.com ♿

Within the Gold Coast Hotel:

**Gold Coast Casino** A large pit dominates the main room, and the din of hundreds of video-poker machines fills another chamber. The 100,000-square-foot casino boasts more than 2,000 slots and video-poker machines. The bingo parlor is a 750-seater, and of the 32 blackjack tables, more than half have two-, three-, or five-dollar minimum bets. ◆ Daily 24 hours. 367.7111

# Volumes on Vegas

Perhaps because Las Vegas has such unique visual appeal, the city has appeared more often as the subject of films and TV shows than literary efforts. Still, more than a handful of authors have parlayed their fascination with the neon oasis into works in print.

## Fiction

*The Desert Rose,* by Larry McMurtry (Simon and Schuster, 1983). Las Vegas is the perfect place for McMurtry to explore his trademark characters: outcasts and dying breeds who never give up hope even when they know better. The title of the novella refers to Harmony, an aging showgirl in the **Stardust**'s *Lido de Paris* review who's in danger of being replaced by her own daughter.

*Fool's Die,* by Mario Puzo (Putnam, 1978). Las Vegas figures prominently in Puzo's best-seller *The Godfather* (in that book, protagonist Moe Green represents Bugsy Siegel), but *Fool's Die* is the book that truly reveals Puzo's passion for gambling and the gaming capital. He weaves sex, wagering, and corruption into a potboiler. (Puzo also penned *Inside Las Vegas,* which is basically a long essay that accompanies a volume of photos.)

*Last Call,* by Tim Powers (William Morrow and Company, 1992). Poker is the link between the science of randomness and the supernatural in this fantasy set in present-day Las Vegas. Powers creates mythology from carefully researched history and weaves in the true story of Bugsy Siegel. A poker game on **Lake Mead** turns out to have cosmic stakes.

*The Stand,* by Stephen King (Doubleday, 1978). When a deadly strain of flu kills most of the world's population in this apocalyptic epic, many of the survivors are drawn to the most wonderful place on earth (Boulder, Colorado), while the bad guys convene in—you guessed it—Las Vegas.

*Vegas: Memoir of a Dark Season,* by John Gregory Dunne (Random House, 1974). The author of *True Confessions* paints a cynical, memorably seedy portrait of the city and three of its inhabitants— a hooker, a private detective, and a lounge comic—in this semiautobiographical book.

## Nonfiction

*Casino Secrets,* by Barney Vinson (Huntington Press, 1997). The author takes readers on an imaginative journey into the world of gaming tables and slot machines. While a breezy read, there are several good suggestions about how to make a smart bet—and hopefully avoid the worst.

*Fear and Loathing in Las Vegas,* by Hunter S. Thompson (Random House, 1972). With the immortal opening sentence "We were somewhere around Barstow on the edge of the desert when the drugs began to take hold," *Rolling Stone* magazine's infamous gonzo journalist launched a surreal first-person account of one wild weekend. Probably the most popular book ever written about Vegas, to the chagrin of civic leaders.

*The Green Felt Jungle,* by Ed Reid and Ovid Demaris (Trident Press, 1963). The hard-boiled prose of this exposé blasts the lid off the history of organized crime in the casino industry. The book created quite a stir in its day, but now serves mainly as a point of contrast to the corporate-run **Strip** of today.

*The Kandy-Kolored Tangerine Flake Streamline Baby,* by Tom Wolfe (Farrar, Straus & Giroux, 1965). Wolfe's lead-off essay in this anthology of prototypical "new journalism" carries the lengthy title "Las Vegas (What?) Las Vegas (Can't hear you! Too noisy) Las Vegas!!!" It offers a manic tour of the Strip in its heyday and a whimsical treatment of a serious theory: the neon landscape of the Strip in the early 1960s was a monument to the freedom of the postwar lifestyle and Las Vegas is the only city in America with an indigenous architectural makeup.

*Las Vegas: As It Began—As It Grew,* by Stanley W. Paher (Nevada Publications, 1971). The city's frontier-era history is detailed in this fascinating account.

*Las Vegas: The Entertainment Capital,* by Don Knepp (Lane Publishing Co., 1987). The Las Vegas News Bureau provided the outside world with some memorable images of the city, including a swim-up craps table and a shot of **Downtown** silhouetted against the backdrop of a nuclear explosion. This coffee-table book filled with photos culled from the bureau's archives focuses on Las Vegas's entertainment history.

*Yes I Can: The Story of Sammy Davis Jr.,* by Sammy Davis Jr. and Jane and Burt Buyar (Farrar, Straus & Giroux, 1965). Davis and Vegas hit their stride at the same time, and their names were forever entwined. But this book is one of few that documents the period when blacks—even well-loved black performers—were barred from casino floors and forced to stay in a ghetto on the city's west side.

*Resort City in the Sunbelt: Las Vegas, 1930–1970,* by Eugene P. Moehring (University of Nevada Press, 1989). This is the definitive, scholarly historical account of the development of Las Vegas and the community's economic and social relationship to casino gambling.

*Running Scared: The Life and Treacherous Times of Las Vegas Casino King Steve Wynn,* by John L. Smith (Barricade Books, 1995). The thoughtful and compelling story behind the rise of Steve Wynn in the gaming industry.

*Vegas: Live and In Person,* by Jefferson Graham (Cross River Press, 1989). This coffee-table book is filled with amusing personality profiles, ranging from those of local movers and shakers to "the little people"—cocktail waitresses, bellmen, and PBX operators. Historical and current photos enliven the thorough, if already dated, overview.

**26 Rio Suite Hotel & Casino** $$$ Since this hotel opened in 1990, it's been a continuous hit; its stunning neon sign immediately supplanted the **Stardust**'s as the town's most popular. Then in 1998, Harrah's Entertainment purchased the property, expanding its US presence in the gaming world to 19 casinos. Locals like the off-Strip location, easily accessible from Interstate 15, and visitors appreciate the festive atmosphere and luxurious accommodations. Each of the 2,415 rooms is a 600-square-foot suite, with a mini-refrigerator, a wet bar, and unobstructed views of the Strip to one side and West Las Vegas to the other (there also are nine 1,000-square-foot suites, one with its own indoor pool). The hotel's 14 excellent restaurants receive rave reviews. At lunch, the **Beach Cafe** and the **All American Bar & Grille** are popular contenders for the best grilled chicken sandwiches in town. The **Pavilion,** a new $80-million convention and special events center, houses 3 grand meeting halls, a registration area, specialty kitchens, and an adjoining business center. The property also includes a sandy beach with its own lagoon, four pools, a salon, spa, and wedding facilities—two chapels, reception areas, and two honeymoon suites.

The hotel's **Masquerade Village** features the spectacular *Show in the Sky* where visitors interact with dancers, musicians, mime, and aerialists in a paradelike atmosphere. This show rotates with other productions, including *South of the Border Carnivale, Venice Masquerade,* and *New Orleans Mardi Gras.* ♦ 3700 W Flamingo Rd (between Industrial Rd and S Valley View Blvd). 252.7777, 800/752.9746; fax 252.7670; www.playrio.com ⎇

Within the Rio Suite Hotel & Casino:

**Rio Suite Casino** An unusual feature in this casino has players seeing double: video-poker machines topped with small TVs. You can catch a football game, your favorite soap opera, or an *I Love Lucy* rerun while you try to beat the odds. ♦ Daily 24 hours. 252.7777

**Fortunes** ★★★$$$$ A new crowd pleaser, this restaurant's kitchen highlights regional Asian cuisine. Try the lettuce-wrapped minced squab to start or giant clams prepared tableside and served with a hot, spicy sauce. Main course favorites include giant scallops spiced with sautéed vegetables served over rice. The dining room is dramatic—museum-quality Oriental art drapes the pastel walls—though not as fancy as the prices. ♦ Chinese ♦ Daily dinner. Reservations recommended. 252.7777

**Antonio's** ★★★$$$ Few Las Vegas restaurants can match the quality, setting, and service found here. The elegant dining room is a mélange of marble and glass crowned with a domed trompe l'oeil ceiling. Veal is the specialty; try the osso buco, veal scallops in a mushroom-wine sauce, or veal piccata. Chicken preparations include parmesan, Marsala, or *melanzana ai pomodori* (with layers of eggplant, provolone, and tomato sauce). And the chef isn't afraid to experiment—pasta with baby artichoke hearts, fresh garlic, and black olives and veal ravioli in a black-walnut cream sauce are just two of his interesting concoctions. Top off your meal with a selection from the extensive wine list. ♦ Italian ♦ Daily dinner. Reservations recommended. 252.7737

# FIORE
Rotisserie & Grille

**Fiore** ★★★★$$$$ This unique dining room sports a gleaming brass-colored open kitchen and such nice touches as an embroidered footstool at each table for purses or briefcases. The restaurant's master sommelier has an extensive background in wine and has created a list that includes some rare bottles priced in the four figures. Rotisseried steaks, chicken, and seafood are the signature dishes. Grilled scallops topped with lemongrass vinaigrette, herbed risotto, braised striped bass with fennel, and spit-roasted, garlic-studded lamb are among the selections that might appear on the seasonally changing menu. ♦ Continental ♦ Daily dinner. Reservations recommended. 252.7702

Tiger Woods won the 1996 Las Vegas Invitational at the Tournament Players Club in Summerlin.

**Buzios** ★★★$$$ The ceiling is draped with striped Roman shades, the floor is marble with wood planks, the massive chandeliers provide a warm glow, and the tall windows offer a view of the hotel's pool and sandy beach. Steamers, chowders, seafood pastas, cioppino, and bouillabaisse are among the many can't-go-wrong choices. The kitchen emphasizes freshness: chowders are created in steam pots while you wait, and fish choices change with the seasons. ♦ Seafood ♦ Daily lunch and dinner. Reservations recommended. 252.7697

**Carnival World Buffet** ★★★$ Part of the new generation of mass-quantity mess halls, this convivial and chaotic room seats 900 diners; not surprisingly, the volume and the variety of food are overwhelming. For lunch and dinner, mini-buffets offer Italian, Mexican, Chinese, Japanese, seafood, steaks, and American dishes, along with salads, soups, breads, and luscious desserts. The jewel of the buffet, however, is the Mongolian grill, where you spoon vegetables and spices into a bowl and hand it to a cook, who adds chicken, beef, pork, or veal and stir-fries it on a grill. And it doesn't close between meals, so you can drop in at any time. During peak hours the room can get extremely crowded; the best bet is to go early for breakfast and dinner and late for lunch. ♦ International ♦ Daily breakfast, lunch, and dinner. 252.7777

**Napa Restaurant** ★★★★$$$$ The stainless steel sculpture and picture windows overlooking the pool give this stunning, wood-paneled dining room a modern feel, while Jean-Louis Palladin's cutting-edge cuisine takes its inspiration from the French countryside. Our favorite is the roasted Muscovy duck prepared with olives. Other excellent choices include tender rack of lamb served with grilled vegetables or Maine lobster with crushed potatoes and asparagus *coulis*. Dessert offerings include homemade chocolate cake and pastries with a good variety of ice creams and sorbets. The wine list is affordable with more than 600 selections to choose from. ♦ French ♦ Dinner W-Su. Reservations recommended. 247.7961

**27 King 8 Hotel & Gambling Hall** $$ For what it's worth, truck drivers swear by this hotel, which is adjacent to the Tropicana Avenue exit off Interstate 15 and surrounded by huge parking lots. The 289 rooms are small and utilitarian, yet comfortable and cool, and are often available at excellent rates, especially at the height of the summer and winter seasons. As for the casino, it's a no-surprise grind joint, with low-minimum blackjack and craps tables and 5¢ video-poker machines. The coffee shop is renowned for its 99¢ breakfast, cheap snow crab leg dinner, and excellent coffee. ♦ 3330 W Tropicana Ave (between Industrial Rd and Polaris Ave). 736.8988

**28 El Paso Kitchens** ★★$ Since it opened a few years ago, this eatery's been such a smashing success that about a dozen branches are now scattered throughout the residential areas of the city. Bench-pressing the hefty burritos provides a pretty good workout. Open around the clock, this is the place if you're craving chips and guacamole or a tasty chorizo-and-bean burrito at 3AM. Lines can get long during the peak lunch and dinner hours. ♦ Mexican ♦ Daily 24 hours. 3720 W Tropicana Ave (between Procyon Ave and S Valley View Blvd). 891.0222

**29 The Orleans Hotel & Casino** $$$ This French Quarter–themed hotel combines French, Spanish, and Plantation influences throughout its 88 acres, including a 40-foot atrium highlighting the sights and sounds of the Crescent City. The oversized 840 rooms and 30 suites have spectacular views of the Strip or mountains. A recent $40-million expansion added a multiplex movie theater, an interactive arcade, a wedding chapel, and child-care center. Guests also enjoy six restaurants, a buffet, and a 70-lane bowling center. ♦ 4500 W Tropicana Ave (between Arville and Cameron Sts). 365.7111, 800/ORLEANS; www.orleanscasino.com

Within the Orleans Hotel & Casino:

**The Orleans Casino** With 92,000 square feet of space, this casino is enhanced by a 40-

foot high ceiling depicting New Orleans street scenes and architecture. Players enjoy more than 2,100 slot machines, video poker, video keno, a poker room, and the latest new generation LED race and sports book. ◆ Daily 24 hours. 365.7111

**Canal Street Grille** ★★★$$$ This elegant restaurant is a favorite of visitors and locals alike. Specialities include crawfish and crab ravioli, ocean scallops in wine sauce, Pacific salmon in lime-ginger sauce, beef topped with crabmeat, and blackened gulf shrimp with pecan rice. A must for carnivores are the prime ribs served with a choice of seven delicious sauces. Desserts are also not to be missed here, especially the bananas Foster. ◆ French/Creole ◆ Daily dinner. Reservations recommended. 365.7111

**30 Young Electric Sign Company (YESCO)** In the late 1920s Thomas Young came to Las Vegas from Ogden, Utah, and had a vision. As he looked at the budding  businesses of Fremont Street, a lightbulb went off—literally. Neon, the new European sign fad, had recently arrived in the States. Within a few years, most of the major clubs on Fremont (and Virginia Street in Reno) had dazzling technicolor displays in their windows, and Young's company had

established itself as the premier sign maker in the state. More than 60 years later, the signs continue to get bigger and brighter. A new technology, whereby cheaper digital message marquees are illuminated by thousands of computer-programmable bulbs, is now taking the industry by storm, and the company has kept up with the pace, its primacy still intact. The neon graveyard in back of the building contains old casino signs and letters, uniquely preserving the city's history. There are no tours of the factory, and visitors aren't allowed to wander around the junkyard, but peeking through the fence will give you a sense of the long and brilliant love affair between YESCO and Las Vegas. ◆ 5119 Cameron St (between W Hacienda and W Reno Aves). 876.8080

**31 Silverton Hotel & Casino** $$ Featuring an Old West mining town theme, this $75-million hotel, casino (formerly **Boomtown**), and RV resort is located five minutes south of Tropicana Avenue on Interstate 15. The property meanders over 62 acres and includes a 300-room hotel, 460-space deluxe recreational vehicle park, 350-seat buffet and chili bar, two specialty snack bars, 100-seat lounge featuring country-western bands that perform nightly, 600-seat theater, 30 table games, 1,100 slot and video-poker machines, and a sports book. ◆ 3333 Blue Diamond Rd (between I-15 and Industrial Rd). 263.7777, 800/588.7111; fax 896.4925

## Bests

### Bill Branon
Author, *Let Us Prey, Devils Hole*

**Gambler's Book Club** to browse the world of books about gambling and Las Vegas. Anecdotes, history, "systems," and technique. It's all there. Print to computer programs. (You better learn if you hope to earn.)

The real raison d'être for Las Vegas isn't gambling. It's the casino buffet. You learn this truth about two years after moving here if you have some neurons left and are still solvent. My vote goes to the off-the-beaten-path (emphasis on "beaten") **Main Street Station.** The cardiac gauntlet at the **Fiesta** rates a close second.

The **Desperado** at **Buffalo Bill's** located a few miles out of town on the highway back to California. This roller coaster was designed by chiropractors. The last nail in the coffin of my denial of old age. But fun? You bet!

If you have to bet a football parlay card, bet the "Mega Teaser/Ties Win" teaser card at the Fiesta Sports Book, especially during the last half of the season. You're using the casino's own computer to beat the numbers. If they know what they're doing, you'll be in action right up to Monday night. Then you hedge that last game, sit back, and look disturbingly clever.

Nicest place to park your winnings: the **Forum Shops** at **Caesars.** Eerie, nostalgic, classy.

Any book on Vegas and casinos by Barney Vinson.

The beautiful, and almost unknown to visitors, **Red Rock Canyon** loop. Head west on **Charleston** until you think you're on another planet. Look for the **BLM Visitors' Center** sign. Drive, bike, hike, climb, snap pictures, have a picnic, fall off a cliff. Early morning sunlight does something to the color of that rock you won't forget. Continue southwest after you leave the loop. Watch out for wild burros on the highway. And don't try to feed them. They're into finger sandwiches—your fingers. If you're a real navigator and know a weatherman, you'll discover how Irish coffee tastes around the circular fire pit at the **Bonnie Springs Ranch** restaurant during a snowfall.

### Stanley W. Paher
Publisher, Nevada Publications

**Fiesta Casino** (Mexican restaurant): Best *chiles rellenos* in Vegas.

**Orleans Casino** (steak house): Great value and exceptional service.

**Carluccio's** at **The Liberace Museum:** Chicken cacciatore is greatest!

# East Las Vegas

You won't see theme parks or artificial volcanoes on the "Eastside," as locals call the area east of the Las Vegas Strip. But you will encounter an eclectic mix of attractions and some middle-class, residential communities (a refreshing reprieve from the gambling palaces on Las Vegas Boulevard).

For the most part low-key and suburban, the Eastside is still idiosyncratic enough to escape blandness. The world's only **Hard Rock Casino** is located in this area, as is the garish **Liberace Museum,** a monument to the late entertainer's love of excess, where his flamboyant cars, furs, rings, and pianos are on display. Visitors in search of some of the city's beautiful people may spot them at **Cipriani,** a favorite lunch spot known for classic Italian cuisine. From there, drive down **Maryland Parkway** to the **University of Nevada, Las Vegas,** home to the town's beloved **Runnin' Rebels** basketball team. And

Nellis Air Force Base, a major Eastside employer, is the site of the Thunderbird Museum, which is chock-full of aeronautical memorabilia.

The Eastside is also the site of Sunrise Mountain, home of the Las Vegas Mormon Temple, a towering white structure built by the Church of Jesus Christ of Latter-day Saints. The peak is still a favorite of residents: each year readers of the *Las Vegas Review-Journal* newspaper vote the mountain the best place to view the nocturnal light show of Las Vegas.

While they lack the flashy facades that pulsate on the Strip, a few good-size casinos in East Las Vegas draw plenty of business from both locals (a combination of military families, retirees, blue-collar workers, and middle-class residents), and tourists. The oldest and tallest, the Showboat, is one of the first casinos that chose to cater to locals, with a combination of decent food, low prices, and a convenient location. Boulder Station, which opened in August 1994, has duplicated the success of its long-popular older brother, Palace Station, on West Sahara. One local rival, Sam's Town Hotel & Gambling Hall, is popular with Eastsiders, who crowd its western dance hall and bowling complex. Adjacent to Sam's Town on Boulder Highway is Nevada Palace, an overgrown motel and casino that has carved out a niche for itself with low-rolling locals and folks who prefer to avoid the crowds next door at Sam's Town.

The Eastside also supports a number of offbeat mom-and-pop businesses. You'll find some of the more interesting places clustered around the intersection of Fremont Street and Charleston Boulevard, such as the funky Green Shack, a saloon and supper club where cholesterol counters plead temporary amnesia when ordering the house specialty, crusty fried chicken. The restaurant sits in the shadow of the Showboat in a building considered prehistoric by Las Vegas standards, dating back to at least 1932.

A great escape from the Strip, East Las Vegas is where you'll meet Las Vegans and see how the residents live.

---

**1 Alexis Park Resort** $$$$ If you're tired of walking by clanging slot machines to get to your room, this understated and elegant hotel might be your kind of place. It's a first-rate resort, and there's not a slot machine or a table game in sight. While each of the resort's 500 rooms is a suite, the property also offers a spate of amenities: a gourmet restaurant, spacious meeting rooms, three pools, a health spa, a beauty salon, a nine-hole putting green, two lighted tennis courts, and all the usual perks found at fine hotels. It's also within walking distance of two of the Strip's brightest intersections. Without a casino to subsidize the hotel, the room and meal prices here are high by Las Vegas standards, but then so is the quality. The rooms, built around a sprawling courtyard, are designed with the business traveler in mind; each includes a desk, and the decor is more sedate than that found at most Las Vegas hotels. Ten two-bedroom suites are also on the property. ♦ 375 E Harmon Ave (between Paradise Rd and La Mar Cir). 796.3300, 800/582.2228; fax 796.0766 ♿

Within the Alexis Park Resort:

**Pegasus Gourmet Room** ★★★$$$$ Fine cuisine is served in a quiet and subtly decorated dining room with a waterfall view. Frequent patrons rave about the oysters Rockefeller and the pasta, which is made on the premises. ♦ Continental ♦ Daily dinner. Reservations recommended for dinner; jacket requested. 796.3300

**2 Hard Rock Cafe** ★$ The ever-expanding restaurant chain known for its trendy T-shirts and rock 'n' roll memorabilia built one of its most novel branches here in 1990. The swanky structure, with a flashy white and gold color scheme reminiscent of Downtown's **Golden Nugget,** is pure Vegas, even if the cuisine is classic California. It boasts one of the city's most striking neon signs: an 82-foot replica of a classic Gibson guitar—billed as the biggest instrument of its type in the world—that has strings that move, as if being strummed by a giant invisible hand. Inside, hundreds of music mementos are on display. They range from a gorgeous 1968 Harley Davidson Electraglide motorcycle once owned by the late Roy Orbison to an autographed album cover from the Irish rock band U2. Of course, the King's presence is felt throughout: Busts of Elvis ring the ceiling, a guitar broken by his Highness is enshrined here, and imitation Graceland gates stand under the "Viva Las Vegas" sign. Tourists pack the place on weekends, crowding a bar that's already a bit small. Few are elders, since the nonstop rock music tends to drive off anyone whose heyday predates the 1960s. But the food's

not bad—if you're lucky enough to get a table. ♦ American ♦ Daily lunch and dinner. 4475 Paradise Rd (at E Harmon Ave). 733.8400

**2 Hard Rock Hotel and Casino** $$$ A recent $85-million expansion has raised the room count to 689 and seen the addition of private bungalows, four more restaurants, a 5,000-square-foot nightclub, and a health club. The progeny of the world-famous cafe also offers a European-style concierge, 24-hour room service—and, of course, a multimillion-dollar collection of rock 'n' roll memorabilia. In addition to the cafe next door there are five restaurants to choose from within the hotel: **Nobu,** with chef Nobu Matsuhisa (who operates restaurants in New York, Beverly Hills, and London); an Italian eatery, **Mortoni's,** which features pizza and huge salads served either indoors or on the garden patio overlooking the pool; and **Mr. Lucky's 24/7,** a coffee shop that is open 24 hours. The **Hard Rock Beach Club,** exclusively for guests and included in the price of a room, features whirlpools, spas, luxury cabanas, and even a sandy beach. The **Athletic Club,** available to guests for a fee, provides an exercise room and personal trainer, outdoor pool, and a 2,000-square-foot clothing, personal electronics, and collectibles store. **The Joint** is a 1,400-seat headliner room that books top-name rock and pop performers. ♦ 4455 Paradise Rd (between E Harmon Ave and E Flamingo Rd). 693.5000, 800/473.7625; fax 693.5010; www.hardrock.com/hotel

Within the Hard Rock Hotel and Casino:

**Hard Rock Casino** A favorite haunt of the under-35 crowd, this high-energy 30,000-square-foot betting palace features a rock 'n' roll theme. Piano-shaped roulette tables and slot machines with guitar-neck handles are just two examples. Other gaming facilities include blackjack, craps, minibaccarat, poker and video-poker machines.

**3 La Strada** ★★★$$$ Old World charm—an intimate dining room with a balcony, mirrored walls, and soft chandelier lighting—is the setting for elegant service and classic Italian fare. Among the sumptuous antipasti are chicken-liver pâté, marinated mussels on the half shell, buffalo mozzarella with basil and sliced tomato, marinated mushrooms, calamari salad, and roasted zucchini. Delectable entrées include calamari *Provença* (with garlic, oregano, wine, and tomato sauce), chicken *Dama Bianco* (with mushrooms, wine, and cream), veal *boscaiola* (with sautéed mushrooms and wine), veal *Strada* (with ham, cheese, and eggplant in wine and tomato sauce) and *spaghettini Vesuvio* (with chicken, capers, olives, garlic, wine, and tomato sauce). ♦ Italian ♦ Daily dinner. Reservations recommended. 4640

Paradise Rd (between E Tropicana Ave and E Naples Dr). 735.0150

**4 University of Nevada, Las Vegas (UNLV)**
Traffic from nearby **McCarran International Airport** runs right into the southern tip of the campus, site of the massive **Thomas & Mack Center,** home of the school's **Runnin' Rebels** basketball team and the **International Hockey League**'s **Las Vegas Thunder.** Most visitors to the campus only see the 18,776-seat, all-purpose arena, which is fitting since many sports fans across the country still think of **UNLV** as a basketball team with a school attached. They're fond of pointing out that more than 20,000 students now attend the school.

Founded in 1957, the university's mostly unremarkable buildings fill the 335-acre campus. One of the most interesting places to visit is the **Marjorie Barrick Museum of Natural History,** which showcases traveling exhibits from the Smithsonian (M-F 8AM-4:45PM, Sa 9AM-2PM). Aside from the **Thomas & Mack,** the other big campus landmark is the huge black-metal *Flashlight* sculpture that points skyward from the plaza at the **Performing Arts Center,** where most of the school's cultural events are held. Not far from the big basketball arena and just outside the **Harry Reid Center for Environmental Studies,** visitors can stroll through an almost-hidden desert garden that symbolizes the school's recent blossoming. But beware: Campus parking can be a problem, as it is at most urban universities. Luckily, the **Citizens Area Transit** bus system runs right along Maryland Parkway, stopping several times an hour in front of the school. ◆ 4505 S Maryland Pkwy (between E Tropicana and Cottage Grove Aves). 895.3011; basketball tickets 895.3900

California residents generate the most trips to casinos, approximately 15 million, according to a Harrah's national survey. Rounding out the top five are Illinois, New York, Pennsylvania, and Wisconsin.

Nevada ranks 49th out of 50 states for the adverse impact of lifestyle factors on health, according to studies by the Nevada State Medical Association. The death rate from smoking is 22 percent higher than the national average, and deaths from chronic liver disease (caused by alcohol) are 62 percent above the national average.

**5 Mamounia** ★★★$$ Romance abounds at this exotic Moroccan restaurant. There are richly decorated pillows to lean back on; a traditional hand-washing ceremony to prepare you for eating with your fingers; a multicourse feast of *harira* (lentil) soup (drunk from a bowl), Middle Eastern salads, kabobs speared into a whole pineapple, couscous, Cornish hen, *pastilla* (chicken pie), and mint tea; and a belly dancer. An à la carte menu is also offered. ◆ Moroccan ◆ Daily dinner. Reservations recommended. 4632 S Maryland Pkwy (between Dorothy Ave and Del Mar St). 597.0092

**6 The Liberace Museum** If ever an entertainer belonged in Vegas, Liberace did. Before he died in 1987, Mr. Showmanship spent much of his career living and performing in Las Vegas and trying to top his own outrageous costumes and audience-pleasing acts. Despite his exaggerated on-stage image, the Wisconsin native born Wladziu Valentino Liberace was actually down to earth, often seen grocery shopping in supermarkets near his home, just a mile or so west of this glitzy museum. Lee, as his friends called him, founded the museum in 1979, and it has since been expanded into an entire complex containing three exhibit areas and a gift shop. The museum has taken over most of **Liberace Plaza** shopping center. The main building houses the many customized cars and pianos Liberace collected during his lifetime. His favorite piano, a Baldwin grand covered with thousands of mirrored tiles, revolves on a stage in the middle of the room. Nearby, his red, white, and blue Rolls-Royce convertible draws big crowds. Some of his wild costumes and gaudy jewelry are on display in the rear of the complex. One highlight is a piano-shaped ring topped with 260 diamonds, a gift from the Hilton Hotel baron Barron Hilton. A third exhibit area includes a library containing Liberace's miniature piano collection, musical arrangements, and family photos. The museum is hard to miss. Just look for the showmeister's oversize signature on the sign out front, the gold lettering on the buildings, and the tour buses lined up in the parking lot. Tickets are tax deductible; proceeds benefit the Liberace Foundation for the Performing and Creative Arts. ◆ Admission. Daily. Liberace Plaza, 1775 E Tropicana Ave (at Spencer St). 798.5595

# Carluccio's
## Tivoli Gardens
### *Family Style Restaurant*

**6 Carluccio's ★★$$** When this place was known as **Liberace's Tivoli Gardens,** it was a frequent hangout of Lee himself. Although it is no longer affiliated with the museum, the restaurant has retained the original decadent design, along with one of Liberace's showpiece mirrored pianos, which anchors the bar. Less formal than in the past and frequented by more locals than ever before, the kitchen still serves Italian preparations of chicken, veal, steak, and pasta. Two highly recommended specialties are the crab-stuffed shrimp and the veal florentine. ◆ Italian ◆ Tu-Su dinner. Reservations recommended for eight or more. Liberace Plaza, 1775 E Tropicana Ave (at Spencer St). 795.3236

**7 Bootlegger Ristorante ★★★$$$** One of the oldest restaurants in town (since 1949) and still run by the same family, its hearty portions and consistent quality make this a popular local dining spot. Turn-of-the-century decor and Italian family portraits provide an attractive setting in which to enjoy complimentary homemade *panetti* (small bread puffs) tossed with garlic, oregano, and oil served with tomato-basil sauce; *mostaccioli* (two-inch-long macaroni tubes), one of the most popular dishes; and eggplant parmagiana. Entrées named respectively for the husband-and-wife owners—veal saltimbocca à la Blackie (with prosciutto and wine) and veal Lorraine (with fresh mushrooms in a wine and cream sauce)—are also first-rate. For the health-conscious, there are such "Project Lean" selections as angel hair *pomodoro* (with fresh tomato and basil sauce) and linguine with clams, shrimp, or calamari. ◆ Italian ◆ Tu-Su lunch and dinner. Reservations recommended. 5025 S Eastern Ave (between E Reno and E Tropicana Aves). 736.4939

Basketball great Kareem Abdul-Jabbar broke the National Basketball Association record for earning the most points in a career during a game in Las Vegas. The Los Angeles Lakers were playing the Utah Jazz on 5 April 1984 at the Thomas & Mack Center at the University of Nevada, Las Vegas campus, when Jabbar swished a long skyhook over Utah center Mark Eaton. The basket gave the legendary Lakers' center 31,421 points for his career, breaking Wilt Chamberlain's record of 31,419.

**8 Pasta Mia ★★★$$** Founded by popular chef Piero Broglia and run by his wife and daughter, this casual, friendly restaurant is known for the scent of garlic and the sounds of Sinatra. The homemade antipasto features roasted peppers, marinated eggplant, and stuffed artichokes. Extra-large portions (doggie bags are de rigueur here) are preceded by superb garlic bread and *pasta e fagioli* (pasta and bean soup) or a hearty romaine salad with garlic vinaigrette. Specialties include tortellini *bolognese* (meat sauce), penne with broccoli and spinach, chicken *angelo* (with artichoke hearts and white wine sauce), orange roughy, and roasted chicken with peppers and onions. ◆ Italian ◆ Daily lunch and dinner. No credit cards accepted. 2585 E Flamingo Rd (between Flamingo Crest Dr and S Eastern Ave). 733.0091

*Cipriani*

**9 Cipriani ★★★★$$$** Outside, a three-story lighthouse complete with beacon sets the mood: French doors with pale salmon-colored drapes, crystal chandeliers, and hanging plants decorate the interior of the elegant dining room. A prime Las Vegas destination for lovers of fine Italian fare, it presents classic cuisine in equally classic surroundings. Among the house specialties prepared in the open kitchen are escargots; steamed clams in herbs, shallots, and garlic; a superb *pasta e fagioli; veal scallopini boscaiola* (with wild mushrooms); fettuccine with fresh salmon, caviar, and a light cream sauce; cioppino (fish and shellfish in a hearty tomato sauce); and such scrumptious desserts as tiramisù, crème caramel, and chocolate mousse. ◆ Italian ◆ M-F lunch and dinner; Sa dinner. Reservations recommended. 2790 E Flamingo Rd (between McLeod Dr and Topaz St). 369.6711

**10 Las Vegas Hilton Country Club** One of only three public golf courses east of Paradise Road, this lush country club is tucked away in one of the area's finer neighborhoods, its borders defined by Eastern Avenue to the east and Desert Inn Road to the north. The course traces its history back to 1961, when it was the **Stardust Country Club.** Until 1967, it hosted the **PGA**'s Tournament of Champions, and from 1969 to 1976 was the site of the Sahara Invitational, won by such golfers as Jack Nicklaus (in 1969) and Lee Trevino (in 1971). The course record of 62 is shared by David Graham and Tom Kite. With 71 bunkers and five lakes, the course is considered challenging by local golfers, but the greens fees are a bit steep. Amenities include two putting greens, one chipping green, a lighted driving range, and a beverage cart. There's also a pro shop, the **Country Club Restaurant,** where breakfast and lunch are served, and a bar. Proper golf attire is required. Due to heavy demand, the management suggests calling or faxing up to three weeks in advance to reserve a tee time. ♦ Admission. Daily 5:30AM-6PM (driving range until 8PM). 1911 E Desert Inn Rd (between S Eastern Ave and Seneca Dr). 796.0016; fax 796.0015

## The Boulevard

**11 The Boulevard Mall** The largest shopping center in Nevada, it boasts 1.31 million square feet of shopping space, 5,825 parking spaces, and 140 stores spread out over 77 acres along Maryland Parkway. Specialty stores in the mall include the Bay Area–based **Nature Company** and the **Sesame Street General Store,** both of which have caught on with kids. The oldest of the city's four major malls, it's a good distance from the local freeway system. But it has a reputation for being less touristy than the Strip's **Forum Shops at Caesars** and **Fashion Show Mall** and less crowded than the rival **Meadows Mall** on the other side of town. ♦ Daily. S Maryland Pkwy (between E Twain Ave and E Desert Inn Rd). 735.8268; www.blvdmall.com

**12 Huntridge Performing Arts Theater** On the corner of Charleston Boulevard and Maryland Parkway, this Las Vegas landmark (ca. 1944) was the city's main movie house for years. Once owned by actress Irene Dunne and frequented by star-studded audiences (including Frank Sinatra and Marlene Dietrich), the movie theater fell on hard times during the 1980s, and the Art Deco building, with its 75-foot-tall tower, eventually closed. Current owner Richard Lenz reopened it in 1992 as a 725-seat concert venue. For four years, it hosted everything from classic films to a performance by rapper Ice T. Soon afterwards, the roof fell in—literally—destroying much of the theater. At press time, the theater was completely repaired and in business once again, offering much the same fare as before. ♦ 1208 E Charleston Blvd (at S Maryland Pkwy). 477.0242

**13 The Green Shack** ★$$ The oldest saloon and supper club in town, it opened back in 1932, when workers bound for Hoover Dam would stop to wet their whistle here before the long drive down dusty Boulder Highway. Up to a decade later, regulars from town were still

riding up on horseback for some hot grub and a cold beer. Current proprietors Jim and Barb McCormick are distant relatives of the club's founder, Jimmie Jones. Despite the fact that the little wooden building is painted green and garlanded with tiny white Christmas lights, its location—next door to the towering **Showboat**—makes it hard to spot. Locals like the Old Vegas atmosphere and famous fried chicken. They hang out, get a peek into the city's past, and enjoy plenty of homespun hospitality. ♦ American ♦ Tu-Sa dinner. 2504 E Fremont St (between Atlantic St and E Charleston Blvd). 383.0007

**14 The Oklahoma Kitchen** ★$ Since 1978, locals have feasted on hearty home cooking at this bare-bones restaurant. The kitchen whips up big breakfasts, chicken-fried steak, and homemade Mexican food, among other specialties. Pictures of western figures such as John Wayne and Willie Nelson grace the dining room walls. ♦ American/Mexican ♦ Daily breakfast, lunch, and dinner. 23 N Mojave Rd (at Contract Ave). 382.2651

## SHOWBOAT

**15 Showboat Hotel** $$ A longtime favorite of Eastside slot players, the **'Boat,** with its big electronic marquee, boasts two specialty restaurants, a buffet, the brightest, freshest, and most comfortable bingo hall in town, a poker room, the New Orleans Square courtyard with an old-fashioned ice-cream shop, and a six-story parking garage. The 495-room hotel—with its famous riverboat/Mardi Gras facade—is still known as a locals' joint with friendly employees, decent food, and fast service. It's also famous for its 106-lane bowling center, the largest in the US. ♦ 2800 Fremont St (between E Oakey Blvd and Atlantic St). 385.9123, 800/826.2800; fax 385.9154; www.showboat-lv.com

Within the Showboat Hotel:

Nevada's so-called Black Book of persons banned from entering casinos has been in existence since 1960, when 11 reputed mobsters were nominated for the list of excluded persons. Since then, only one person nominated ever has been removed while still alive—hotel operator Ruby Kolod.

# Crime Story

The tale of organized crime syndicates' involvement in Las Vegas reads like an epic parable in which the evil villains eventually meet their nemesis: justice.

By the time 37-year-old Benjamin "Bugsy" Siegel first set foot in Las Vegas in 1942, he'd been a gangster and a ranking member of New York's criminal underworld for more than 20 years. In the early 1920s, after Prohibition—the constitutional amendment that declared the production, distribution, and possession of alcohol illegal—Bugsy and his mob partners helped unite the nation's criminal syndicates, masterminding the large-scale illegal production of liquor. Smugglers, bootleggers, and urban street gangs, protected by corrupt police and politicians, supplied 300,000 speakeasies nationwide with the demon drink.

## The Way It Was

The underground liquor business funneled enormous sums of untaxed dollars to a new class of gangster millionaires, including Siegel, Cleveland's Morris "Moe" Dalitz, and Chicago's Al Capone. When federal legislators finally repealed Prohibition in 1933, the well-organized and well-capitalized underworld networks run by these mobsters were ready to exploit other criminal vices, such as drugs, prostitution, loan-sharking, and gambling.

Gambling proved especially profitable. It had nearly as large a customer base as bootlegged booze, and it was highly portable: games such as craps and blackjack could be set up almost anywhere and taken down in a moment's notice. Gaming was also subject to widely varying laws enforced by local police, who could be easily "persuaded" with bribes. However, gambling was often a target of moralistic crusaders who periodically mounted successful political campaigns to shut down the back-room games.

Despite the efforts of self-righteous lobbyists to eradicate betting, gamblers gained one safe haven in the country in 1931, when Nevada legislators legalized casino gambling in the state. Suddenly, men who would have been arrested and jailed for operating games of chance or betting joints elsewhere in the nation had

only to cross the Nevada line to become legitimate entrepreneurs.

## Dawn of the New West

It took a decade for underworld gambling-hall operators to recognize that Nevada, and Las Vegas in particular, could be the promised land. When Siegel made his fateful trip to Vegas in the early 1940s, **Fremont Street** consisted of a motley collection of saloons with Wild West facades, sawdust floors, cigars, whiskey, and poker. Their small-time owners (unlike the powerful operators working in Reno at the time, including Bill Harrah, Raymond "Pappy" Smith, and several well-established ranching families) proved no match for the notorious East Coast gangster, who quickly muscled into the Downtown joints, then helped himself to pieces of fledgling businesses on the seminal Las Vegas **Strip.**

Then came Bugsy's ill-fated obsession: the fabulous **Flamingo.** Although he invested $1 million of his own money in building his grandiose casino-resort, he eventually needed $6 million to finish the project. Some think that Bugsy's mobster partners believed he was skimming funds borrowed from them for construction and decided to stop him—permanently. Another hypothesis has it that Siegel's Las Vegas mob associates had him eliminated out of fear that his notorious hysteric outbursts—he wasn't known as Bugsy for nothing—might give gambling a bad reputation. Whatever the reason, in 1947 Bugsy Siegel's body was found in a Beverly Hills mansion with two bullets in the head (an unwritten mob code held that no one was to be eliminated in Las Vegas). Once Siegel was conveniently out of the picture, the mob emerged with a trophy: its first wholly owned Las Vegas casino.

Moe Dalitz, old-time bootlegger and gambling boss in Ohio and Kentucky, opened the **Desert Inn** in 1950. Over the next eight years, underworld cash supplied by mobsters from New England, New York, New Orleans, Miami, Chicago, Dallas, and the West Coast financed seven major Las Vegas hotel-casinos. By 1958, the mob controlled a dozen of the 15 major casinos on the Strip and **Downtown.**

## All in the Family

By all accounts, the 1950s were the mob's heyday in Las Vegas, an era that arouses nostalgia among many old-timers. Frank Sinatra, who owned a piece of the **Sands,** performed there regularly; his friends in the "Rat Pack" (Dean Martin, Joey Bishop, Peter Lawford, and Sammy Davis Jr.) held court all over town, sometimes stealing the stage from lesser-known lounge performers to give impromptu shows. Tourists shot craps with visiting mobsters. A little "juice" (in other words, knowing the right people) ensured complimentary food, rooms, shows, and even chips for visitors with influential connections. Floating crap games (literally played in the pool), cheating gamblers buried unceremoniously in the desert, and couriers transporting paper bags stuffed full of cash were a few of the mythic highlights that occurred during the mob's zenith.

Throughout most of the 1950s the Nevada Tax Commission, headquartered in Carson City, 400 miles from Las Vegas, oversaw the casino industry. Individual licenses were granted by city and county officials, who could be relied on to turn a blind eye toward criminal records and associations. Since gambling wasn't a crime in Nevada, the locals preferred to let these mobsters-turned-executives—the only people who had the money, muscle, and experience to control gaming—handle the volatile business.

By the early 1960s, the state Gaming Control Board had been established to batten down the licensing hatches and police casinos. Robert Kennedy, the new attorney general, fired up the federal heat on the Las Vegas underworld. In addition to this pressure, the price of opening a casino was skyrocketing. Hotels that cost $3 million, $6 million, even $10 million to build in the mid-1950s now ran $20 to $30 million, too much for even a gangster syndicate to afford. Because banks and other conventional sources of capital refused to finance gambling, which they considered a pariah industry, the only source of adequate funding for mob-owned Las Vegas casinos between 1958 and 1966 was the Midwest Pension Fund of the Teamsters Union, controlled by Jimmy Hoffa. The union used the pensions of thousands of truck drivers to float tens of millions of dollars in unsecured loans to mobsters to operate and expand properties, and build new ones.

When **Caesars Palace** opened in 1966 (financed primarily by Hoffa), Las Vegas casino owners, with or without underworld associations, were sweating under state, federal, and media pressure. Almost daily, officials and reporters denounced Las Vegas as the most mob-infested, crime-ridden city in the country.

## Vegas Soars with Hughes

That's when Las Vegas's eccentric savior, Howard Hughes, snuck into town on a private midnight train. Hughes, who had decided to transform Las Vegas into the western gateway for the supersonic jets that he predicted would soon be flying all over the world, took over an entire floor of the **Desert Inn.** Moe Dalitz, owner of the hotel, saw the perfect opportunity to escape increasing police surveillance and make a tidy profit in the bargain. He sold the **Desert Inn** to Hughes, who then purchased a total of eight casinos, an airport, a TV station, and millions of dollars worth of undeveloped Las Vegas property. Hughes bought out a number of mobsters, replacing them with his own corporate executives. The reclusive billionaire's four-year presence in Las Vegas, along with the $300 million he invested, helped legitimize the gambling industry in the eyes of big business. The media, along with local officials, tagged him a savior, and soon thereafter, Hilton Hotels became the first major legitimate corporation to license a hotel-casino. Holiday Inn quickly followed suit.

Meanwhile, the FBI, IRS, and the Gaming Control Board, along with other agencies, were engineering a massive, nationwide purge of organized crime. In 1978, Nevada auditors uncovered a large-scale slot-machine-skimming operation at the **Stardust** and the **Fremont** (the unreported cash making its way to mob bosses in Chicago, Kansas City, and St. Louis), and hidden underworld ownership of the **Dunes** and the **Aladdin.** Even as recently as the mid-1980s, the Midwest mob's continuing interest in Las Vegas was overseen by Tony "the Ant" Spilotro, a well-known and ruthless local figure. But internal power struggles, along with informers, wiretaps, and dogged pursuit by police, weakened the mob's ability to siphon off undeclared cash from casinos. Spilotro turned up in a shallow grave in Indiana in 1985 after a failed coup against his Chicago bosses, who themselves were subsequently either murdered or imprisoned. By the late 1980s, the last vestigial traces of the underworld were gone, ending organized crime's 45-year relationship with Las Vegas.

**Showboat Casino** While not as crowded as most popular locals' casinos, this one seems to have picked up steam after lagging for a while. In the last several years, an expansion has widened the aisles and made this sprawling complex one of the most comfortable. ♦ Daily 24 hours. 385.9123

**Bowling Center** This cavernous bowling palace founded in 1959 has its own snack bar and a lounge that sports plenty of TVs and bowling memorabilia. The 106-lane center is also the oldest stop on the Pro Bowlers Tour and home of the High Roller Bowling Tournament. ♦ Daily 24 hours. 385.9123

**Coffee Shop** ★$ Around the clock, the hotel's coffee shop serves traditional and inexpensive specials such as steak and eggs. ♦ American ♦ Daily 24 hours. 385.9123

**Di Napoli** ★$$ The **Showboat** seems an unlikely place to find fine cuisine from southern Italy, but the hotel made a valiant effort when it built this restaurant. The setting includes Roman columns, statues, a domed, trompe l'oeil ceiling painted to look like the sky, and a fountain in the center. Vintages from the ample wine list suit the refined menu of pasta, veal, chicken, and beef dishes. The veal parmagiana and the eggplant *rollatini* are highly recommended, as is the family-style feast offered from 2 to 10PM Sunday. ♦ Italian ♦ M-Sa dinner; Su brunch and dinner. Reservations recommended. 385.9123

**Plantation** ★$$ Next door to **Di Napoli,** the room features a Southern plantation decor, but you won't find corn bread and grits here. Specialties include mesquite-grilled steaks and fresh seafood flown in daily. The lobster tails are Australian and reasonably priced, the king crab leg special is one of the best in Las Vegas. ♦ American ♦ Daily dinner. Reservations recommended. 385.9123

**Captain's Buffet** $ One of the more popular feasts in town, the buffet features fair food at better-than-fair prices. On any day the generous spread could include ham, shrimp, cooked-to-order omelettes, barbecued chicken, crab legs, and corned-beef hash. ♦ American ♦ Daily lunch and dinner. Second floor. 385.9123

Suburban Las Vegas has come to resemble the stucco-and-tile residential sprawl of Southern California for a reason. A substantial number of southern Californians have relocated here. Of all the out-of-state driver's licenses collected by the Department of Motor Vehicles, about 36 percent belong to transplanted Californians.

Restaurants/Clubs: Red   Hotels: Blue
Shops/♣ Outdoors: Green   Sights/Culture: Black

**16 Boulder Station Hotel and Casino** $$ Looking much like its older, West Las Vegas sibling, **Palace Station,** this 15-story hotel features 300 rooms and five full-service restaurants. The casino offers more than 2,000 slot machines, 40 gaming tables, a 70-seat keno lounge, 10 poker tables, and a 240-seat race and sports book. Among the restaurants are the 24-hour **Iron Horse Cafe;** the "Feast," featuring an all-you-can-eat buffet; a steak and seafood restaurant called **The Broiler;** the **Pasta Palace;** and the **Guadalajara Bar & Grille.** The lounge rocks nightly with regulars on the large dance floor, and there's also a multiplex movie theater showing first-run films. ♦ 4111 Boulder Hwy (between S Lamb Blvd and I-515). 432.7777; 800/683.7777; fax 432.7754; www.stationcasinos.com ♿

**17 Sam's Town Hotel and Gambling Hall** $$ Long a favorite with locals, founder Sam Boyd's place is a bit off the tourist track, but its location, about six miles east of the Strip, is convenient for most Eastsiders. All 650 rooms and 33 suites are decorated in Old West style. In addition to the two-floor casino, the hotel's attractions include two RV parks (with total room for 1,000 RVs), **Calamity Jane's Ice Cream Shop and Coca-Cola Museum,** and a 56-lane bowling center with a playroom for the kids. There's also a spectacular 25,000-square-foot atrium and indoor park complete with trees, a creek, footpaths, and a 50-foot waterfall. The atrium features a variety of shops, including a western attire shop called **Cowboy Christmas** (open year-round) and a general store. There are 10 restaurants, including the Italian **Papamios** and the steak house **Billy Bob's,** as well as an international food court. At press time, a $78-million expansion and renovation was underway, which would add a 1,200-seat special events center, new buffet, video game arcade, and child-care center.

Lucky gamblers can blow their take at the **Western Emporium,** which carries a wide selection of western wear, art, jewelry, candy, and other souvenirs. Parking is available (though sometimes scarce) at various locations within the 58-acre property or in the five-story parking barn. And Sam's Town has room for 1,000 RVs in two parks with full hook-ups. ♦ 5111 Boulder Hwy (between E Harmon Ave and S Nellis Blvd). 456.7777, 800/634.6371; fax 454.8060

Within Sam's Town Hotel and Gambling Hall:

**Sam's Town Casino** The bustling, two-story casino covers 58,000 square feet and is crammed with slot machines. Most of the high-stakes action takes place on the ground floor, where gamblers play to the sounds of live country music blaring from **Roxy's Saloon,** an action-filled lounge located between the coffee shop and the race and sports book. There are more than 30 hand-dealt blackjack tables, a busy poker room, and a 590-seat bingo parlor. After dining and gambling, aspiring two-steppers can take free lessons nightly in the western-style dance hall on the second floor. ♦ Daily 24 hours. 456.7777; www.vegas.com/samstown/lasvegas

**Diamond Lil's** ★★$$$ Mesquite-grilled steak and seafood are served politely and in plentiful portions here, and the quiet atmosphere is Old West elegance at its best. Try the 18-ounce porterhouse or the stuffed lobster special, or—even better—the Champagne brunch on Sunday. ♦ American ♦ W-Sa dinner; Su brunch and dinner. Reservations recommended. 454.8009

**Smokey Joe's Cafe & Market** $ A country market atmosphere greets hungry gamblers within earshot of the action in the main casino. The coffee shop is always busy. The midnight breakfast and prime rib specials are among the best bargains in town. ♦ American ♦ Daily 24 hours; closed 11PM Thursday to 6AM Friday. 456.7777

**Willy & Jose's Mexican Cantina** ★★$$ Diners here can wash down authentic Mexican food with massive margaritas in this casual cantina. They have all the standard dishes, including tacos, burritos, and enchiladas. You can eat for free on your birthday. ♦ Mexican ♦ Daily dinner. Reservations recommended. 454.8044

**Mary's Diner** ★$ Fans of the 1950s come to this Art Deco diner to feast on bacon and eggs, burgers, and great milk shakes. Breakfast is served around the clock Thursday through Saturday. Service can be slow, but the thick malts and milk shakes amply reward your patience. ♦ American ♦ Daily breakfast, lunch, and dinner. Second floor. 456.7777

**The Great Buffet** $ Its name notwith-standing, this buffet is merely good, offering an abundance of breakfast, lunch, and dinner specialties. The prices are so reasonable that

they *almost* make it a great buffet. ♦ Buffet ♦ Daily breakfast, lunch, and dinner. Second floor. 456.7777

**18 Nevada Palace Hotel-Casino** $$ Founded in 1981, this overgrown motel, RV park, and casino clings to its massive neighbor **(Sam's Town),** luring locals, truckers, and overflow crowds with a combination of cheap food, reasonable rooms, and low-cost gaming options. Like **Sam's Town,** it offers live country music and free dance lessons Tuesday through Saturday nights in its **Silverado Saloon & Dance Hall.** The 210 rooms, though of the typical roadside motor-lodge variety, are clean and quiet. The hotel is less than four miles northwest of the **Sam Boyd Stadium,** site of **UNLV** football games and the occasional rock concert. ♦ 5255 Boulder Hwy (at E Harmon Ave). 458.8810, 800/634.6283; www.nvpalace@vegas.quik.com ♿

Within the Nevada Palace Hotel-Casino:

**Nevada Palace Casino** This 13,000-square-foot casino provides the perfect place to try your luck when your bankroll isn't as big as you'd like: there's two-dollar blackjack, one-dollar roulette, and 50¢ keno here. All the basic casino games are offered, as well as bingo and giveaways, such as a $1-million drawing in which contestants guess which numbers will come up in the California lottery. ♦ Daily 24 hours. 458.8810

**Boulder Cafe** ★$ The hotel's inexpensive 24-hour coffee shop serves the basic sandwiches and burgers, plus such full-course meals as a steak and snow crab special, grilled beef liver with bacon strips and onions, and a big prime rib plate. For the amount most places charge for a muffin and coffee, diners can choose one of seven copious breakfast specials on Monday through Friday mornings; night owls can enjoy the same breakfast bargains any Sunday through Thursday night. ♦ American ♦ Daily 24 hours. 458.8810

In 1960, during the filming of *Ocean's Eleven*, the movie's stars—Frank Sinatra, Dean Martin, Sammy Davis Jr., Joey Bishop, and Peter Lawford—appeared onstage nightly at the Sands Hotel's Copa Room in what's been called the "most celebrated talent event in supper-club history." Senator John F. Kennedy showed up for the festivities. In the movie, the five casinos on the Strip that the Rat Pack's characters rob are the Sahara, the Riviera, the Sands, the Desert Inn, and the Flamingo.

La Bella Pasta ★$$ Although primarily Italian cuisine is served in a country-and-western setting here, on Sunday night this is the site of a $5.95 Bavarian buffet, which features roasted baron of beef (two loins of sirloin joined at the backbone and carved to order—very popular in Las Vegas)—veal loaf, baked *leberkäse* (liver sausage), and bratwurst. On Monday night, there's a western buffet for the same price.
♦ Continental ♦ Daily dinner. 458.8810

**19** **Las Vegas Super 8 Motel** $$ This 150-room, bare-bones motel also features the popular **Longhorn Casino & Restaurant.** The casino boasts a handful of blackjack tables and **Leroy's Sports Book.** There's also a small bar and the modest **Chuck Wagon** coffee shop. ♦ 5288 Boulder Hwy (between Sun Valley Dr and E Harmon Ave). 435.8888, 800/825.0880

**20** **Desert Rose Golf Course** Although this modest, 147-acre course isn't the most scenic in town, it is one of the cheapest, and it does overlook nearby Sunrise Mountain. But the view is blocked by an unsightly power plant to the east of the links. Some golfers steer clear of this course because it's watered in part with treated wastewater. Still, it's crowded all year long, especially from February to June, when golfers should call a week in advance to reserve a tee time. Amenities include a pro shop, a clubhouse, a driving range, two putting greens, a small restaurant, and a bar. ♦ Fee. Daily sunrise to sunset. 5483 Clubhouse Dr (between Abarth St and Winterwood Blvd). 431.4653; fax 431.7910

**21** **Las Vegas Mormon Temple** The 60,000-square-foot temple, surrounded by an iron fence, sits on 12 well-manicured acres at the base of Sunrise Mountain, which forms the eastern boundary of the Las Vegas Valley. Since it was built in 1989 by the Church of Jesus Christ of Latter-day Saints, the $18-million structure has become one of the area's most recognizable pieces of architecture. The public is allowed to tour the grounds but may not enter the temple. Even many Mormons have to content themselves with viewing the stately exterior, which features a copper roof

*Las Vegas Mormon Temple*

and six cast-stone towers. The tallest tower rises 125 feet above the east entrance and is topped by a 10-foot-tall, gold-leaf statue of Moroni, the angel Mormons believe helped the prophet Joseph Smith to "usher in the restoration of the gospel of Jesus Christ." Unlike the dozens of Mormon churches in Vegas, this temple is, according to church leaders, "a special place where couples are married for eternity, where families are joined together forever, and where members receive sacred instruction." To many locals, including some 100,000 Mormons in Nevada and portions of Arizona and California, the temple is also a symbol of the historical importance and political power the church holds in the state. ♦ Call to find out when the grounds are open. 827 Temple View Dr (at E Bonanza Rd). 452.5011

**21 Nellis Air Force Base** The largest and busiest base in the Air Combat command covers about 12,000 square miles of airspace and approximately three million acres of land northeast of Las Vegas. More than 5,000 military and civilian employees work at the base, which was established in 1941 as the Las Vegas Gunnery Range. While the base is not open to the public, the hangar that houses the famed Thunderbirds air demonstration squadron is usually open for free 90-minute guided tours on Tuesday and Thursday. The tour begins at 2PM and includes a brief lecture on the history of the team and a 13-minute film showing the red, white, and blue jets in action. It concludes with a walk through the **Thunderbird Museum,** which also is open only for tours. The museum thrills aeronautics buffs with its collection of photos and memorabilia of the T-Birds and the pilots who have flown them. If you're lucky and the Nellis-based daredevils aren't performing somewhere, you'll get a close-up view of one of the team's F-16 jets. Unfortunately, air shows are not part of the package. To take the tour, visitors must check in at the **Nellis Visitors' Center** between 1:30 and 1:45PM to receive a vehicle pass and directions to the hangar. Groups of 20 or more can request their own tour by calling the **Thunderbird Public Affairs Office** at least a month in advance. ♦ Free. Tu-Th 2PM. Las Vegas Blvd N and E Craig Rd. 652.4018

## Bests

### Barbara Molasky
Administrative Officer/City of Las Vegas, Special Projects

Meandering through the fabulous display of neon signs in the outdoor sculpture walkway known as the "Neon Museum" located in **Downtown** Las Vegas on **Fremont Street.**

Feeling "laked out" after a great day of boating on **Lake Mead.**

Meeting friends and having dinner at **Piero's.** Make sure you say hello to the owner, Freddie Glusman.

Attending the *Distinguished Lecture Series* at **UNLV** and hearing interesting speakers such as Hillary Rodham Clinton, Henry Kissinger, Sam Donaldson, and Leah Rabin, to name a few.

Picnicking at the outdoor concerts at **Hills Park** in **Summerlin.**

Enjoying the beautiful desert sunsets when everything looks clear and still.

Driving up to **Mount Charleston** and experiencing all of the seasons.

### Anthony N. Cabot
Lawyer, specializing in Gaming Law/Lionel Sawyer & Collins

See more stars than you ever thought existed by sleeping on top of a houseboat on **Lake Mead.**

The only way to see the **Strip** is in a convertible at about 3AM on a warm summer night.

No crowd is like a fight crowd, grab the cheap seats, get there early and see everyone from the Hollywood elite to the rappers.

Eat lunch outdoors inside the **Forum Shops** at **Bertolini's,** an Italian restaurant in the most impressive modern, er, ancient mall in the world.

If you like gambling and want to learn more about it, the only place you need to go is the **Gambler's Book Club.** If a book was written on gambling, you will likely find it among the thousands there.

There is still romance in baseball, only it's found in the minor leagues. Buy a general admission ticket to a **Las Vegas Stars** game, grab a beer and a Memphis barbecue sandwich, sit near the visitors' bullpen and talk to tomorrow's major league stars.

### John Chambers
Manager, Adaptive Recreation Division, Department of Parks & Leisure Activities, City of Las Vegas

A drive in beautiful **Red Rock Canyon** and a spring picnic at dusk.

A trip up the **Stratosphere Tower.**

A summer concert in **Hills Park** at **Summerlin.**

The tigers at **The Mirage,** the pirate show at **Treasure Island,** and the light show on **Fremont Street.**

A visit to **The Liberace Museum.**

A trip to the **Ethel M. Chocolate Factory.**

Dinner at **Binion's Ranch Steak House** in **Downtown** Las Vegas, overlooking the city.

The buffet at the **Rio.**

# Gambling

Gambling is as old as civilization itself. Even before the advent of written records, a Neanderthal carved the first dice from ankle bones of sheep. Later, another of our ancestors devised one of the first practical applications for paper: the playing card. Gambling myths are common in most ancient religions. Indeed, gambling can be considered a theological by-product, if you subscribe to the idea that divine authority controls luck, fate, and destiny. And though mass public gambling has evolved into its current sanitized manifestation—a high-volume, corporate-profit assembly line, euphemistically known as gaming—it's still monotheistic. Nowadays, though, the Higher Power, the Great Pit Boss in the Sky, is represented by a simple mathematical concept: the house advantage.

Let's face it. Every game in every casino in the world yields the advantage to the house. The house advantage is an invisible, automatic, and efficient system that ensures that the casino reaps a commission from every dollar the players win. All the pennies, nickels, dimes, and quarters that the casino "rakes" (takes off the top) from all winning wagers eventually grind bettors' bankrolls into dust. This process, in gambling lingo, is known as a "long-term negative expectation." In layman's terms, it's called "going broke."

Players can make nearly a hundred types of wagers in a casino. (Craps alone accounts for a couple of dozen.) The house advantage for each of these bets is calculated as a percentage, the difference between the true odds of a winning wager (what the wager would pay if the casino were not deducting a profit) and what the casino actually pays.

For example, since a roulette wheel has 38 numbers, the odds of choosing the correct number are 37 to 1. Therefore, the true odds would call for a $37 payoff for a one dollar bet on a winning number. However, the casino only pays $35. This two dollar difference between the true odds and the actual payoff amounts to a house advantage of 5.26 percent. The house recoups a little more than a nickel commission from every dollar it pays out.

The house percentage ranges from zero—with perfect play at blackjack (when the player makes no mistakes) and on some video-poker machines—up to a whopping 30 percent on a typical keno wager. This averages out to a casino "hold," or pretax profit margin, of 20 percent (holds vary only slightly since most casinos operate under similar game rules). This opulent hold is evident throughout Las Vegas. It pays the massive hotel-casino overhead and subsidizes bargain room rates, rock-bottom food prices, and "comps" (complimentary accommodations, meals, and drinks). It helped finance the construction of megaresorts such as **The Mirage, Luxor, Stratosphere, MGM Grand, New York–New York, Mandalay Bay, Paris–Las Vegas, Bellagio**, and **Venetian**—and still continues to bankroll newer and bigger monuments to the almighty house advantage.

# Betting Smart

Sticking to bets that yield the lowest percntage to the house gives you an advantage over less discriminating gamblers. If you win, you contribute a smaller portion of your winnings to the casino's 20 percent profit margin.

Listed below (in order) are the five best and worst casino wagers from a bettor's perspective. Refer to the sections on each individual game (beginning on page 88) for further explanation.

**Five Best Bets**

**1** any cash wager augmented with a casino coupon (which supplements your return if you win)

**2** single-deck blackjack using perfect basic strategy

**3** maximum-coin bet on a full-pay deuces wild video-poker machine with a $4,000 royal flush jackpot

**4** placing a bet on either player or banker at baccarat

**5** making line bets with full odds at craps

**Five Worst Bets**

**1** any bet at keno

**2** any bet on the money wheel

**3** proposition bets at craps

**4** nickel reel slots

**5** tie at baccarat

# Mastering the Basics

The best way to increase your chances of winning is to learn the rules, odds, and etiquette of casino games before you attempt to play. You can choose from countless books covering all aspects of gaming, from probability theory and how to play slots to shuffle variations at blackjack and professional tournament strategy. **Gambler's Book Club** (630 S 11th St, Las Vegas, NV 89101; 382.7555) has the most complete selection of titles on gambling in the US and will send books by mail. Call to order their free catalog of titles.

Interactive computer software that simulates

blackjack, craps, or video poker can help develop strong gambling skills. You can purchase a range of gambling software from **Huntington Press** (3687 S Procyon Ave, Las Vegas, NV 89103; 252.0655, 800/244.2224).

Most of the large casinos provide free gambling lessons during slack periods in the day. Here you can gain some experience and insight on how to play. Show up early so that you're close to the "layout" (the playing area of the table games) to take full advantage of this free service.

# In the Casino

Always begin gambling, especially at the live table games (those with a dealer), with all of your powers of observation on alert. There are many customs and rules of etiquette, and until you master them, you're an obvious novice. From the outset, don't be shy about asking questions of dealers or pit personnel. It's perfectly acceptable to ask a craps dealer what the odds are on a particular bet or a blackjack dealer what the basic strategy is for a certain hand. Dealers should be polite and helpful. If they're not, leave.

A friendly dealer can help provide an enjoyable, and sometimes unforgettable, gambling experience. An occasional "toke" (tip) or bet for the dealer will quickly loosen up a mechanical and impersonal game. Dealers earn little more than minimum wage and depend on tokes for a large portion of their income. You can either give the dealer a chip by placing it on the layout (never hand it over directly), or making a side bet for the dealer. If the player hand wins, the dealer takes the wager and winning payoff

for him or herself; if the dealer hand wins, the house gets the wager.

Remember, the whole idea of a trip to the casino is to have fun (at least for nonprofessionals). If you consider gambling recreation, you'll be willing to spend money for the enjoyment of it, just as you would pay for the pleasure of a meal or a concert. Be patient and courteous with the people around you. Remain friendly and gracious even when you're losing.

# BACCARAT

Named after an Italian word meaning zero, baccarat (*bah*-kah-rah) made its way from Italy to France, where, in the late 15th century, it evolved into *chemin de fer*, a game enjoyed primarily by the French nobility. In the late 1950s, Las Vegas casinos imported *chemin de fer* and adopted the original name. Today, baccarat is one of the simplest, and at the same time most exclusive, casino table games. It's easy to learn and play, and is as thick in tradition, glamour, and exclusivity as it is thin in substance and nuance. And while the house advantage is minor (a little more than one percent), the minimum bet (usually $20 to $25) is major. Thus, neither the casino nor the players take baccarat lightly. Though it offers excellent odds and takes little skill, it requires a large investment.

## How to Play

The object of baccarat is to come as close as possible, with two or three cards, to a hand that totals nine. Picture cards, 10s, and cards that together total 10 are treated as zero. Ten is subtracted from a hand that totals more than 10. Aces count as one. Therefore, a three and a four add up to seven; eight and seven add up to five; a king and ace together count as one; a jack, a five, and a nine add up to four. A hand totaling eight or nine is called a natural.

Baccarat involves obscure ritual, orchestrated by the "caller," one of the three casino employees who run the game. Two dealers handle the betting; the caller oversees the dealing. Eight decks of cards are shuffled by a dealer, and the cards are placed in a "shoe" (card-holding device). The cards are dealt from the shoe by the players themselves, who, when they're dealing, are known as the bank. The caller instructs the players as to the proper sequences of the dealing ritual. The simplicity of the game lies in the fact that there are only three bets to baccarat: player, bank, and tie. The whole idea is to bet on which hand, bank or player, will come closest to nine. The player bet has a house edge of 1.36 percent, the bank bet 1.17 percent; the casino collects a 5 percent

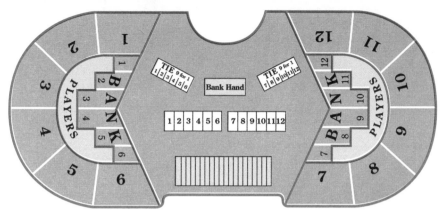

commission on winning bank wagers. The tie bet has a 14 percent edge, which means you'll lose your money 14 times faster than if you stick to player or bank bets.

Two cards are dealt to each hand (usually face down, but some casinos deal them face up). Depending on their totals, it may be necessary for one or both hands to draw a third card, governed by a specific set of rules. If both hands total eight or nine, no cards are drawn, and the nine beats the eight; in a tie, the hands are redealt. The winning hand is paid off at even money (ties are paid at eight to one).

## Player's Rules

| Hand | Action |
|---|---|
| 1, 2, 3, 4, 5, 10 | draw a third card |
| 6, 7 | stand (hand stands as dealt) |
| 8, 9 | natural (wins or ties) |

## Bank's Rules

| Hand | Draw if third card is: | Stand if third card is: |
|---|---|---|
| 3 | 1, 2, 3, 4, 5, 6, 7, 9, 10 | 8 |
| 4 | 2, 3, 4, 5, 6, 7 | 1, 8, 9, 10 |
| 5 | 4, 5, 6, 7 | 1, 2, 3, 8, 9, 10 |
| 6 | 6, 7 | 1, 2, 3, 4, 5, 8, 9, 10 |
| 7 | stand | |
| 8, 9 | natural (wins or ties) | |

## Mini-baccarat

While baccarat is played in its own ritual-laden pit with a table minimum of $20 to $25, mini-baccarat (see below) takes place in the main blackjack pit, with none of the ritual and a two- to five-dollar table minimum. One dealer handles dealing the cards, taking the bets, and receiving the commissions; the rules and house advantage are the same as with baccarat. It's a faster game and much more casual—a good training ground for anyone who aspires to play at the big table.

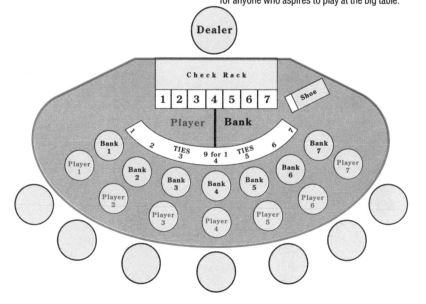

# BLACKJACK

On one hand, blackjack is an easy game. You play at least two cards to come as close to 21 as you can without "busting" (going over). You always have four choices for playing your cards: stand, hit, double down, or split (see "Blackjack Glossary," on page 92). You may have a fifth option of surrendering immediately after the deal and losing half your bet. And sometimes you have the option of buying insurance if the dealer is showing an ace. On the other hand, strategies for playing blackjack can be as complicated as a pro football offense, and the action can be nearly as intense.

*Hard Hand*

Here's a typical scenario for a round of blackjack. Several players sit around a blackjack table facing the dealer, who deals two cards to each person, including herself. The players' cards are dealt face down, but one of the dealer's cards is face up; it's an 8. The players look at their hands to see how close their two cards have brought them to the magic number: 21. (Cards are tallied at face value, except for

*Natural*

face cards, which count as 10, and aces, which can be worth either 1 or 11.) The player with two jacks stands. The player whose hand totals 16 hits (asks the dealer for a card), receives a king, and busts; he throws his two other cards toward the dealer, who collects the cards and the bet. The guy who holds two 4s hits, receives a 10, and stands on 18. The woman with 11 doubles down and receives a single card, face down.

Now the dealer turns up the hole card (unexposed card) and shows a queen, for a total of 18. The dealer pays even money to the player with a 20. To the player with 18, the dealer says "Push," meaning a tie, and no money changes hands. The dealer turns over the card that's face down for the player who doubled down: It's a 3, for 14, and the dealer collects the bet. The dealer quickly places all the used cards in the discard tray and starts dealing another hand. The whole round takes less than a minute.

Ever since Dr. Edward O. Thorp wrote and published *Beat the Dealer* (Vintage Books,

*Soft Hand*

1960), in which he described a system for "counting" the cards that have been dealt and determining if the remaining cards are advantageous or detrimental to the player, the blackjack table has been the fiercest battleground in the casino, with players facing off against dealers and pit bosses. Knowledgeable players have invented, tested, and refined strategies to the point that they can sometimes reduce the house advantage to mere fractions of a percentage, even it out, or in some cases turn it in their favor.

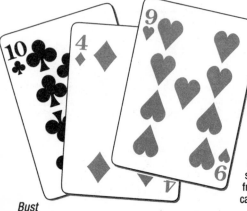

*Bust*

Because a player who counts cards can achieve a long-term advantage, however slight, over the house, professional gamblers play blackjack; people actually earn a fair living doing a daily shift at the 21 table. Of course, establishing a career as a card counter can require up to a year of advanced study and practice, a substantial financial stake, and facing risk every minute on the job. In short, it's not for everyone. Luckily, you can learn a less demanding blackjack strategy in a day, which can tilt the odds in your favor so that you're in the rare position of being on a level playing ground in the casino.

| H — Hit | S — Stand | D — Double Down | P — Split |
|---------|-----------|-----------------|-----------|

|        | The Dealer's Up Card |   |   |   |   |   |   |   |    |   |
|--------|---|---|---|---|---|---|---|---|----|---|
| Your Hand | 2 | 3 | 4 | 5 | 6 | 7 | 8 | 9 | 10 | A |
| 8      | H | H | H | H | H | H | H | H | H | H |
| 9      | H | D | D | D | D | H | H | H | H | H |
| 10     | D | D | D | D | D | D | D | D | H | H |
| 11     | D | D | D | D | D | D | D | D | D | H |
| 12     | H | H | S | S | S | H | H | H | H | H |
| 13     | S | S | S | S | S | H | H | H | H | H |
| 14     | S | S | S | S | S | H | H | H | H | H |
| 15     | S | S | S | S | S | H | H | H | H | H |
| 16     | S | S | S | S | S | H | H | H | H | H |
| 17     | S | S | S | S | S | S | S | S | S | S |
| A,2    | H | H | H | D | D | H | H | H | H | H |
| A,3    | H | H | H | D | D | H | H | H | H | H |
| A,4    | H | H | D | D | D | H | H | H | H | H |
| A,5    | H | H | D | D | D | H | H | H | H | H |
| A,6    | H | D | D | D | D | H | H | H | H | H |
| A,7    | S | D | D | D | D | S | S | H | H | H |
| A,8    | S | S | S | S | S | S | S | S | S | S |
| A,9    | S | S | S | S | S | S | S | S | S | S |
| A,A    | P | P | P | P | P | P | P | P | P | P |
| 2,2    | H | H | P | P | P | P | H | H | H | H |
| 3,3    | H | H | P | P | P | P | H | H | H | H |
| 4,4    | H | H | H | H | H | H | H | H | H | H |
| 6,6    | H | P | P | P | P | H | H | H | H | H |
| 7,7    | P | P | P | P | P | P | H | H | H | H |
| 8,8    | P | P | P | P | P | P | P | P | P | P |
| 9,9    | P | P | P | P | P | S | P | P | S | S |
| 10,10  | S | S | S | S | S | S | S | S | S | S |

## Basic Strategy

This system for blackjack was developed by mathematicians and statisticians using high-speed computers to run simulations of hundreds of millions of blackjack hands. They've analyzed every possible combination of cards you might wind up holding against every possible dealer's up card and have determined the strategy for each play that optimizes your chances of winning the round. The chart above shows the proper play for the cards in your hand against the dealer's up card. Memorize the entire chart and practice with cards, then review the chart periodically until you play optimum blackjack automatically.

## Six Basic Rules

What if you're reading this in your Las Vegas hotel room, about to go down to the casino to play a little blackjack, and you don't have time to memorize the chart? Take the chart with you; casinos allow gamblers to consult basic strategy while playing. Another option is to memorize the following rules, which will see you through all but the most advanced doubling and splitting situations.

1 When you hold 12 to 16 and the dealer's up card is 2 to 6: stand.

2 When you hold 12 to 16 and the dealer's up card is 7, 8, 9, 10, or ace: hit.

3 Stand on 17 to 21.

4 Double down on 10 and 11 against the dealer's up cards 2 to 9.

5 Always split aces and 8s.

6 Never take insurance (a real sucker bet).

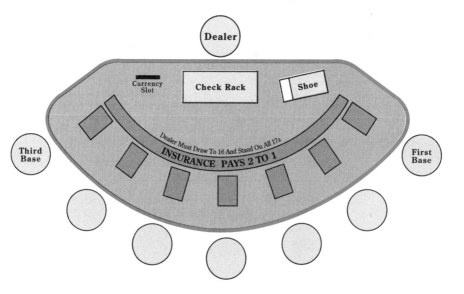

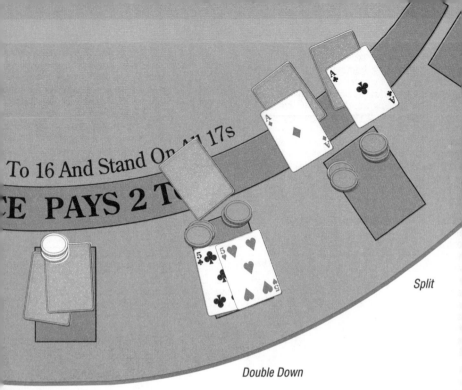

To 16 And Stand On All 17s

E PAYS 2 T

*Split*

*Double Down*

*Stand*

## Blackjack Glossary

**Burn** A ritual in casinos; the dealer places one or more cards at the bottom of the deck or in the discard tray just after shuffling (to confuse card counters)

**Bust** Any hand that exceeds 21

**Card counting** An advanced blackjack strategy that tracks the cards played to determine if the remaining pack is favorable or unfavorable to the player

**Double down** Doubling the bet on the first two cards of the hand

**Flat bet** Betting the same amount each time

**Front loading** When the dealer inadvertently exposes the hole card to a player

**Hard hand** A hand totaling 12 or more that includes an ace

**Hit** Take another card

**Hole card** The dealer's unexposed card

**Insurance** This side bet, made when the dealer's up card is an ace, is a wager—half your original bet—that the dealer won't have a natural blackjack

**Natural** A two-card 21

**Push** A tie

**Round** One complete hand, start to finish

**Shoe** Multiple-deck card holder

**Soft hand** Any hand containing an ace valued at 11

**Split** Dividing two like cards into two hands

**Spooking** Catching a glimpse of the dealer's hole card

**Stand** Don't take another card (see "Hit" above)

**Stiff** A hand totaling 12, 13, 14, 15, or 16

**Surrender** Folding a hand after viewing the first two cards

**Tells** Dealer mannerisms after checking the hole card

**Warp** Slightly bent card

# Child's Play

For decades, Las Vegas has enjoyed a reputation as the playground for adults. But whether in response to baby boomers with babies in tow or simply because it is trying to shed its anything-but-PG rating, southern Nevada is increasingly designing attractions specifically with children in mind. From animal displays to water parks, Las Vegas is doing its best to provide parents with ammunition to stave off the inevitable mid-vacation "What do we do now?" blues.

Although kids can pass through casinos, they must always be accompanied by an adult; as long as you keep moving, you'll be all right (waiting in line to get into a buffet or coffee shop is okay, too). But, in a growing number of casinos, youngsters are seldom far from games, shows, and other on-site activities tailored to provide them with a few lasting memories of their trip.

And unlike grown-ups, kids don't have to blow their allowances to have fun.

**1** **Bonnie Springs Ranch/Old Nevada** offers a petting zoo with a full complement of the usual creatures (including rabbits, deer, a donkey, baby goats, and a buffalo), a duck pond, an aviary, horseback riding, and exhibits highlighting the history of this stopover point for California-bound wagon trains during the mid-1800s.

**2** **Circus Circus** is the circus-themed hotel-casino and the granddaddy of child-friendly Las Vegas venues. There's **Grand Slam Canyon,** an indoor amusement park complete with a water ride and a roller coaster. There's also the second-story **Midway,** where kids will find plenty of video games and a variety of carnival activities (basketball tosses, pitching games—the usual amusement park mainstays), plus aerialists, acrobats, and other strolling circus performers.

**3** **Lake Mead** is the largest man-made lake in the US and has more than 550 miles of shoreline. The lake has become a popular recreational area and features boating, swimming, water skiing, and fishing.

**4** **Las Vegas Natural History Museum,** a local favorite, offers tableaux of stuffed animals ranging from antelope to yaks. The centerpiece of the *Prehistoric Life* exhibit is an animated dinosaur, which emits an impressive roar with ear-numbing frequency. Aquariums teeming with live sharks are crowd pleasers in the **Marine Life** gallery.

**5** **Las Vegas Stars,** the Triple-A farm team of the **San Diego Padres** baseball team, play from April to Labor Day at **Cashman Field** in what is generally considered one of the cleanest and best-designed minor-league ballparks in the country.

**6** **Lied Discovery Children's Museum** features more than 100 hands-on exhibits that illustrate principles of nature and science. Kids—and adults who aren't afraid of acting like kids—can construct buildings out of cardboard boxes, encase themselves in giant bubbles, buy "groceries" by withdrawing money from a pretend automated teller machine, and even design and fly paper airplanes. Who says science isn't fun?

**7** **MGM Grand Adventures Theme Park** features seven rides, including the **Lightning Bolt, Deep Earth Exploration, Backlot River Tour, Parisian Taxis, Over the Edge,** and **Grand Canyon Rapids.** But the greatest attraction at this park is **SkyScreamer,** where thrill seekers don a harness, pull a ripcord, and free-fall from the top of a 220-foot tower.

**8** **Omnimax Theater** at **Caesars Palace** is a super-marvel of theater technology and allows people to watch movies that are larger and louder than any they've seen before. The curved Omnimax screen is 82 feet high and 82 feet wide, and audio is provided through 89 hi-fi speakers, enveloping the audience in sight and sound.

**9** **The Mirage Hotel**'s **Tigers** and **Dolphins** are two separate exhibits. The white felines belong to magicians Siegfried and Roy. When the Bengals aren't working in the duo's act, they are on view at no cost 24 hours a day, lazing, prowling, and otherwise doing typical tiger things in a glassed-in habitat off the main casino.

**10** **Wet'n Wild** is the perfect remedy for Las Vegas's hellish desert afternoons. The water park is open daily from early April to early October.

# CRAPS

Dice! Those magical spotted cubes that have been the cause of exultation and desolation among gamblers since Zeus won the heavens from Hades and Poseidon in an Olympian crap shoot. "Bones" (slang for dice) have been around for thousands of years, and the American game of craps is descended from *hazard*, a French dice game that evolved from *az-zahr*, an Arabic dice game inspired by *ish-char*, the Sanskrit word for, you guessed it, dice.

The craps table is where the fastest moving and rowdiest action in the casino takes place. Craps is a complicated game that offers a couple dozen betting options. It's possible to have thousands of dollars—on a score of different wagers—riding on a single roll of the dice. The dealers double as human calculators, the cocktail waitresses keep one eye out for flying objects, and the players lose track of their bets often enough that vociferous arguments over stray chips are not uncommon. Fortunately, you can learn craps in increments and start by playing a satisfying (and low-risk) version when you know only the basic, most common wagers on the layout.

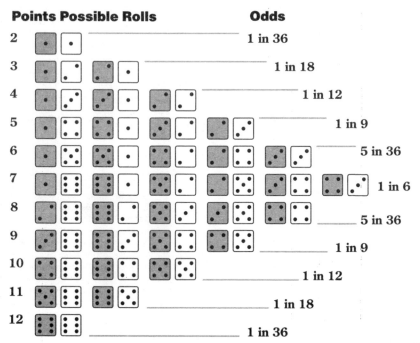

| Points | Possible Rolls | Odds |
|---|---|---|
| 2 | | 1 in 36 |
| 3 | | 1 in 18 |
| 4 | | 1 in 12 |
| 5 | | 1 in 9 |
| 6 | | 5 in 36 |
| 7 | | 1 in 6 |
| 8 | | 5 in 36 |
| 9 | | 1 in 9 |
| 10 | | 1 in 12 |
| 11 | | 1 in 18 |
| 12 | | 1 in 36 |

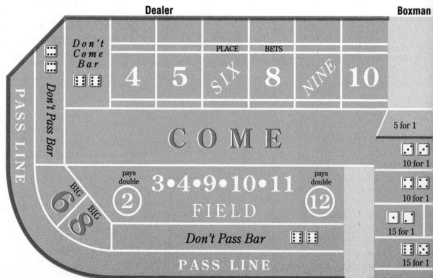

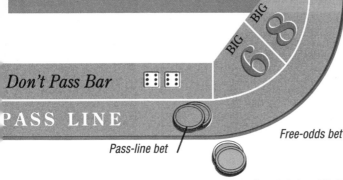

*Don't Pass Bar*

PASS LINE

Pass-line bet

Free-odds bet

## For the Beginner

Even beginners can make simple bets, which have the lowest house advantage, by playing the "line."

Watch a crap game until you hear the stickman (he who wields the stick that moves the dice) call "seven out," and the dealers sweep up most of the chips on the layout (shown below). The pair of dice then goes to a new shooter (player), whose first roll is called the "come-out" roll. On the come-out, everyone places a bet on either the pass line (betting *with* the shooter) or the don't-pass line (betting *against* the shooter). If the come-out is a 7 or 11, those who bet the pass line win. If it comes up "craps" (2, 3, or 12), they lose. If a 4, 5, 6, 8, 9, or 10 is rolled, that number becomes the shooter's "point," and to win he must continue rolling until hitting it again.

Betting on the pass line means you think the shooter will roll his point before "sevening out" (rolling a seven, an automatic loser). If you bet on the don't-pass line, you wager that the shooter will seven out before he rolls his point. Both bets are wagered against the house.

**Pass line:** Wins even money with a 7 or 11 on the come-out roll; loses on a 2, 3, or 12.

**Don't-pass line:** Wins even money if the come-out roll is a 2 or 3, and loses on a 7 or 11; 12 is a tie—no money changes hands.

**Point (4, 5, 6, 8, 9, or 10):** If the point is rolled before a 7, a bet on the pass line wins even money. A bet on the don't-pass line loses. If a 7 is rolled before the point, a pass-line bet loses and a don't-pass-line bet wins. A black-and-white plastic "buck" marks the point on the layout.

**Come:** Same as a pass-line bet, except it's made after a point has been established. A 7 or 11 wins; a 2, 3, or 12 loses; and any other number is a second point. If the newly established point is rolled before a 7, you win even money; if a 7 is rolled first, you lose.

**Don't come:** The opposite of the come bet. A 7 or 11 loses; 2, 3, and 12 win. If a 7 is rolled first, you win even money; if the point is rolled first, you lose.

**Odds:** One of the best bets is taking the "true odds" on a line bet (many players don't realize it exists since it's not marked on the table). Any pass/don't pass or come/don't come bettor can make a side bet equal to or greater than his previous bet—after the point has been established—that the shooter will roll his point before sevening out. You "back up" your line bets with odds by placing your chips behind the line bet (see above). If the point is rolled, the true odds pay off at two to one on the 4 and 10; three to two on the 5 and 9; and six to five on the 6 and 8 (as opposed to even money). (See page 96 for odds on the come bet.)

**Dealer**

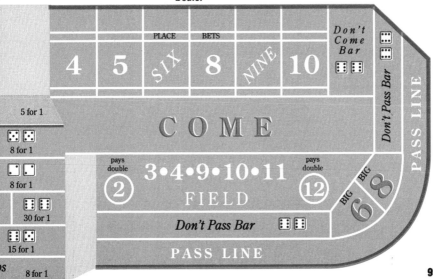

95

*Dealer places free-odds bet atop original bet but offset to distinguish from come or don't-come bet*

Don't-come and free-odds bet

Come and free-odds bet

**Field:** This bet is won or lost on each roll. A 3, 4, 9, 10, or 11 pay even money; a 2 or 12 pay 2 to 1. You lose on a 5, 6, 7, or 8. (See page 96.)

| Bet | Payoff | House Advantage |
|---|---|---|
| Pass line/come | 1 to 1 | 1.4 percent |
| Don't-pass line/ Don't come | 1 to 1 | 1.4 percent |
| With single odds | true odds | .8 percent |
| With double odds | true odds | .6 percent |
| With triple odds | true odds | .4 percent |
| Field | 1 to 1 | 5.5 percent |
| Field (when 12 plays triple) | 2 to 1 on 2; 3 to 1 on 12 | 2.7 percent |

## For the Advanced

Once you've played craps a few times and are familiar with the line bets and table etiquette, you can start to place more advanced and complicated wagers. The more money you have down on the table, the harder it is to keep track of it all, which is why you should be quite conversant with the game before you get into "placing" and "buying" points. However, even the most experienced craps shooters occasionally lose track of some of their bets. Fortunately, the dealers almost always have a handle on the layout and will make sure you get the money that's coming to you.

**Place:** Similar to a come bet, except that instead of waiting for a point to be rolled, you place a bet directly on any point other than the pass-line point. You win if the place-bet point is rolled before a 7. Winning bets are paid at house odds (as opposed to true odds) of nine to five on the 4 and 10; seven to five on the 5 and 9; and seven to six on the 6 and 8.

**Buy:** Similar to a place bet, except the odds paid off are true, and the house charges a five percent commission on winnings.

**Lay:** Similar to a buy bet, except that you bet against

the shooter. A 7 wins, and the point loses.

| Bet | Payoff | House Advantage |
|---|---|---|
| Place 6/8 | 7 to 6 | 1.5 percent |
| Place 5/9 | 7 to 5 | 4 percent |
| Place 4/10 | 9 to 5 | 6.7 percent |
| Buy | true odds less 5 percent | 4.7 percent |
| Lay 6/8 | 5 to 6 less 5 percent | 4 percent |
| Lay 5/9 | 2 to 3 less 5 percent | 3.2 percentt |
| Lay 4/10 | 1 to 2 less 5 percent | 2.4 percent |

Seven
5 for 1                    5 for 1
10 for 1                   8 for 1
10 for 1                   8 for 1
15 for 1    30 for 1    30 for 1
15 for 1                  15 for 1
8 for 1     Any Craps    8 for 1

## For the Sucker

"Proposition" bets are those made in the center of the layout, handled by the stickman. They all have a punishing house advantage of at least nine percent and can go nearly as high as 17 percent. A lot of craps players make these sucker proposition bets for excitement and the rare payoff; if you can't resist long-shot odds, join in—but be prepared to lose your money nearly as fast as you can play it.

**Big 6/big 8:** Paid off at even money if 6 or 8 are rolled before a 7 (9.09 percent).

**Hardways:** When the same number is rolled on each die two 3s for a hardways 6, two 4s for a hardways 8, etc.). These bets pay nine to one on the 6 and 8 (9.09 percent) and seven to one on the 4 and 10 (11.1 percent). (See illustration above.)

**Any 7:** Pays five to one when the next roll is a 7 (16.7 percent).

**Any craps (2, 3, or 12):** Pays seven to one when the next roll is a 2, 3, or 12 (11.1 percent).

**2 or 12:** Pays 30 to 1 when the next roll is either of those numbers (13.9 percent).

**3 or 11:** Pays 15 to 1 when the next roll is either of those numbers (11.1 percent).

**C and E (craps and 11):** Pays three to one on any craps; seven to one on 11 (11.1 percent).

pays double
(2)

3•4•9•10•11

FIELD

pays double
(12)

# KENO

A variation on an ancient Chinese form of bingo, keno was imported to the US by Chinese immigrants in the mid-1800s. Americanized, it's now played with 80 numbered Ping-Pong balls contained in a round plastic bowl (sometimes a wire mesh cage) called a "goose." A "blower" (powerful electric fan) mixes the balls and forces them, one at a time, into two long plastic tubes that hold 10 balls each. A caller announces the numbers, which are also illuminated on electronic keno boards throughout the casino.

It's hard to believe, but the house advantage for keno is even higher than it is for the money wheel: an astronomical 25 to 35 percent! You can expect to throw away roughly 30¢ for every dollar that you bet. On the other hand, it's a slow game. The action is protracted, so your dollar tends to go farther. Thus keno is convenient if you want to relax and drink in the keno lounge or add some excitement to a meal in the coffee shop. Also, keno offers substantial jackpots, often $50,000. If you can't resist a long shot or you're hoping total dumb luck will strike, this may be your game.

## How to Play

Get a keno ticket and, using one of the black crayons provided, mark your lucky numbers. You can mark any number of "spots" from 1 to 15, and sometimes 20, but the lowest house advantage is on the 8-spot wager. You can use a straight, split, way, or combination betting scheme. (See below.)

Make the appropriate notations in the right-hand margin, depending on the type of ticket you play. Then write the amount of your wager in the box in the upper right-hand corner. The average minimum bet is $1.

Present your ticket and bet to a keno runner (circulating throughout the casino) or at the keno counter. You'll receive a duplicate ticket with the date, game number, and serial number.

*Blank Keno ticket*

As soon as you've placed your bet, watch any keno board for the numbers drawn and match them with the spots you've selected. Payoffs are listed in booklets displayed near the tickets and crayons. If enough of the casino's numbers match yours (depending on how many spots you've played), collect your payoff immediately. The numbers from the current game remain on the board for about five minutes; as soon as they're erased in preparation for a new game, you forfeit any payoff you haven't collected.

*Straight ticket*

## Types of Keno Tickets

**Straight ticket:** The simplest and most common keno play. You mark from one to 15 numbers (out of a possible 80) and make a single bet on them. (See illustration, page 97.)

*Split ticket*

**Split ticket:** Contains a number of straight bets on the same ticket. Draw a circle around different combinations of numbers and place a bet on each combination. By circling, for example, four sets of three numbers and marking 4/3 in the margin, you are making four three-spot straight bets, the same as if you used four different tickets and marked one three-spot bet on each. At one dollar each, your total action would be four dollars (shown above).

**Way ticket:** A complicated and fancy way to lose money. You circle three or more equal groups of numbers and then play them by betting on all the different ways that the

numbers can come up. For example, if you circled three groups of three numbers each, you'd make a notation of 3/6 in the margin, meaning the three ways to make a six spot, or the three ways that six different numbers could be called. With a betting unit of one dollar, your total bet would be three dollars. Large way tickets can get very complex and expensive. (See illustration above.)

**Combination ticket:** Adds another dimension to the way ticket. Using the three-groups-of-three example, you could bet them separately as three spots, in which case you would be making a one dollar bet on each of the three spots, and you'd mark the margin 3/3 (total bet: three dollars). You could also bet them as three six spots, in which case you would be making a one dollar bet on the three different combinations of six numbers, and you'd mark the ticket 3/6 (total bet, now six dollars). Finally, you could also bet one dollar on all the numbers together as one nine spot, and you'd mark the ticket 1/9 (total action on the three different combinations: seven dollars). (See illustration, below)

*Combination ticket*

**Replay ticket:** Simply a ticket from a prior game that's reused.

Las Vegas is home to all manner of microbreweries, where visitors can drink their fill of specialty beers. One of the first beers sold in the city was bottled under the American Beauty label—during Prohibition.

A 1996 national survey by Harrah's found that 61 percent of Americans found casino entertainment to be "acceptable for anyone" while another 30 percent found it acceptable for others—but not for themselves.

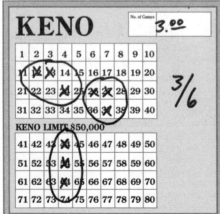

*Way ticket*

# THE MONEY WHEEL

Also known as "big six" or "wheel of fortune," the money wheel is a legacy of carnival midways that has somehow insinuated itself into the casino pit. Anyone who's ever watched Merv Griffin's popular TV game show "Wheel of Fortune," with Pat Sajak and Vanna White, will be instantly familiar with the basics. The big wheel (usually six feet in diameter) is divided into nine sections. Each section is further divided into six monetary denominations from $1 to $20. There are 24 $1 segments, 15 $2 segments, seven $5 segments, four $10 segments, two $20 segments, and two jokers. Posts protruding from the circumference of the

wheel separate the segments. The posts click against a leather or wood pointer at the top of the wheel as it spins; when it stops, the pointer indicates the winning denomination.

The layout (the area on the table where you place your bets) displays the same denominations as the wheel. Players place their bets on the $1, $2, $5, $10, $20, or joker options; the denominations also determine the payoff (i.e., a $1 bet on the $2 spot wins $2; a $5 bet on the $20 spot wins $100).

The player disadvantage on the money wheel is so prohibitive (from 11 percent on a $1 spot up to 24 percent on the joker) that most wheels and layouts need a dusting every few days. Still, if you've never been in a casino, are about to make your first bet ever, and don't know how to play any other game, you might consider putting a buck or two on the money wheel.

ROLANDO CORUJO

# ROULETTE

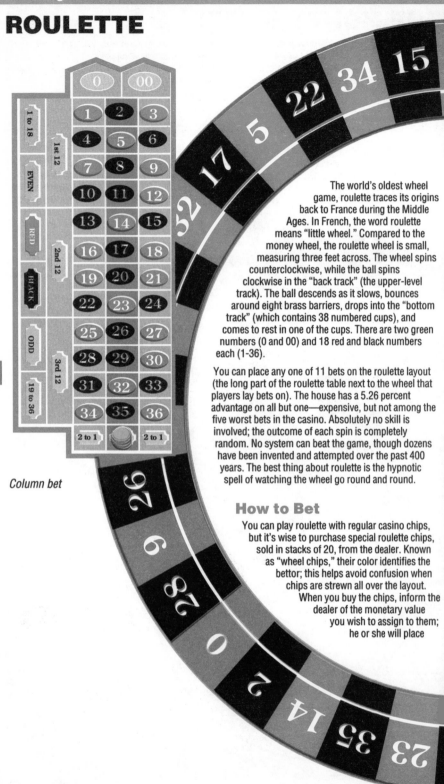

*Column bet*

The world's oldest wheel game, roulette traces its origins back to France during the Middle Ages. In French, the word roulette means "little wheel." Compared to the money wheel, the roulette wheel is small, measuring three feet across. The wheel spins counterclockwise, while the ball spins clockwise in the "back track" (the upper-level track). The ball descends as it slows, bounces around eight brass barriers, drops into the "bottom track" (which contains 38 numbered cups), and comes to rest in one of the cups. There are two green numbers (0 and 00) and 18 red and black numbers each (1-36).

You can place any one of 11 bets on the roulette layout (the long part of the roulette table next to the wheel that players lay bets on). The house has a 5.26 percent advantage on all but one—expensive, but not among the five worst bets in the casino. Absolutely no skill is involved; the outcome of each spin is completely random. No system can beat the game, though dozens have been invented and attempted over the past 400 years. The best thing about roulette is the hypnotic spell of watching the wheel go round and round.

## How to Bet

You can play roulette with regular casino chips, but it's wise to purchase special roulette chips, sold in stacks of 20, from the dealer. Known as "wheel chips," their color identifies the bettor; this helps avoid confusion when chips are strewn all over the layout. When you buy the chips, inform the dealer of the monetary value you wish to assign to them; he or she will place

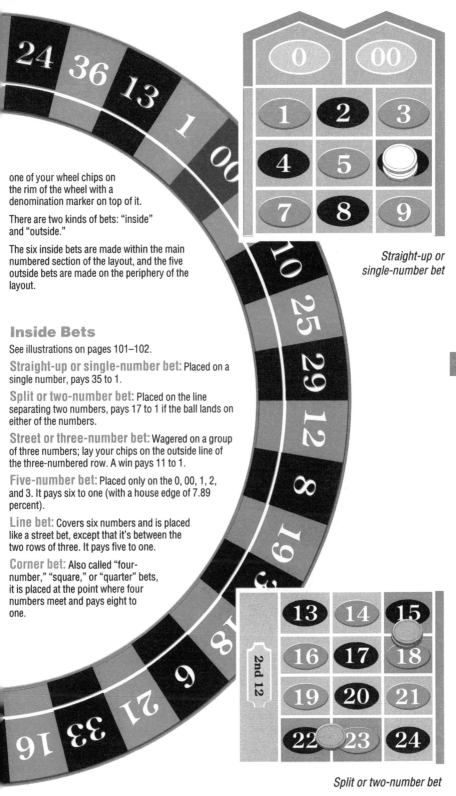

one of your wheel chips on the rim of the wheel with a denomination marker on top of it.

There are two kinds of bets: "inside" and "outside."

The six inside bets are made within the main numbered section of the layout, and the five outside bets are made on the periphery of the layout.

## Inside Bets

See illustrations on pages 101–102.

**Straight-up or single-number bet:** Placed on a single number, pays 35 to 1.

**Split or two-number bet:** Placed on the line separating two numbers, pays 17 to 1 if the ball lands on either of the numbers.

**Street or three-number bet:** Wagered on a group of three numbers; lay your chips on the outside line of the three-numbered row. A win pays 11 to 1.

**Five-number bet:** Placed only on the 0, 00, 1, 2, and 3. It pays six to one (with a house edge of 7.89 percent).

**Line bet:** Covers six numbers and is placed like a street bet, except that it's between the two rows of three. It pays five to one.

**Corner bet:** Also called "four-number," "square," or "quarter" bets, it is placed at the point where four numbers meet and pays eight to one.

*Straight-up or single-number bet*

*Split or two-number bet*

## Outside Bets

**Column bet:** Placed on 12 numbers at the base of the column, pays two to one.

**Dozen bet:** Also a 12-number bet, but numbers are bet to appear consecutively, 1-12, 13-24, or 25-36, and placed on the first, second, or third group of 12 numbers. Payoff is two to one.

You also can lay a chip on 1 to 18 or 19 to 36; red or black; and even or odd. This bet pays even money, or one to one.

*Line bet*

*Street or three-number bet*

*Split or two-number bet*

*Five-number bet*

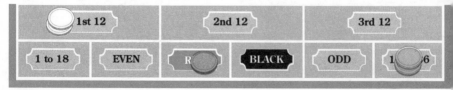

# SLOTS

Mechanical "reel" slots, the kind with three, four, or more spinning reels with various symbols on them (fruit, bars, and sevens are most common), were invented and originally used in San Francisco's notorious Barbary Coast neighborhood at the turn of the 20th century. The fruit symbols corresponded to the flavor of the gum that was delivered as the prize. With the exception of a few minor variations, the original slot-machine design remained unchanged for 65 years. Electric slots were introduced in the mid-1960s, complete with lights and noisemakers. The miracle of electronics revolutionized the slot-machine industry in the mid-1970s, introducing a vast array of sizes, symbols, and payouts, all controlled by microprocessors. For example, nickel video slots (using a screen instead of reels) can feature 24 symbols with a complicated payout based on a variety of symbol patterns. Likewise, Megabucks is a one dollar, four-reel slot that's connected by modem to hundreds of other Megabucks machines throughout Nevada; each time a player inserts a dollar, the giant "progressive" jackpot grows by a nickel. By the time a player lines up all four Megabucks symbols, the jackpot can be as high as $10 million to $12 million. Nickel slots rank as one of the five worst bets in a casino, with a hold of around 25 percent. Dollar slots can be as low as five percent. With such odds, how they manage to earn casinos more money than all table games combined due to heavy play is one of life's biggest mysteries.

## Tips on Playing Slots

One of the great myths of slot machines is that they become "due," or overdue to hit a big jackpot. Slots fall under the "independent event" category of probability theory (as opposed to games like blackjack and poker, where the odds continually change, depending on what cards are in or out of play). Each spin of the reels has absolutely nothing to do with the last spin nor the next. Don't spend hours on a machine that you think is "ready."

To be eligible for the highest jackpot, you must play the maximum number of coins that a machine will accept. Megabucks slots, for example, have three paylines, each corresponding to a one dollar bet. To win the $5-million plus jackpot, you must line up the four Megabucks symbols on the three dollar payline. Imagine lining up the symbols on the three

dollar payline when you've only played one dollar and winning nothing, instead of millions.

Dollar slots pay back at a higher percentage than quarters, which pay back at a higher percentage than nickels. Machines with smaller jackpots pay back smaller amounts more frequently than machines with larger jackpots. So you get more action for less money.

Always join slot clubs, which you can find in most of the large casinos. To join, simply fill out an identification form at the slot club booth, at which time you receive a membership card. You still play with coins, but you insert your card into a digital reader on the machine, which tracks the amount and number of your bets and converts them into points. The more points you accumulate, the more discounts on rooms and food, various comps, gifts, and sometimes even cash are returned to you. Best of all, slot clubs are free.

# SPORTS BETTING

The large room, generally off to one side of the casino, with long rows of tables and chairs, banks of TV and video screens on the wall, and a big board covered with team names and hieroglyphic notations is called the sports book. In Nevada, you can bet on all major league baseball, basketball, football, and hockey games, college football and basketball (except for **University of Nevada** teams), as well as boxing matches and horse races from around the country.

Sports books didn't appear in casinos until the mid-1970s, but over the past 20 years sports betting has become a billion-dollar adjunct to the casino industry. The **Super Bowl** (professional football) and the **Final Four** (**NCAA** basketball) are the two largest sports betting events of the year; together they generate more than $100 million in action.

The complicated world of sports betting involves handicapping (attempting to predict the winner of a game or race), point spreads (the number of points by which one team beats the other), money lines (the odds of one team beating another), and commissions (the sports book rake). If you don't understand the terminology or procedures, the ticket writers behind the counter where you place your bets are generally helpful in determining what kind of wager you're trying to place. So don't be afraid to walk up cold and bet on a game that you've been following. The minimum bet is usually 5 or 10 dollars.

The best introductory book on sports betting is *Sports Betting 101,* written by Arne K. Lang and published by Gambler's Book Club.

# VIDEO POKER

There are only two "bank" games (played against the house, unlike poker, in which you are up against other players) that people play professionally: video poker and blackjack. You can learn, practice, and apply an exact strategy to video poker for optimum results. In addition, unlike reel slots, video-poker machines can be handicapped. In other words, you can tell just by looking at them what the house advantage is. Furthermore, with perfect play (making the correct decision for every hand) on the best machines, you can reduce the house advantage to zero; occasionally, opportunities arise in which you have an edge over the casino.

There is a large, and growing, variety of video-poker machines, including jacks or better, bonus and double bonus, joker wild, deuces wild, loose deuces, double-down stud, double-down high card, and second chance. They come in penny, nickel, quarter, $1, $5, $25, and even $100 denominations, with "flat-top" (fixed) or progressive jackpots for the royal flush.

## Playing Your Cards

For anyone familiar with the nuances of poker, proper play will be nearly automatic on the draw machines (though not on the joker or deuces machines); in other words, you'll keep cards that have the best potential for achieving pairs, three of a kind, straights, flushes, etc. However, the few basic differences in strategy between regular and video poker are important, since mistakes can be costly. The best way to learn video-poker strategy is on your home computer. A program such as *Stanford Wong's Video Poker* simulates draw, joker poker, deuces wild, and joker/deuces; tutors you on correct play; and calculates the house advantage for each hand. After an hour or two with this software, you'll be playing video poker in all its variations on a nearly professional level.

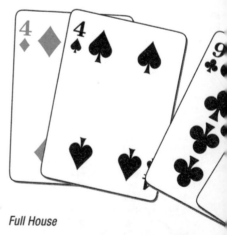

*Full House*

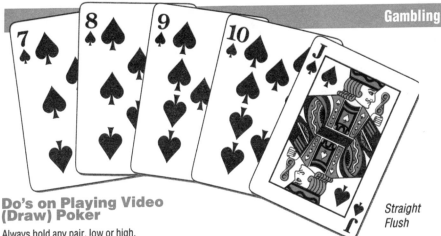

*Straight Flush*

## Do's on Playing Video (Draw) Poker

Always hold any pair, low or high.

In the absence of a pair, hold a picture card or an ace (or two).

In the absence of pairs, picture cards, or four-card straights or flushes, draw five new cards.

Always hold a high pair rather than drawing one card to a straight or flush.

## Don'ts on Playing Video (Draw) Poker

Don't hold a "kicker" (unpaired high card) with a low pair.

Don't draw to an inside straight (i.e., if you have 2, 3, 5, 6, and 9, don't discard the 9 hoping to get a 4).

Don't hold three cards to a straight or flush (you probably won't get the two cards needed to complete either hand).

Never hold two cards to a straight flush.

## Video-Poker Payout Schedules

Playing your cards properly is only half the challenge of video poker. The other, more important half is knowing which machine to play. Surprisingly, you can determine this with complete accuracy in a matter of seconds, by analyzing the payout schedule posted on the machines. The following rules apply to jacks or better draw machines.

Make sure the machine pays back your bet on a pair of jacks or better.

Determine that the maximum wager is five coins.

Check the payout column for one coin: A full house should return nine coins, and a flush should return six. This is known as a 9/6 machine.

Determine the payout for a royal flush with five coins played: It should return 4,000 coins.

| Full House/Flush Payout (Draw) | Expected Return |
| --- | --- |
| 10/6 | 100.7 percent |
| 9/7 | 100.8 percent |
| 9/6 | 99.5 percent |
| 8/5 | 97.3 percent |
| 7/5 | 96.2 percent |
| 6/5 | 95.1 percent |

# Excursions

No one really blames the tourist who still thinks a trip to Las Vegas begins and ends at the Strip. But locals know better, and they're quick to tell you that within an hour's drive of Las Vegas lies—well, Nevada: mountains, lakes, and colorful desert landscapes that offer stunning contrasts to the city's famous nightlife.

Face it. You've got to be fairly lucky, ridiculously wealthy, or unhealthily hooked to gamble for more than three or four hours at a stretch. Even experienced players, wise to the rhythms of cards and dice, would agree that it's occasionally necessary to escape the lights and sounds of the casinos. Nerve-soothing getaways can be found just a short drive away in almost any direction.

There's boating and fishing at **Lake Mead**, rock climbing and hiking at **Red Rock Canyon National Conservation Area**, and striking natural sculpture at the **Valley of Fire State Park**. And that shrine to human ingenuity—**Hoover Dam**—endures. Many visitors are surprised to learn they can even go skiing on **Mount Charleston** and be back by sundown to answer the siren call of the casinos.

You can easily visit many of these attractions in a day, and you need not make extra arrangements beyond renting a car (or in some cases hopping on a bus). But some Las Vegas visionaries are hoping vacationers realize there's more to Nevada than a three-day blowout. Even as resorts such as **New York–New York**, **Treasure Island**, and the **MGM Grand Hotel and Theme Park** vie for the family market, the city is also promoted as home base for an

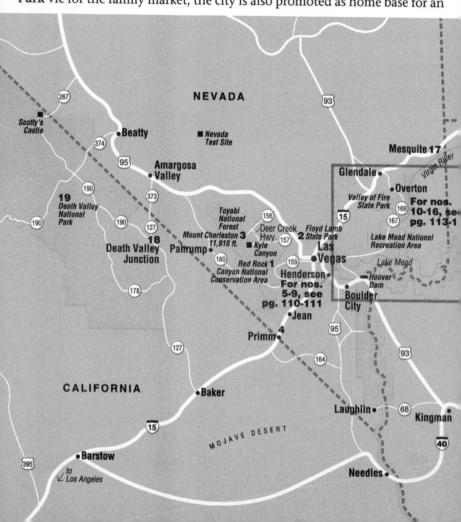

extended tour of the region. McCarran International is the closest airport to the **Grand Canyon**, one of the most spectacular natural wonders of North America. With **Death Valley, Zion, and Bryce Canyon National Parks**, plus the booming river town of **Laughlin** within reach, Las Vegas is no longer simply a so-called "adult Disneyland," but a multifaceted vacation destination to rival any other.

---

**1 Red Rock Canyon National Conservation Area** It's amazing to think that less than 20 miles from the chaos of Las Vegas there is a serene landscape of giant sandstone formations, rolling desert valleys, craggy hilltops, and—late in the day, when most people have gone—incredible, peaceful silence.

When touring one of Las Vegas's most popular off-Strip tourist attractions, many people begin at the **US Bureau of Land Management Visitors' Center,** located just inside the park entrance. Maps, trail guides, and other information about the park's amenities are available. A short videotape and displays detailing the geology and history of the canyon also whet the newcomer's appetite for what awaits.

Most visitors then hop into their cars for a trip along the 13-mile, one-way scenic roadway that circles the canyon's inside perimeter. The route features several spots where you can leave your car, stretch your legs, perch on a rock, drink in the sight of thousands of feet of red sandstone jutting into the sky, and listen to the eerie sound of the wind whistling through the rocky corridor.

Millions of years ago, everything now visible here was covered by the warm waters of a shallow sea. The multicolored shale and sandstone that form the outcrops, escarpments, cliffs, and caves are products of this era, created as the sea dried up and erosion worked its artistry on the rock faces.

**Calico Hills,** a series of rust-colored cliffs about a mile past the visitors' center, is the visual centerpiece of the canyon. It's also a favored challenge among rock climbers, who can be seen each day inching up the bluff as sightseers breathlessly chart their progress from a nearby scenic lookout point.

Farther along the picturesque loop are picnic areas, trailheads for several hiking paths, and vistas where drivers can park and bask in the unadorned peace of nature. Those wanting to enjoy a more intimate experience can take one of the dozen-plus trails within the 83,100-acre conservation area, which range from an easy one-mile trek suitable for children to strenuous hikes that involve a bit of rock scrambling. Checking in at the visitors' center is advisable, since some areas of the canyon are prone to flash flooding, and the environment is harsh and unforgiving for unprepared outdoors enthusiasts.

Backpacking is not permitted along the scenic loop drive. Backcountry backpackers must check in at the visitors' center to obtain permits; camping is allowed but restricted. Car campers may use primitive campsites at **Oak Creek,** situated on Route 159 three miles south of the visitors' center, and **Black Velvet Canyon,** off Route 160.

From March through June, the park becomes a palette of colors, thanks to the red, orange, purple, and yellow wildflowers blossoming throughout. The roster of wildlife includes scorpions, Gila monsters, and three varieties of venomous rattlesnakes.

But the desert dweller that visitors will most likely see is the friendlier wild burro. About 70 wild burros make their home in the canyon area. Despite their benign appearance and rather endearing tendency to beg from slow-moving vehicles, burros can be mean, ornery, and temperamental critters. Visitors should

to Salt Lake City

**22 Bryce Canyon National Park**

**UTAH**

**21 Zion National Park** 15 89 9

**Hurricane** 59 89

St. George Lake Powell

**Fredonia** 389 89A **Marble Canyon**

**Jacob Lake** 89

67

Colorado River

**Grand Canyon National Park 20**

64

180

**ARIZONA** 180

64

40 **Williams** **Flagstaff** 17

N

km 50 100
mi 25 50

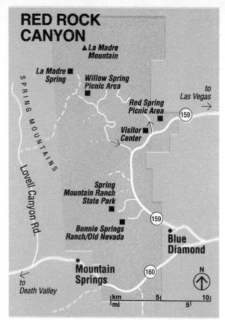

## RED ROCK CANYON

▲ La Madre Mountain

La Madre ■ Spring

Willow Spring Picnic Area

Red Spring Picnic Area

Visitor Center

to Las Vegas →
159

SPRING MOUNTAINS

Lovell Canyon Rd.

Spring Mountain Ranch State Park

Bonnie Springs Ranch/Old Nevada

159

Blue Diamond

Mountain Springs
160

← to Death Valley

N

|km          5|          10|
|mi        5|

not play with them, and there is a $25 fine for those caught giving them food. Rangers report that numerous people are bitten each year. ♦ Admission. Visitors' Center daily; scenic loop roadway daily 9AM-sunset. For information, contact US Bureau of Land Management (PO Box 26569, Las Vegas, NV 89126). Rte 159 (west of S Town Center Dr). 363.1921

Within Red Rock Canyon National Conservation Area:

### Spring Mountain Ranch State Park

Famed billionaire and eccentric Howard Hughes and German heiress Vera Krupp are two past owners of this historic 520-acre patch of grass and trees.

Thanks to a spring-fed stream, the ranch property spent much of its early days as an encampment for passing wagon trains, horse thieves, outlaws, and various travelers. In the 1880s, it became a working ranch, and in the 1940s it was purchased by Chester Lauck, also known as "Lum" of the "Lum & Abner" radio show. The Laucks maintained it as a working cattle ranch and their private vacation retreat until 1955, when they sold it to Vera Krupp, wife of German munitions magnate Alfried Krupp von Bohlen und Halbach.

Krupp lived at her ranch until 1967, when she sold it to Hughes Tool Company. In 1972, two California businessmen purchased the ranch from owner Howard Hughes with plans to build a condominium project. However, after two years of public opposition to their plans, they sold the property to the state.

A picnic area with barbecue pits, grassy spaces, picnic tables, and other amenities takes up a portion of the now public park. Intriguing guided tours of the ranch are offered on weekends and holidays. Visitors can see the main house—preserved as it appeared during the Lauck/Krupp years—the swimming pool added by Krupp, a fish pond, a family cemetery, cabins that date from the mid-1800s, a blacksmith shop, and even a shed once used by a long-ago owner as part of a chinchilla-breeding operation.

During the summer, hundreds of Las Vegans lug blankets and picnic baskets to an outdoor amphitheater on the grounds to watch plays and concerts. Special events such as nature walks, nighttime hikes, lectures, children's activities, and photography and art exhibits are offered on a regular basis. ♦ Per-car entry fee. Daily 8AM-sunset. Guided tours leave from the ranch house on weekends and holidays. For information, contact Spring Mountain Ranch (PO Box 124, Blue Diamond, NV 89004). 875.4141

**Bonnie Springs Ranch/Old Nevada** These adjacent examples of Old West nostalgia are aimed primarily at visitors, although locals often drop by after an excursion to **Red Rock Canyon** or **Spring Mountain Ranch**.

**Bonnie Springs Ranch,** built in 1843, was originally a stopover point for California-bound wagon trains. For more than three decades it's been a tourist attraction, complete with horseback-riding stables, a petting zoo, and a family-style restaurant offering basic meals (breakfast, lunch, and dinner) suitable for kids, but hearty enough for grown-ups.

**Old Nevada** is a working re-creation of a frontier town, featuring historical exhibits (including a smithy) and more theatrical attractions, such as staged hangings and gunfights. The **Miner Restaurant** serves the usual snack-joint fare for breakfast, lunch, and dinner—from sandwiches and hot dogs to salads. ♦ Bonnie Springs, free; Old Nevada, admission. Daily. 875.4191

Within Bonnie Springs Ranch/Old Nevada:

**Bonnie Springs Motel** $$ This clean, basic motor lodge offers family units with kitchens, as well as rooms with one king-size or two double beds. All told there are 50 rooms. Kids, of course, will like the pool. ♦ 875.4400

**2 Floyd Lamb State Park** Originally known as **Tule Springs State Park,** this simple, cozy patch offers picnic areas with barbecue grills, easy nature walks, and four lakes suitable for fishing and feeding the resident ducks and geese. ♦ Per-car entry fee. 9200 Tule Springs Rd (northeast of N Durango Dr). 486.5413

**3 Mount Charleston** A 45-minute drive from Las Vegas, Mount Charleston, a 316,000-acre chunk of **Toiyabe National Forest,** attracts more than two million visitors per year. The Mountain—for locals, no additional description is needed—has long been a favorite escape for desert-weary Las Vegans lusting after trees, scenic vistas, and temperatures 20 to 30 degrees cooler than in the city.

Mount Charleston is the highest peak in the **Spring Mountains,** which comprises the western border of the Las Vegas Valley. During the summer, this is a prime spot for hiking, camping, picnicking, and horseback riding, with skies blessedly free of polluted air.

Hikers can explore almost a dozen trails, from one to 10 or more miles in length and ranging in difficulty from sweat-free to strenuous. However, all guarantee excellent views of mountains, wooded areas, and, on the **Mary Jane Falls Trail,** a waterfall. Be aware, though, that this is serious woodland, and it pays to be prepared for quick weather changes and occasionally tricky terrain. (For weather conditions, call 736.3854.) No sanitary facilities or water are available during the winter months, and rangers recommend cold-weather excursions only for experienced hikers. Sledding and tubing runs are available at the **Fox Tail Snow Play Area** in Lee Canyon on Route 156, about one mile northeast of the **Las Vegas Ski & Snowboard Resort** (see at right). In the winter, the ski runs at the resort are open and equipment may be rented.

Now, the downside: The mountain gets incredibly crowded on weekends. Parking is often difficult at the **Mount Charleston Hotel** and the **Mount Charleston Lodge,** the slope's two prime sources of rest and refreshment (see at right). And, from November to April, the roads can be all but inaccessible to anything but four-wheel-drive vehicles and

cars equipped with tire chains. ♦ For trail maps, forest-use regulations, and general information about hiking and recreational activities, contact the Toiyabe National Forest Las Vegas Ranger District (2881 S Valley View Dr, Suite 16, Las Vegas, NV 89102, 873.8800)

On Mount Charleston:

**Mount Charleston Hotel** $$$ Halfway up the mountain, this hotel offers 63 rooms (including suites), a full-service but affordable restaurant, and some of the most breathtaking landscapes in southern Nevada. The best vantage is from the third-floor rooms at the back of the hotel. You'll pay a few bucks more, but the view is well worth the extra tariff. ♦ 2 Kyle Canyon Rd (west of Hwy 95). 872.5500, 800/794.3456; www.mtcharlestonhotel.com

# Mount Charleston Lodge

**Mount Charleston Lodge** $$$ Locals know this woodsy, laid-back establishment simply as "The Lodge." You pass through the lodge to get to the restaurant, but many never make it that far. It's the perfect place to relax in front of a fireplace and enjoy a Mount Charleston coffee—a spirit-lifting mixture of Drambuie, coffee, brandy, and whipped cream. The restaurant serves hearty breakfasts and exotic wild game at dinner. A charming addition, adjacent to the restaurant and lodge, is the cluster of 24 A-frame log cabins built on a terraced hillside with unobstructed views of the forest. There are 20 480-square-foot cabins and four 750-square-foot ones—perfect for a large clan. The cabins feature log furniture—a dining table, chairs, king-size bed, and a sofa bed—plus fireplaces, whirlpool baths, and showers. ♦ Kyle Canyon Rd (west of Hwy 95). 872.5408

**Las Vegas Ski & Snowboard Resort at Lee Canyon** For serious downhillers, this small ski operation offers well-groomed slopes (snowmaking machines augment what Mother Nature has supplied), three double chairlifts, a lounge, and a gift shop. Thirteen runs are available for beginning, intermediate, and advanced skiers. Weekend nighttime skiing is scheduled occasionally. Snowboarding is allowed on weekdays and at night only. ♦ Free shuttle bus service from Las Vegas is available from the Plaza Hotel and the Santa Fe Hotel & Casino (reservations required). Call Las Vegas Ski Resort Rentals (646.0008) for general information and shuttle reservations. For ski conditions, call 593.9500. Rte 156 (southwest of Deer Creek Hwy). 872.5462

# Primadonna®
## CASINO RESORTS

**4 Primadonna Casino Resorts** $$ Forty miles south of Las Vegas on both sides of Interstate 15 is an exciting entertainment and hotel complex, consisting of **Buffalo Bill's Resort & Casino, Whiskey Pete's Hotel-Casino,** and the **Primm Valley Resort & Casino.** The headline attractions include the $10-million **Desperado** roller coaster, the **Adventure Canyon Water Flume** ride, two motion-simulator theaters, and a giant Ferris wheel.

Recently expanded, **Buffalo Bill's** now boasts 1,200 rooms within its 16 floors. On-site attractions include a 200-seat Victorian-style movie theater and a 6,500-seat special events arena to host rodeos, boxing matches, and concerts. The 777-room **Whiskey Pete's** hotel boasts the **Silver Spur Steak House** and a 700-seat showroom featuring weekend performances by the likes of Ronnie Milsap,

America, and Mickey Gilley. Among **Primadonna**'s highlights are the excellent **Skydiver** steak and seafood restaurant and **Gary's Garage,** a buffet by day and, on weekend evenings, a 750-seat showroom spotlighting such stars as Gordon Lightfoot, Patti Page, and Helen Reddy.

On the thrilling **Desperado,** with more than 6,000 feet of track, passengers experience near-zero gravity three times during the two-minute ride. The steel-track coaster has a lift height of 209 feet with a 225-foot drop, the longest coaster drop in the world. Passengers are hurled 80 miles an hour at a maximum gravity force of three Gs (one or two is usual). ◆ I-15, Primm. Buffalo Bill's 382.1111, Whiskey Pete's 382.4388, Primadonna 382.1212. All three: 800/386.7867; fax 874.1079; www.primadonna.com

**5 The Sports Club/Las Vegas** This member of the lavish body-buffing emporiums (NY and LA) offers over 136,000 square feet of tracks, courts, and $1.5-million worth of state-of-the-art exercise equipment. Carpeted aerobics rooms, steam rooms, saunas, whirlpools, and toiletries complete the picture. There are two restaurants plus valet parking available. ◆ 2100 Olympic Ave (between Mountain Vista St and N Green Valley Pkwy), Henderson. 454.6000

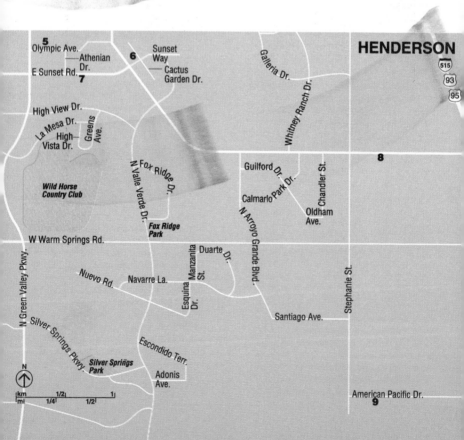

**6 Ethel M. Chocolate Factory** It's a pretty safe bet that at least one-third of the people taking the tour here on any given day are locals sprinting through just to get the free sample each visitor receives when it's all over.

True, that is one of the benefits of making the trip to the nearby town of Henderson, where the luscious sweets are made. But it's not the only one, unless you think a table filled with gooey chocolate fudge is a sight that makes Hoover Dam absolutely irrelevant.

Founded by the reclusive Forrest Mars (head of the Mars candy empire) to make strictly gourmet chocolates, the small but well-known company sells its wares nationally via mail order, and in Las Vegas at shops located in casinos, malls, and inside **McCarran International Airport.** Favorites range from simple milk chocolate coins to foil-wrapped, liqueur-filled morsels. The company prides itself on using only the finest ingredients, thus the expensive price tags for their treats: The special two-pound "Taste of Las Vegas" costs $35.

Tourgoers watch the candymaking process from lip-smacking start to finish through plate glass windows while videos playing on TV monitors along the route explain in delectable detail what is happening.

Work off those newly ingested calories from the free piece of candy by strolling through the two-and-a-half-acre cactus garden just outside the building. More than 350 species of cacti, succulents, and desert plants are artfully arranged along concrete paths. A cactus-themed gift shop is also on the premises. ◆ Free. Daily. Cactus Garden Dr (just north of Sunset Way), Henderson. 458.8864

**7 Renata's** ★★★$$$ On the borderline of Las Vegas and the posh master-planned community of Green Valley, this elegant restaurant was created by two former **Caesars Palace** employees—an Asian food and beverage director and a French chef. Families enjoy the options this mix provides—kids can order Chinese while their parents order continental, or vice versa. Such exquisite appetizers as dumplings filled with pork and water chestnuts, escargots with garlic butter and Pernod in phyllo cups, and lobster ravioli served with gulf prawns make this place worth the trip. You won't be disappointed with any main dish, but among the favorites are lobster Cantonese served with slivers of green scallions in a fermented black bean sauce, Hong Kong steak (marinated strip sirloin,

sliced and served atop a bed of stir-fried vegetables with *hoisin* sauce, a sweet, spicy mixture of garlic, chili peppers, and soybeans), broiled lamb chops with peppery goat cheese and rosemary garlic demiglace, and seared breast of duckling with huckleberry sauce. Both the Bailey's caramel flan and the truffle chocolate cake are standouts. There is also a lounge and bar open 24 hours a day; in addition to typical bar food, it serves treats like beef teriyaki on a stick, fried wontons, and eggs and waffles all day long. ◆ Continental/Asian ◆ Daily dinner. Reservations recommended. 4451 E Sunset Rd (between Mountain Vista St and N Green Valley Pkwy), Henderson. 435.4000

**8 Sunset Station Hotel/Casino** $ Favored by those looking for a place away from the madding crowd, this Mediterranean-inspired hotel offers comfort at a good price. Opened in 1997, the newest member of the growing Sunset Station Hotels features 448 spacious rooms and suites furnished in soft desert hues complete with king- and queen-sized beds. Iron balconies, exposed brick walls, and lots of windows make the 80,000-square-foot casino more like a stroll through a Spanish village. Guests also get to enjoy a multiplex movie theater, five restaurants (including **Ben & Jerry's Scoop Shop** and **Sunset Brewing Co.** microbrewery), and an amphitheater. ◆ 1301 W Sunset Rd (between I-515 and Stephanie St). 888/SUNSET9, 800/544.2411; www.sunsetstation.com

**9 Cranberry World West** Ocean Spray Cranberries Inc. opened this 10,000-square-foot visitors' center adjacent to its juice-processing and distribution plant in 1995. Offering an educational, entertaining, and mouthwatering look at an exclusively American fruit, the center includes a theater, exhibit hall, gift shop, and demonstration kitchen. Visitors are shown the cranberry's life cycle from planting through harvesting and quality-control testing. Picture windows overlook the fully automated activity on the floor of the processing plant. You'll get to taste juice, cranberry pastries, and Craisins (sweetened, dried cranberries)—just three of the surprising array of products into which the berry is made. Free recipes and cups, pens, and key chains with the company's logo are given as souvenirs. ◆ Free. Daily. 1301 American Pacific Dr (between N Gibson Rd and Stephanie St), Henderson. 566.7160

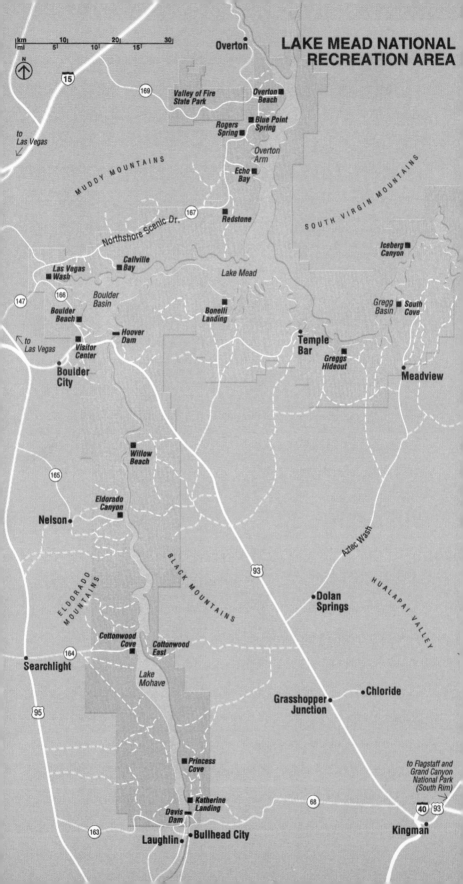

**10 Lake Las Vegas Resort** Scheduled to open in 2001, this $4-billion residential/resort community will feature a 320-acre man-made lake, a custom Mediterranean-inspired village, the 200-room **Grand Bay Hotel,** the 496-room **Hyatt Regency Resort,** golf, tennis, hiking, fishing, swimming, boating, horseback riding, and more. ♦ Lake Las Vegas Pkwy (north of E Lake Mead Dr), Henderson. 564.1600, 800/564.1603

**11 Railroad Pass Hotel & Casino** $ If there is such a thing as a generic hotel-casino, this is it. Not nearly as appealing as the nearby **Sunset Station Hotel/Casino,** this property's bland, institutional white exterior is your first clue that it's by no means a must-see. It's just convenient as one of many truck stop–casinos common to rural Nevada and benefits from a well-trafficked location near the Highway 95 turnoff to Laughlin. The serviceable complex on the outskirts of Henderson boasts no themes or gimmicks beyond 120 low-priced rooms and several restaurants. There's a steak house, a buffet, and a 24-hour coffee shop. ♦ 2800 S Boulder Hwy (southeast of Wagon Wheel Dr), Henderson. 294.5000, 800/654.0877

**12 Laughlin** Don Laughlin had a vision. A Minnesotan who operated slot machines in gas stations and Elks clubs until it became a felony in his home state, Laughlin decided to head west in 1952. He ended up on the Colorado River border between Nevada and Arizona, 95 miles south of Las Vegas, where he opened a roadside rest stop. Laughlin watched the town that bears his name grow into a gaming mecca that drew almost 4.5-million visitors in 1998. Many compare it to Las Vegas in its 1950s boom days; nearly half of the city's 10,000-plus rooms have been built since 1988.

Today, Laughlin isn't so much an added attraction for Las Vegas visitors as it is an alternative destination. Nearly 20 percent of its tourists come from Phoenix, 215 miles away; another 33 percent come from the Los Angeles area. Laughlin also has become a winter refuge for snowbirds fleeing cold climates in recreational vehicles, since there are plenty of RV parks. In recent years the town has become a bargain-shoppers mecca with the opening of the 250,000-square-foot **Horizon Outlet Center** on Casino Drive. Another attraction for lovers of country/western activities is the annual **Laughlin Rodeo Days**—competition takes place on the banks of the Colorado River (see "The Main Events," page **10**).

Despite its expanding skyline, Laughlin still draws people who are attracted to its small-town feel, its low prices, and lack of high-roller pretension. You won't find jackets or ties, themes or gimmicks, and there's not much in the way of big-name entertainment. But what distinguishes Laughlin from Vegas is its scenic river setting. Many of the casinos have picture-window views, something unheard of in Las Vegas. **Harrah's Laughlin** has a recreational beach, and the **Flamingo Hilton** uses the river as a backdrop for outdoor concerts in early and late summer. For those who don't bring their own craft to cruise the river or Lake Mohave, some casinos offer riverboat rides. As you enter Laughlin from Route 163, you'll first see Don's place: the **Riverside Resort,** the start of the casino strip. The Riverside has the town's only movie theater and celebrity showroom. The rest of the strip includes the 2,000-room **Flamingo Hilton,** Laughlin's largest hotel; the **River Palms Regency** (formerly the **Gold River**); Circus Circus Enterprises's **Edgewater** and **Colorado Belle; Ramada Express; Golden Nugget;** and **Harrah's.** ♦ www.lasvegas24hours.com

**13 Boulder City** This lakeside community of 13,000 sprang to life in 1931 as an instant city to house the men who built Hoover Dam. Nowadays, it has the distinction of being the only city in southern Nevada where gaming is *not* legal. Instead, the city lures tourists with antiques and gift shops and a major art festival held outdoors every September.

Within Boulder City:

**Boulder Dam Hotel** $$ The focal point of the town square is this hotel, built in 1933 to accommodate dignitaries—including US presidents Hoover and Roosevelt—visiting Hoover Dam. The hotel has expanded twice since it opened and now has 61 rooms, a pool, and a gift shop. Guests will also enjoy the restaurant and the bar located on the lower level. ♦ 1305 Arizona St (between Utah St and Nevada Hwy). 293.3510

---

Restaurants/Clubs: Red    Hotels: Blue

Shops/♥ Outdoors: Green    **Sights/Culture:** Black

**14 Lake Mead** Although Hoover Dam was built for a no-nonsense purpose—to control drought and flooding in California's farmlands—it also created one of southern Nevada's most cherished playgrounds when it backed up the Colorado River into this massive lake, with its 550 miles of shoreline. Most of that is accessible year-round, albeit only by boat. Dozens of coves enable houseboats to dock overnight in virtual seclusion.

Landlubbers aren't completely out of luck, however, since the lake has nine developed areas. Amenities vary, but the majority offer picnic sites, marinas, camping, RV parking, and swimming. Most commercial activity—boat and scuba rentals and lake excursions—is centered around Boulder City and the **Visitors' Center,** four miles northeast of Boulder City on Highway 93 (open daily 8:30AM-4:30PM; 293.8990). Attendants at the center can direct you to the remote regions of the lake, which extend as far north as the **Valley of Fire** and as far east as the edge of **Grand Canyon National Park.** ♦ For information, contact Lake Mead National Recreation Area, 601 Nevada Hwy, Boulder City, NV 89005. 293.8907; www.Laughlin.net/gambill

At Lake Mead:

**Hoover Dam** While the casinos try to keep your attention with white tigers, artificial volcanoes, and Roman centurions, a water and power plant 30 miles from Las Vegas is still Nevada's No. 1 tourist attraction. This 726-foot concrete monolith remains a civil engineering marvel undiminished by the high-tech revolution.

Guided tours of the dam draw about 750,000 people per year, and since 1936, more than 30 million have seen its sights. Each day, thousands of visitors line up along the Highway 93 bridge to plunk down two dollars for a 45-minute tour that offers a spectacular view or two and a painless briefing on the principles of engineering. A 44-story elevator inside the dam takes you and two dozen of your closest friends to the base, where you see some of the administration area (which looks as though it's straight out of a 1930s movie) and a few of the massive electrical generators. Then you step outside for a neck-craning, awe-inspiring, one-of-a-kind perspective from below.

The trip back to the top includes a stop at the tunnel that diverted the river while the dam was under construction. Of course, the escort is making your head spin with statistics the entire time: the dam contains 6,600,000 tons of concrete, enough to pave a two-lane road from New York to San Francisco. And no tour passes without the guide fielding two morbid questions: How many people were killed during construction? (96). And how many of those bodies are entombed inside the concrete? (None, they insist.)

The dam was dedicated in 1935 after four-and-a-half years of construction by a labor force that peaked at 5,250 workers. Its chief purpose was to control the flood-prone **Colorado River,** thus ending cycles of drought and flooding in Southern California farmland. Electricity was considered a mere by-product of the project, but it proved lucrative in its own right; power sales recouped the original $175 million expenditure with interest. A walkway under the highway bridge leads to the **Visitors' Center,** and a 530-foot elevator shaft through the Nevada wall of Black Canyon (to the side of the dam) has been completed. Two 50-passenger elevators have replaced the lifts in the dam, doubling their capacity.

Two-thirds of the dam's visitors come on bus tours from Las Vegas hotels. The excursions are heavily advertised on the Strip and average in price from $16 to $30, depending on whether they include other stops such as the **Ethel M. Chocolate Factory.** If you have six people in your party willing to share the bill (or one magnanimous benefactor), consider renting a limousine; not only do the rates compare favorably to the buses, but you won't have to conform to their schedules; the chauffeur is at your disposal. ♦ Admission. Daily. For information, contact Hoover Dam Visitors Services (PO Box 60400, Boulder City, NV 89006-0400). Hwy 93 (east of Rte 166). 293.8367

**15 Valley of Fire State Park** Centuries of erosion carved this sculptural valley of stunning red sandstone named for the glowing crimson hues at sunset (not the temperature). Nevada's oldest state park, established in 1935, encompasses 56,000 acres of unusual rock formations both enormous and minuscule, from chunks of petrified wood to Swiss-cheese-like boulders tailor-made for climbing. Visitors approach via a nondescript desert road into an environment that gradually descends into an immense and slightly surreal garden of stones. The otherworldly effect is heightened by the drop in elevation, which varies by 1,500 feet from one end of the park to the other, sometimes obscuring the horizon.

About 300,000 visitors come to the park each year, most of them between March and May and October and November. The valley is open from sunrise to sunset; overnight campers are allowed to remain after dark only at designated campsites, which are available on a first-come, first-served basis.

Almost everyone strolls **Petroglyph Canyon Trail,** a quarter-mile sandy path that offers the most colorful geology in the park as well as its highest concentration of petroglyphs—symbols left on the rock by prehistoric Indians from the Lost City, a pueblo village now

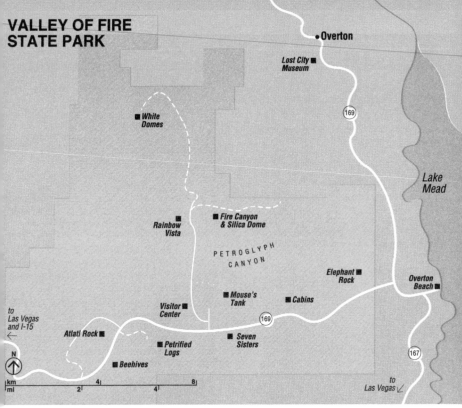

# VALLEY OF FIRE STATE PARK

Overton

Lost City Museum

169

White Domes

Lake Mead

Fire Canyon & Silica Dome

Rainbow Vista

PETROGLYPH CANYON

Elephant Rock

Overton Beach

Visitor Center

Mouse's Tank

Cabins

169

to Las Vegas and I-15

Atlati Rock

Seven Sisters

Petrified Logs

167

N

Beehives

km
mi

2

4

4

8

to Las Vegas

submerged in Lake Mead. The trail ends at **Mouse's Tank,** a watering hole in the truest sense: the secluded basin was frequented by a renegade Paiute Indian dubbed "Mouse," who eluded authorities at the turn of the century.

For those making a full day of it, there's no need to backtrack upon leaving the park. Keep going on Route 169 out the Lake Mead side of the park and cool off at the swimming beach at the **Overton Beach** marina four miles east, or head back to Interstate 15 via Overton, with a stop at the **Lost City Museum** (see below). ♦ Free. Daily sunrise-sunset. Visitors' Center daily 8:30AM-4:30PM. Rte 169 (southeast of I-15). 397.2088

**16 Lost City Museum** While Hoover Dam was being built, a team of archaeologists excavated a Pueblo ruin; after the dam created Lake Mead, the site was submerged. Artifacts salvaged from the **Pueblo Grande de Nevada** (popularly known as the "Lost City") are preserved in this modest museum in **Overton.** Exhibits are devoted to the dig itself as well as a reconstruction of the village and displays of

pottery and hunting tools. ♦ Admission. Daily. 721 S Moapa Valley Blvd (south of W Alma Ave), Overton. 397.2193

**17 Mesquite** Even in the middle of the desert the exact location of the Nevada state line is usually obvious, because the first casino or slot machine haven usually looms no more than a few yards away. This highway hamlet of 6,000 residents offers the first taste of Nevada gaming for those coming in from Utah or the last chance for Nevadans on the way north. The three major hotel-casino complexes in this otherwise sleepy burg are **Si Redd's Oasis,** the **Casablanca Hotel Casino Golf and Spa,** and the **Virgin River Hotel/Casino/Bingo** (see pages 117-118). Smaller properties include **Budget Inn & Suites** (800/463.6303), **Holiday Inn** (800/346.4611), **Best Western Mesquite Star Hotel Casino** (800/411.DRAW), and **Mesquite Springs Motel** (800/319.2935). Mesquite Boulevard is the main east-west road through town, and a ride from one end to the other takes you past old Mesquite, which is primarily made up of motels, bars, and antique service stations and the newer part of town consisting of shopping centers, banks, and billboards advertising the many condo developments in the area. There are also three good golf courses: the **Casablanca, Oasis,** and **Palms** (see 118).

# Reels of Fortune: Vegas Goes to Hollywood

The gaudy rhinestone Las Vegas skyline has long provided a visually irresistible backdrop for movies, advertisements, rock videos, and TV series.

The following list contains the most significant movies filmed in Las Vegas, plus a few that were supposedly set here but were actually shot elsewhere.

**The Amazing Colossal Man** (1957) This laughably camp thriller offers amazing footage of the **Strip** when the title character—an Army officer turned into a giant by a nuclear explosion—decides to go for a stroll. The final showdown takes place at **Hoover Dam.** See it back-to-back with *Honey, I Blew Up the Kid.*

**Black Moon Rising** (1996) In this suspense thriller, the feds hire Tommy Lee Jones to infiltrate and get the goods on a corrupt Las Vegas corporation. The intrigue is compounded when Linda Hamilton—a member of an auto theft ring—robs the car in which Jones hid the damaging evidence.

**Bugsy** (1991) The riveting story of charismatic gangster Benjamin "Bugsy" Siegel (Warren Beatty) and his vision of Las Vegas could not be filmed here—except for a closing shot of the **Flamingo Hotel**—simply because nothing in Las Vegas looks as it did in 1946.

**Casino** (1995) The glitter and glamour of the 1970s is brought to the screen in this Martin Scorsese film starring Robert DeNiro (Ace Rothstein) and Joe Pesci (Nicky Santoro) as two mobsters who move to Vegas to strike it rich. The **Riviera Hotel and Casino** were used for location shots.

**City Slickers II** (1994) The sequel starring Billy Crystal and Jack Palance continues the story of male bonding out West. Although Palance expired in the original, the Oscar winner comes back as his own brother.

**Con Air** (1997) Nicholas Cage, John Cusack, and John Malkovich star as imprisoned convicts who get their revenge and wreak havoc once they're airborne in a federal marshall's flight over Las Vegas.

**Cool World** (1992) A Las Vegas comic book artist (Gabriel Byrne) and his fantasy-girl-come-to-life (Kim Basinger) share adventures in this combination live-action and animation film created by Ralph Bakshi *(Fritz the Cat).*

**Diamonds Are Forever** (1971) For James Bond fans, there's skullduggery in **Circus Circus,** a car chase on **Fremont Street,** and agent 007's (Sean Connery) ascent to the villain's head-quarters on top of "The Whyte House."

**The Electric Horseman** (1979) The romantic pairing of Robert Redford and Jane Fonda when both were at the height of their appeal was a hit. Redford's the fallen rodeo champ who saves a racehorse from corporate evildoers by riding it through **Caesars Palace.**

**The Gauntlet** (1977) Clint Eastwood plays a dim-witted cop sent to Las Vegas to bring back a hooker (Sondra Locke) to testify against corrupt police officers.

**Heat** (1987) Burt Reynolds is a Las Vegas bodyguard with a compulsive gambling problem.

**Honey, I Blew Up the Kid** (1992) Disney's comic sequel to *Honey, I Shrunk the Kids* revisits the climax to *The Amazing Colossal Man,* setting a giant baby loose on Fremont Street.

**Honeymoon in Vegas** (1992) A charming sleaze ball (James Caan) tries to woo away the fiancée (Sarah Jessica Parker) of a commitment-shy detective (Nicolas Cage). The memorable climax features a team of Elvis impersonators parachuting into the **Bally's** parking lot.

**Indecent Proposal** (1993) Robert Redford is the smooth-talking gambler who comes between a young couple (Demi Moore and Woody Harrelson) by offering the wife $1 million to spend the night with him. Locations include the **Las Vegas Hilton.**

**Kill Me Again** (1988) A private eye (Val Kilmer) follows a mysterious woman (Joanne Whalley) from Reno to Las Vegas, **Lake Mead,** and the **Valley of Fire,** all of which are shown to good effect amid the violent plot twists.

**Las Vegas Story** (1952) Gambler Vincent Price takes his wife (Jane Russell) to Las Vegas, where she runs into her former-lover-turned-detective (Victor Mature). Howard Hughes produced this melodrama more than a decade before he moved to Vegas.

**Leaving Las Vegas** (1995) In his Oscar-winning role, Nicolas Cage plays a down-and-out writer who travels to Las Vegas where he plans to drink himself to death. Along the way, he meets and falls in love with a prostitute (Elisabeth Shue). The city is a backdrop for this touching drama.

**Lost in America** (1985) The **Desert Inn** is the unfortunate stop for a yuppie couple who decide to drop out of the rat race and travel across America by motor home. This cult classic directed by Albert Brooks includes a hilarious argument at Hoover Dam.

**Meet Me in Las Vegas** (1956) Cyd Charisse is a French ballerina lured to the glamour of the showrooms of Las Vegas. She is romanced by Dan Dailey in this MGM musical. Showroom stars Lena Horne and Frankie Laine make guest appearances.

*Melvin and Howard* (1980) Perennial loser Melvin Dummar (Paul Le Mat) gives a scruffy, nameless hitchhiker (Jason Robards) a ride to Las Vegas. He later produces a will supposedly written by Howard Hughes, a.k.a. the hitcher, that leaves him $156 million.

*Ocean's Eleven* (1960) Frank Sinatra, Sammy Davis Jr., Dean Martin, and Peter Lawford lead a group of war buddies planning to rob five casinos at once on New Year's Eve.

*Oh God! You Devil* (1984) In this pleasant but forgettable comedy, a musician sells his soul to the devil for success. Portraying both God and the Devil, George Burns works his old **Caesars Palace** haunts (Burns himself was a Vegas showroom performer for five decades).

*One From the Heart* (1982) The film that sent Francis Ford Coppola into bankruptcy eschews the real **Glitter Gulch** for a stylized soundstage mock-up that's the way people wish **Downtown** could be.

*Rain Man* (1988) A hostile young man (Tom Cruise) gets to know his long-separated autistic brother (Dustin Hoffman) on a cross-country road trip in this Oscar-winning drama. **Caesars Palace** looks dazzling as the site of their triumph at the card table.

Scenes of rural America were shot in nearby Nevada.

*Rocky IV* (1985) Props from the *Jubilee!* show at **Bally's** turn up in James Brown's "Living in America" musical number in this Sylvester Stallone boxing film. Stallone returned to Las Vegas for an arm-wrestling tournament in the equally silly *Over the Top* (1987).

*Sister Act II* (1994) Whoopi Goldberg, a nightclub performer, hides from the "bad guys" in a convent.

*Starman* (1984) A road-flick/science-fiction romance pairs a stranded alien (Jeff Bridges) with an earthling companion (Karen Allen). The couple taps some slots in Las Vegas during their quest to get him home.

*Star Trek: Generations* (1994) Shot in the colorful **Valley of Fire,** this time-travel story pairs retired Starship *Enterprise* Captain Kirk (William Shatner) with the future's Captain Picard (Patrick Stewart) to save a planet from destruction.

*Vegas Vacation* (1997) The Griswald family pack their bags for their annual vacation—this time into the neon lights and casinos of Las Vegas. The comedy stars Chevy Chase and Beverly D'Angelo along with a cast of characters including Wayne Newton and Christie Brinkley.

*Viva Las Vegas* (1964) One of the best Elvis movies, thanks to costar Ann-Margret and a title tune that gave the city an anthem.

---

At Mesquite:

**Si Redd's Oasis** $$$ This popular weekend getaway for Las Vegans also serves as a launching point for excursions to southern Utah destinations such as **Zion** and **Bryce Canyon National Parks.** The resort (with 728 rooms and 10 suites) prides itself on its three golf courses, six swimming pools, health club, four restaurants, and a RV park. The grounds are lush and immaculately groomed, living up to the resort's image of a desert oasis. The interior decor is vintage casino: border neon, black ceiling, and millions of dollars worth of silk trees, ferns, and flowers. ♦ 897 W Mesquite Blvd (just east of I-15). 346.5232, 800/621.0187; www.oasisresort.com, www.siredd.com

At Si Redd's Oasis:

**Garden Room Coffee Shop** $ A glade of leafy artificial trees and strategically placed mirrors give this crowded casino coffee shop the surprising feel of a relaxing hideaway. The prime rib and steak plates are the featured attractions. Don't be misled by the lack of a line outside. During busy times, patrons put their names on a waiting list and go off to gamble until they're paged. ♦ American ♦ Daily 24 hours. 346.5232, 800/621.0187

**The Redd Room Steak House** ★★$$$ The bustling atmosphere slows down inside this dinner-only restaurant, complete with uniformed waiters proffering a respectable wine list. The wait is usually short since the bargain-minded favor the specials at the coffee shop. In addition to variations on its

namesake, the menu includes lemon chicken (at the low end of the price range) and veal Oscar (sautéed veal medaillons topped with crabmeat, asparagus, and béarnaise sauce) and saltimbocca (at the high end). ◆ Steak house ◆ M-Sa dinner; Su brunch and dinner. 346.5232, 800/621.0187

**The Paradise Buffet & Grill** ★★$$ The masking fake foliage of the coffee shop is also found in this buffet, giving the room a less institutional feel than many of its counterparts and much better food. ◆ Buffet ◆ Daily breakfast, lunch, and dinner. 346.5232, 800/621.0187

**Oasis Golf Club** Arnold Palmer designed this 18-hole, par 72 golf course. Voted one of the best 10 courses in the country by *Golf* magazine, it is laid out to provide duffers with exceptional views of the lovely lakes from every hole. ◆ 851 Oasis Blvd (north of Pioneer Blvd). 800/621.0187; www.siredd.com

## THE PALMS GOLF CLUB

**The Palms Golf Club** This world-class, 18-hole championship golf course, which takes its name from the 200-some palm trees that grace its fairways, suits golfers of all levels. The extended fairways on the front nine holes provide contrast to the hilly fairways and breathtaking views on the back nine. ◆ 711 Palms Blvd (off Hillside Dr); 800/621.0187. www.siredd.com

**Casablanca Hotel Casino Golf and Spa** $$$ Each of the 500 spacious rooms and 18 suites here boasts beautiful views of the Virgin River Valley, mountains, or the resort's swimming pool. Accommodations are nicely decorated and feature king- or queen-size beds, coffeemakers, hair dryers, and TVs. Guests have unlimited use of the mineral spa, steam room, and exercise facilities. Also available are massage and aromatherapies, mud baths (using nearby Virgin River mud), and facials. The outdoor pool has a rock centerpiece with a 30-foot waterfall and water slide. The casino sports keno, blackjack, roulette, and other favorites. And for those who would rather feast there are two restaurants, a coffee shop, and buffet. There also are 200 motor lodge rooms with kitchenettes on the property. Duffers will enjoy the 18-hole, Cal Olsen–designed, par 72 golf course with its challenging back holes. ◆ 930 W Mesquite Blvd (at I-15). 346.7529, 800/896.4567; fax 346.7103; www.casablancaresort.com

**Virgin River Hotel/Casino/Bingo** $ While **Si Redd's** tries to sport an uptown Las Vegas look, this 400-room, bland, vanilla-colored complex stays true to the more modest country trappings of rural Nevada. The owners let their better-known neighbor do all the advertising, then they catch the overflow customers, as well as those seeking lower room rates. There's no golf course or health spa here. The guest rooms, in several adjacent buildings surrounding a large pool, are modern, clean, and well maintained. They're nicer than what you might expect after visiting the compact casino, which packs in as many tables and slot machines as the laws of physics allow. On the other hand, the bingo hall and race and sports book are quite expansive. The round-the-clock restaurant is comfortable, decorated with wooden beams and modern Western art. Diners can choose from a regular menu or the buffet. ◆ 915 N Mesquite Blvd (at I-15). 800/346.7721

**18 Death Valley Junction** A unique way station, this "town" has seven full-time residents. It's known mainly as the home of the historic **Armargosa Opera House,** where New York–born ballerina Marta Becket stages one-woman dance and performance-art shows in the hundred-seat theater. Becket has lived and performed here for more than 25 years, and averages about 95 productions per year.

**19 Death Valley National Park** In the summer, visitors swarm over the **Grand Canyon,** but winter is the peak season here. With average winter temperatures between 52 and 59 degrees and summer days routinely topping 110 degrees, the mercury readings tell the tale.

Before approaching the valley, make sure your car is in trustworthy condition for covering a desert that, at 3,231 square miles, is larger than the state of Delaware. Trail signs and monuments tell the stories of prospectors and miners who came to best the wilderness and sometimes failed—fatally. The stark, silent vistas prove there is beauty in nature even at its cruelest extremes.

If you're visiting from Las Vegas, this monument to the American spirit and to the spirit of pioneers merits at least an overnight stay. It's a long drive from one end of the valley to the other (140 miles), and there's plenty to view along the way, including spectacular sunrises and sunsets.

At the **Furnace Creek Visitors' Center,** you can pick up brochures and maps explaining how to take self-guided auto tours. There are also slide shows and other activities.

Death Valley is actually a dry lake bed; crunching along this crystallized white salt flat at twilight is an otherworldly experience. There

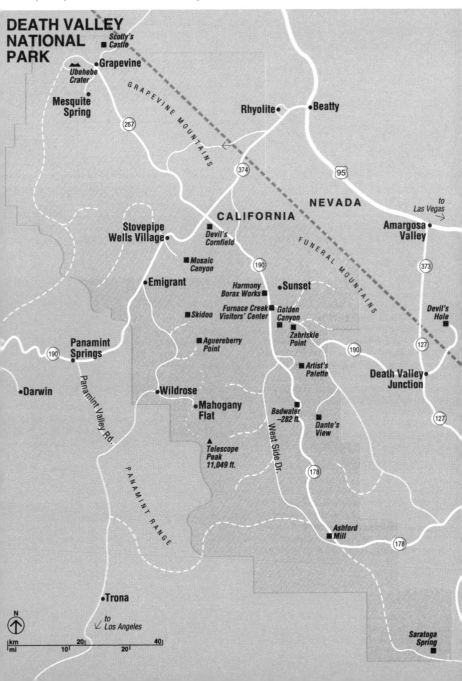

are trails for both casual walkers and hearty hikers. Most people like to visit **Badwater,** officially the lowest point in the US at 282 feet below sea level. The **Harmony Borax Works** is a quarter-mile trail leading to the ruins of a borax mine that dates back to 1883. (Death Valley supplies most of the world's borax, a crystalline compound with industrial uses in washing powders, water softeners, and soaps.) Those up for a more challenging trek can try the five-mile round-trip from **Golden Canyon** to **Zabriskie Point,** a panoramic overlook and photo spot that's especially popular with Europeans, who are more daring than Americans when it comes to summertime exploration of the valley. Park rangers report many Germans and French visit in mid-summer and don't mind soaking up the full heat of the sun since there is no comparable season on their cool continent. ♦ Nominal per-vehicle entry fee is valid for seven days. For information, contact Death Valley National Park (c/o Superintendent, Death Valley, CA 92328) Information 760/786.2331, camping 800/365.2267. Furnace Creek Visitors' Center: Rte 190

Within Death Valley National Park:

**Scotty's Castle** This 25-room Mediterranean-style mansion, formally known as the **Death Valley Ranch,** was built in the 1920s by Albert Johnson, a Chicago insurance investor, who lived there with his wife, Bessie. It takes its more common name from Walter Scott, a former Wild West show cowboy and storyteller who bragged that the house was his. The owners treasured their privacy, so the misnomer was fortuitous.

The castle is near a stream that supplies it with water and hydroelectric power. The interior reveals elaborate craftsmanship, such as ornate tile work, wrought-iron fixtures, and intricate wood carvings. The tours, conducted on the hour year-round, are a "living history" experience given by rangers dressed in period garb. Tour groups are limited to 19 at a time, so there is usually a one- to two-hour wait after purchasing tickets; this gives you time for a self-guided tour of the grounds and castle exterior. ♦ Admission. Daily. North Hwy. 760/786.2392

Las Vegas celebrity weddings in the 1950s and 1960s included Joan Crawford and Alfred Steel at the Flamingo in 1955; Paul Newman and Joanne Woodward at the El Rancho in 1958; Jane Fonda and Roger Vadim at the Dunes in 1965; Xavier Cugat and Charo at Caesars Palace in 1966; Elvis Presley and Priscilla Beaulieu at the Aladdin in 1967; and Ann-Margret and Roger Smith at the Riviera in 1967.

## FURNACE CREEK
### INN & RANCH RESORT

**Furnace Creek Ranch** $$$ An unlikely sister to the oh-so-elegant **Furnace Creek Inn** (see below), this recently refurbished rustic lodging includes 224 motel-type rooms. Guests are afforded an 18-hole golf course, horseback riding stables, and tennis courts. The two spring-fed swimming pools (the water is 84 degrees year-round) are gathering spots by day—you'll hear a number of languages spoken around the decks. In the evening there's good company in the **19th Hole Bar & Grill,** which will toast a mini-pizza for you if you fail to get back before closing time at any of the compound's five restaurants. Or if you feel like grilling your own steak or nibbling on snack food in your room, visit the **General**

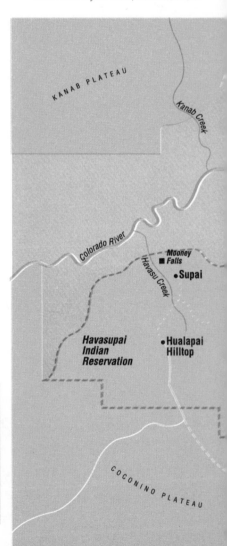

**Store,** which carries everything from fresh food to camping gear (open daily 7AM-9PM). ◆ 760/786.2345

**Furnace Creek Inn** $$$$ Of the many surprising sights in Death Valley, the most incongruous may well be this exclusive 68-room resort where jackets are required for dinner. With a long-standing reputation for luxury that defies its stark surroundings, the recently refurbished inn gets heavily booked in the winter. Rooms feature rich wood furnishings with sand-colored walls and soft-muted tapestry fabrics. The lobby boasts cozy sitting areas with fabulous views of the Panamint Mountains. There's also a lounge with a glass etching that depicts the 20-mule team traversing the Grand Canyon. Amenities include tennis, golf, a swimming pool, bicycle rentals, and a gourmet dining room. ◆ 760/786.2361 or 760/786.2345;

800/236.7916; www.FurnaceCreekResort.com

**Stovepipe Wells Village** $$ Though not centrally located in relation to the better-known sites within Death Valley, this 85-room hotel duplicates most of the services within **Furnace Creek Ranch.** There's a dining room, a pool, a saloon, a general store, and a variety of accommodations. ◆ Rte 190. 760/786.2387

**20 The Grand Canyon** Artists have long sought to capture the majesty of nature's crown jewel of the Southwest—one of the most famous landmarks in the US. A few skilled photographers have caught the vast perspective, but most cameras flatten it, reducing its immensity to something our senses can easily comprehend. It's one of the last awe-inspiring spectacles in this seen-everything world, whether you're a nature lover who wants to absorb its splendor or a

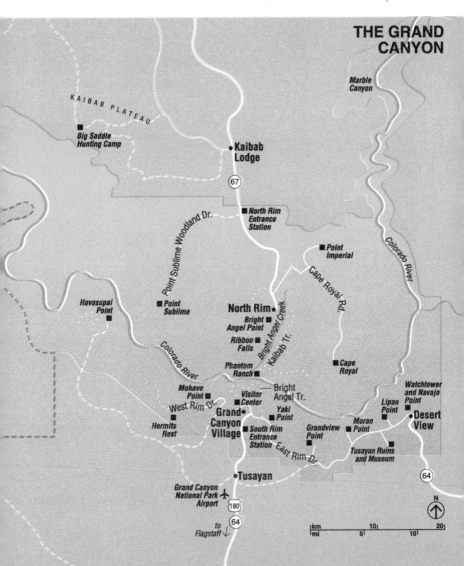

THE GRAND CANYON

city slicker looking to escape the urban melee. No matter how many photos of the canyon you've seen, it's only when you stand here in person that you finally face the humbling notion that there are still some things greater than humankind and its technological achievements.

The canyon is 277 miles long, 10 miles wide, and in some places a mile deep from the rim to the Colorado River. **Grand Canyon National Park** covers 1.2 million acres, which explains why it only *looks* close to Las Vegas on a map; it's about a five-hour drive to either the North or South Rims.

Unfortunately, the canyon has become almost too popular for its own good. Park officials say the growth of Las Vegas and Phoenix has taxed the limits of their ability to accommodate tidal waves of visitors. From a practical standpoint, this means planning well ahead—particularly if you want to camp or stay overnight in the lodges within the park. And the famous rafting trips and muleback rides now accept reservations as much as *two years* in advance. ♦ Per-vehicle entry fee. Visitors center about six miles inside the South Rim entrance (520/638.7888). For advance information, contact Grand Canyon National Park (PO Box 129, Grand Canyon, AZ 86023; www.grandcanyon.com). To incorporate as much casino action as possible, take a slightly longer route to the park through Laughlin, via Hwy 95

Within the Grand Canyon:

**South Rim** Most canyon visitors head to the South Rim, which is open year-round and offers greater lodging opportunities than the North Rim. How much of the canyon you ultimately see depends on how hard you want to work. Those willing to settle for a cursory visit can stick to the rim of the canyon. Those who want to spend their time in the car rather than on the trail can take the 26-mile **East Rim Drive** (Rte 64, open year-round), from the park's east entrance to the cluster of lodges known as **Grand Canyon Village.** A more popular route is the eight-mile **West Rim Drive,** from the village to the landmark known as **Hermits Rest,** but park officials close that road from late May through September to moderate the effects of exhaust fumes. Still you needn't miss out on the sights—during that period there's a free shuttle bus.

If you have a bit more stamina, start walking down one of the trails into the inner canyon. The **Bright Angel Trail,** near the lodge of the same name, is the most popular, a steep but gradual 4.5-mile trek to the bottom. Unlike many hikes, the walk down, though murder on the knees, is a lot easier than the trudge back up. A more strenuous path is the **South Kaibab Trail,** which covers 1.5 miles each

way. No permits are required for day hiking, just common sense.

The round trip from rim to river is usually an overnight affair, so if you decide to journey to the bottom, you should arrange to stay at one of two sites below the rim: **Indian Gardens,** on Bright Angel Trail (520/638.2401), or **Phantom Ranch,** a campground along the Colorado shared by hikers, mule riders, and white-water rafters (520/638.2401). Reservations are required for both. All other campers who wish to stay either in the canyon or in undeveloped areas on the rim need a permit from the **Backcountry Reservations Office** (PO Box 129, Grand Canyon, AZ 86023). Reservations are accepted by mail only, and sometimes must be made a year in advance.

There also are established campgrounds at the top of the rim: the **Mather Campground** (for tents and recreational vehicles without hookups) in **Grand Canyon Village,** the adjacent **Trailer Village** (hookups available), and the **Desert View Campground** (no hookups) 25 miles east of **Grand Canyon Village.** Reservations are strongly encouraged (contact **MISTIX,** PO Box 85705, San Diego, CA 92186-7505, 800/365.2267).

Advance reservations are mandatory for those staying at lodges inside the park. One service now books all the accommodations inside the South Rim: **Grand Canyon National Park Lodges** (PO Box 699, Grand Canyon, AZ 86023, 520/638.2401; fax 520/638.9247). There are no individual addresses or phone numbers for the lodges, and none of them has a pool. Procrastinators may have better luck checking out one of five lodges in **Tusayan,** six miles south of the South Rim, before resigning themselves to staying in Williams or Flagstaff. Tusayan accommodations include **Grand Canyon Squire Inn** (520/638.2681, 800/622.6966); **Moqui Lodge** (520/638.2424); **Quality Inn** (520/638.2673, 800/221.2222); **Red Feather Lodge** (520/638.2414, 800/538.2345); and **Seven Mile Lodge** (520/638.2291).

---

Keno, developed in China, has survived in one form or another for more than 3,000 years; it remains one of the worst bets in any casino.

---

The least crowded, and therefore least expensive, time to visit Las Vegas is between Thanksgiving and Christmas. The most hectic periods are on Super Bowl weekend and during the three largest conventions: Consumer Electronics Show (second week of January), Construction Manufacturers Association (third week of March), and COMDEX—the Computer Distribution Expo—(third week of November).

# Planning the Grand Tour

Teddy Roosevelt described the **Grand Canyon** as "the one great sight which every American should see." Assuming you've taken his advice to heart, deciding which way you choose to see it is the next step. Below are some of the more imaginative ways to take in the awesome expanse that will afford a view unmatchable by foot or car.

For a bird's-eye perspective on the canyon, consider taking a flyover tour on a chartered plane or a combination air/bus tour, which runs about $175 per person. Charter services advertise heavily on the **Strip.** Companies include:

**Adventure Airlines** . . . . . . . . . . . . . . . . . . 631.7100

**Eagle Airlines** . . . . . . . . . . . . . . . . . . . . . . 736.3333

**Grand Canyon Sightseeing** . . . . . . . . . . . 471.7155

**Gray Line Tours** . . . . . . . . . . . . . . . . . . . . 384.1234

**Las Vegas Helicopters** . . . . . . . . . . . . . . . 736.0013

**Interstate Tours** . . . . . . . . . . . . . . . . . . . . 293.2268

**Lake Mead Air** . . . . . . . . . . . . . . . . . . . . . 293.1848

**Las Vegas Airlines** . . . . . . . . . . . . . . . . . . 647.3056

**Scenic Airlines Inc.** . . . . . . . . . . . . . . . . . 739.1900

**Sundance Helicopters** . . . . . . . . . . . . . . . 597.5505

**Tristar Airlines, Inc.** . . . . . . . . . . . . . . . . . 732.8400

While Americans may have had a harder time getting to the **Grand Canyon** in Roosevelt's day, the best way to appreciate its immensity even today is by exploring it on the back of a mule. To do so, you must plan almost a year ahead; reservations are accepted 11 months in advance, and quotas fill up quickly. These rides are coordinated through **Grand Canyon National Park Lodges** (602/638.2401).

Of all the ways to see the canyon, none is more thrilling than rafting the raging **Colorado.** Not only is the view of the canyon towering above you magnificent, but you also experience the excitement of shooting some of the most powerful rapids in the world.

Don't plan a rafting excursion on the spur of the moment, however, since the **National Park Service** carefully regulates the number of permits given to commercial operators for Colorado River trips through the canyon—and the waiting lists can get very long. Private tour operators include:

**Adventures West, Inc.**

Phoenix, Arizona . . . . . . . . . . . . . . . . 800/828.9378

**Arizona Raft Adventurers, Inc.**

Flagstaff, Arizona . . . . . . . . . . . . . . . . 800/786.7238

**Colorado River & Trail Expeditions, Inc.**

Salt Lake City, Utah . . . . . . . . . . . . . . 800/253.7328

**Western River Expeditions, Inc.**

Salt Lake City, Utah . . . . . . . . . . . . . . 800/453.7450

On the South Rim:

**El Tovar Hotel** $$$$ The grande dame of the **Grand Canyon** was built in 1905 and originally staffed by the famed Harvey Girls of story, song, and cinema, who were known for their starched white aprons and impeccable training. The handsome stone and Douglas fir building is famous for its 65 atmospheric period rooms, including five suites with balconies overlooking the canyon. On the National Registry of Historic Places, the most elegant of the village's lodgings offers fine dining in its restaurant. ♦ Grand Canyon Village

**Bright Angel Lodge** $$$ This building, designed to blend in with rather than distract from the canyon, features 50 cozy cabins, some historic, and some with fireplaces. More moderately priced than **El Tovar,** the restaurants are more basic here: there's a steak house and a dining room serving typical coffee shop fare. ♦ Grand Canyon Village

**Kachina and Thunderbird Lodges** $$$ These twin two-story lodges of 47 and 53 rooms respectively are newer than **El Tovar** and **Bright Angel** and offer good service and comfort. There are two double beds per room and a cafeteria in each lodge. ♦ Grand Canyon Village

**Yavapai Lodge** $$ This 348-room motel is not in Grand Canyon Village, but a bit to the west across from the Visitors' Center. Similar in service, comfort, and style to **Kachina and Thunderbird,** this lodge also has two double beds per room and a cafeteria.

---

In the wake of the Kefauver gambling hearings of the early 1950s, the federal tax on sports betting was increased to 10 percent, which quickly drove many southern Nevada sports books to the brink of bankruptcy. The tax eventually was reduced.

"One night at a dinner in Los Angeles, sometime in 1946, a friend of mine said to me, 'Why don't we run up to Vegas and look at this new town?' I said, 'For what?' He said, 'Let's just look around.' The next day we jumped aboard a DC-3 and landed at McCarran Field, hired a car, and proceeded to drive around. There was nothing. Not even a coyote. We stopped at a corner where there was a sign stuck in the ground that said 'For Sale.' My friend went to a phone, called the number on the sign, and found out what it was all about. It turned out to be a piece of property containing a thousand acres at one dollar an acre. So, the great wheeler and dealer that I was, I said to my friend, 'What the hell are we gonna do with it?' He replied, 'Let's hang on to it, it's cheap enough.' I said, 'Don't be ridiculous!' We never made the deal."

Frank Sinatra

---

 **North Rim** If you're coming from Las Vegas, you should not rule out the North Rim. Visitors from the Phoenix area face an extra 150 miles of driving to get here, but those departing from Las Vegas can choose a drive comparable to the one to the South Rim, which lasts approximately five hours. However, the North Rim is a thousand feet higher in altitude—8,000 feet above sea level versus 7,000 for the South Rim—and because of the colder temperatures is only open from mid-May through late October. A drawback: there's only one hotel, and camping facilities aren't as abundant as at the South Rim. There are also fewer choices outside the park's boundaries, making reservations essential. Visitors from Las Vegas drive about 270 miles by heading into southern Utah on Interstate 15. The cozy town of **Hurricane** (pronounced *Hur*-Kin), Utah, on Scenic Byway 9 is at the crossroads for those either planning to go on to **Zion National Park** or head south on Route 59 to the North Rim (another option is to see Zion first, then go south on Route 89). ♦ Fee. Daily mid-May–mid-Oct. For North Rim lodging reservations, contact **TW Recreational Services** (451 N Main St, Cedar City, UT 84720, 801/586.7686). For camping reservations, contact **MISTIX** (PO Box 85705, San Diego, CA 92186-5705, 800/365.2267)

**21 Zion National Park** Though a neighbor to **Bryce Canyon National Park,** with a common geological history, a simple rule of thumb separates these southern Utah parks: To see the splendors here you look up; at **Bryce** you look down. While the precipices of **Bryce** are more akin to those of the **Grand Canyon,** here you enter at the canyon floor, and most of the trails take you skyward. The 229-square-mile park offers rugged and contrasting beauty, from barren sandstone cliff walls and arches to the cottonwoods and ash trees lining the cooling Virgin River. In warm months, visitors can wade into the latter and will be strongly tempted to do so: The park is south of Utah's ski country, and summer temperatures can reach 105 degrees.

There are 11 trails here, ranging from easy half-hour walks to taxing 16-mile treks requiring backcountry permits. Most people start at the **Emerald Pools Trail** directly across from the **Zion Lodge;** it gives you a repre-sentative taste of the park, with a trail leading to waterfalls and impressive elevations (there's an optional mile to an upper pool for the hardy). Another favorite is **Gateway to the Narrows,** a pleasant walk along a narrow trail ending at the river, which invites those who don't mind wading to keep going (wear old tennis shoes—it's a rocky traverse).

For those who prefer the comfort of their car, it's fun to pass through the 1.1-mile tunnel to the east entrance when the park's not too

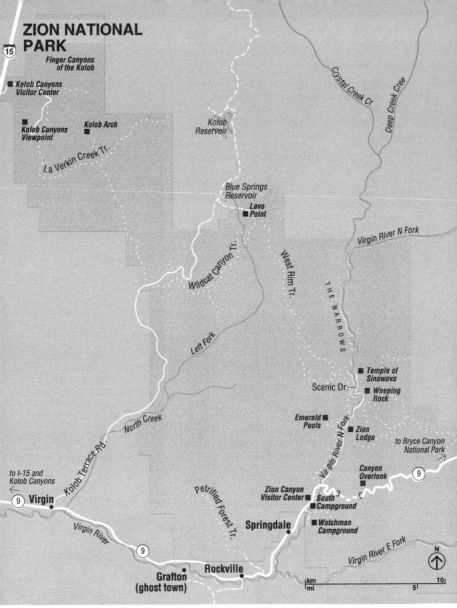

## ZION NATIONAL PARK

15

Finger Canyons
of the Kolob

Kolob Canyons
Visitor Center

Kolob Canyons
Viewpoint

Kolob Arch

La Verkin Creek Tr.

Kolob
Reservoir

Crystal Creek Cr

Deep Creek Cree

Blue Springs
Reservoir

Lava
Point

Virgin River N Fork

Wildcat Canyon Tr.

West Rim Tr.

THE NARROWS

Left Fork

Temple of
Sinawava

Scenic Dr.

Weeping
Rock

Emerald
Pools

Zion
Lodge

North Creek

Virgin River N Fork

to Bryce Canyon
National Park

9

Kolob Terrace Rd.

Canyon
Overlook

to I-15 and
Kolob Canyons

9  Virgin

Petrified Forest Tr.

Zion Canyon
Visitor Center

South
Campground

Virgin River

9

Watchman
Campground

Springdale

Virgin River E Fork

Grafton
(ghost town)

Rockville

N

km
ml

5

10

---

crowded (when it *is* crowded, you can get stuck behind an RV waiting for clear passage through the one-way tunnel). Here you'll find plenty of rocky cliffs, and visitors tend to stick to their autos rather than exploring the precipitous terrain by foot. Drivers will have to keep their attention on the sharp curves of the winding road; however, there are turnouts for those who want to stop and take in the view.

The park itself has only one lodge, which is open year-round. For lodging information, contact the **Utah Parks Division (TW Recreational Services,** 451 N Main St, Cedar City, UT 84720, 801/586.7686). More lodging is available outside the south entrance in **Springdale,** which is lined with motels and bed-and-breakfasts. A free magazine called *Color Country,* which gives information on

southern Utah's scenic routes, parks, recreation, and food and lodging choices, is available from **Color Country Travel Region** (PO Box 1550, St. George, UT 84770-1550, 800/233.8824). ♦ Per-car entry fee. Daily; extended hours in the summer. Visitors' Center about a mile inside south park entrance; open daily except Christmas Day; 435/772.3256

Here are some examples of Las Vegas–speak: A "george" is a player who tokes (tips) the dealer; a "stiff" doesn't tip. A "grind" is a one-dollar or two-dollar bettor. A "plunger" or "screamer" increases his bets when he loses. And a "turkey" is an unpleasant player.

# Laugh Tracks

Las Vegas is a funny town: if you don't believe it, take a look at the lineup of comedy clubs that dot the **Strip** featuring headliners who have made millions laugh for as long as Milton Berle has been stealing jokes!

### In the Beginning...

The city's comic heritage dates to the postwar expansion of the mid-1940s, when the **Strip** began to take shape with the construction of Ben "Bugsy" Siegel's posh **Flamingo.** It was Jimmy Durante who helped Siegel open his showroom, but even the Schnozz couldn't keep the infamous Bugsy's mob partners smiling while the club lost money. Fortunately for generations of funny men and women, other owners were much more successful. At about the same time Siegel was paying the ultimate price for "upsetting" his fellow investors, the Hartmans husband-and-wife dance and comedy team was yakking it up at the **Flamingo.**

At **El Rancho Vegas** gimmick groups such as hurling cyclists Gaynor and Ross and Professor Backwards (who told jokes and tossed out trivia while speaking in reverse) were headlining popular shows. For zany laughter with a musical theme, there was the Spike Jones–style mimicry of the Hoosier Hot Shots band.

A decade later, as the city was approaching its Golden Age and Sinatra and the "Rat Pack" had become international headliners, comedians such as Shecky Greene, Buddy Hackett, and Don Rickles were starting to gain a reputation for keeping lounge audiences in stitches. Rickles made the **Sahara**'s **Casbah Lounge** his personal "insult factory."

The 1960s saw the emergence of Bill Cosby and George Carlin as comic forces not only in the mainstream mediums such as television and recordings, but in Las Vegas showrooms as well. More than three decades later, they continue to remain among the city's few enduring showroom performers.

Continuing in the tradition of Johnny Carson, who headlined in Las Vegas when he wasn't making the nation laugh as the host of "The Tonight Show," comic Jay Leno makes the city an annual stop and when he is in town takes up residence at the **MGM Grand.**

After three generations, Las Vegas still attracts its share of off-beat comedians in the showrooms, including the watermelon-smashing Gallagher and the eccentric Carrot Top and Bobcat Goldthwaite.

### Where to Find the Wise Guys

The city's one-liner policy continues to evolve, and today there are plenty of places to laugh out loud. Here are some of our favorites:

**Harrah**'s *An Evening at the Improv* This place capitalizes on its reputation as a showcase for up-and-coming as well as established comics such as Milo Tremley, Bop Kubota, and Greg Travis.

**Maxim**'s *Comedy Max* Here three comedians share the stage: Look for such headliners as Joe Restivo, John McDowell, and Jeff Nease or Willie Tyler & Lester, Jon Borchers, Greg Schwem. The **Maxim** also offers *Comedy Magic,* which combines one-liners with sleight of hand each afternoon.

**MGM Grand**'s *Catch a Rising Star* A perennial proving ground for the country's best comics wannabes, this place changes three times a week. (It is the best buy of an affordable bunch; the other clubs charge a few dollars more, but offer two drinks in the price of each ticket.)

**Riviera**'s *Comedy Club* "Tonight Show" regular Kip Addotta and Mickey Manners headline in an intimate room. The program features late shows on Friday and Saturday and VIP seating for those who want to risk becoming the subject of improvisational material.

**Tropicana**'s *Comedy Stop* This place is a regular stop for comedians who have hit it big with their own shows on television, such as Kathleen Madigan, Ray Romano, and Jimmy "J.J." Walker.

---

**22**  **Bryce Canyon National Park** The growth of southern Nevada has threatened the ecological harmony of both the **Grand Canyon** and **Zion National Park,** but this park is a relative oasis (over 200 miles from Las Vegas). While **Zion** gets hot, this northern park stays cool—perhaps too much so for those coming to Las Vegas to escape the chills of winter—thanks to elevations that range from 6,600 to 9,100 feet. And though it is a canyon, and most certainly grand, with no cliff wall on the far side, it doesn't resemble the more famous Arizona crevasse. The park is perched at the top of a precipice overlooking a vast, magnificent valley of hoodoos (eroded limestone towers) that

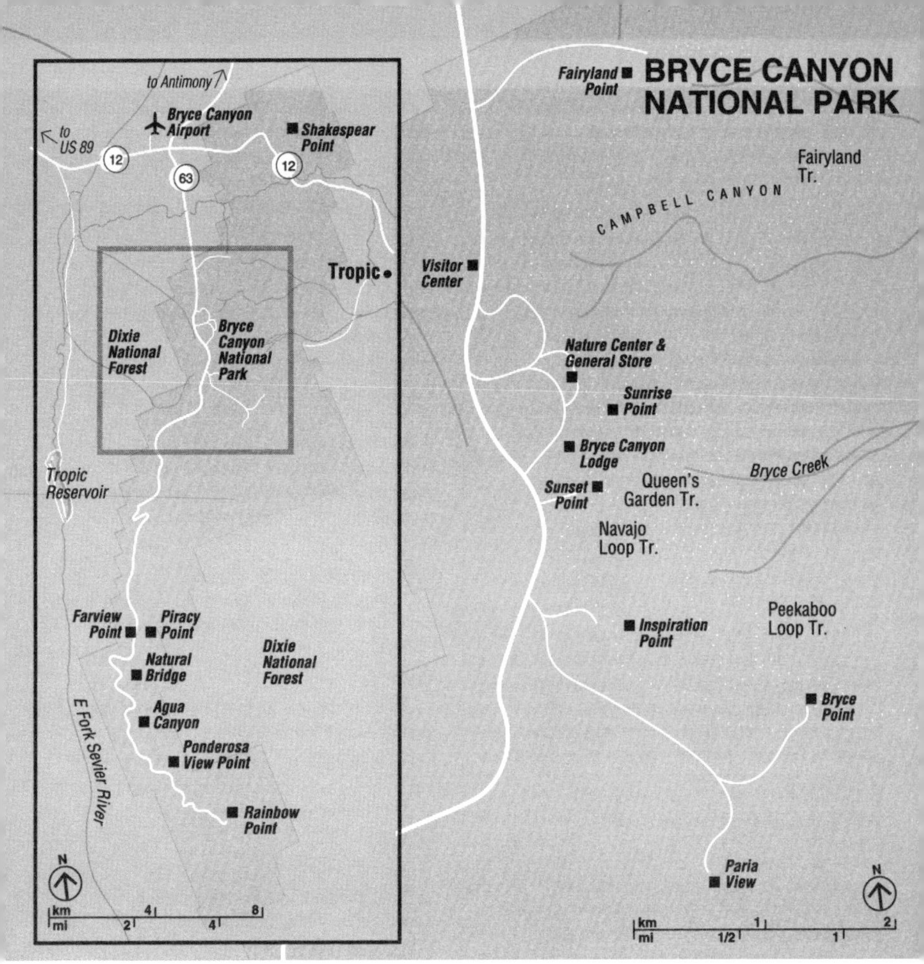
BRYCE CANYON NATIONAL PARK
to Antimony
Bryce Canyon Airport
to US 89
12
63
12
Shakespear Point
Tropic
Dixie National Forest
Bryce Canyon National Park
Tropic Reservoir
Farview Point
Piracy Point
Natural Bridge
Dixie National Forest
Agua Canyon
E Fork Sevier River
Ponderosa View Point
Rainbow Point
N
km 4 8
mi 2 4
Fairyland Point
Fairyland Tr.
CAMPBELL CANYON
Visitor Center
Nature Center & General Store
Sunrise Point
Bryce Canyon Lodge
Sunset Point
Queen's Garden Tr.
Bryce Creek
Navajo Loop Tr.
Inspiration Point
Peekaboo Loop Tr.
Bryce Point
Paria View
N
km 1 2
mi 1/2 1

gradually give way to the green hills and fields of southern Utah.

In fact, looking at the hoodoos here is the earthbound equivalent of finding shapes in puffy white clouds. While some view this natural amphitheater and see a collection of medieval fortresses, towers, or chess pieces on a vast playing board, others see Gothic cathedrals in multihued combinations of brown, red, orange, and gold.

Most exploration stems out from **Bryce Canyon Lodge,** which is between the **Sunrise Point** and **Sunset Point** lookouts. Visitors can walk along the rim between and beyond these points or take a more physically demanding hike to the bottom of the canyon. The **Queen's Garden Trail** takes you out and away from the rim to look back, while the steeper **Navajo Loop Trail** leads hikers down into what seems like the mouth of a cavern. The short drive from the lodge to **Inspiration** and **Bryce Points** is worthwhile—the increase in altitude renders the view even more dramatic. ♦ Admission. Visitors' center daily 8AM-8PM. 801/834.5322, mule rides 800/834.5219

Within Bryce Canyon National Park:

**Bryce Canyon Lodge** $$ The only lodging in the park is this charming and quiet (no TVs) retreat perched just one hundred yards from the canyon rim. The original establishment, listed on the National Register of Historic Places, includes a restaurant, gift shop, and 40 rustic cabins. A pair of newer two-story buildings adds a combined 70 units near **Sunrise** and **Sunset Points,** bearing their respective names. The excellent restaurant is open for breakfast, lunch, and dinner with a basic menu of hearty fare that tastes particularly good after a day on the trail. This lodge follows the solar clock: things get quiet soon after dark, and the dining room closes by 10PM, but dawn brings a crowd to the rim to watch the sunrise. Advance reservations are recommended for a room and are encouraged for dinner. ♦ Closed November to May. For reservations, contact TW Recreational Services, 451 N Main St, Cedar City, UT 84720. 801/586.7686

Approximately three percent of the 30 million visitors who come to Las Vegas each year arrive from outside the US, according to the State Gaming Control Board.

# History

Circa AD 500 The Anasazi (Navajo for "Ancient Ones") inhabit the area. They live in pit homes (shallow excavations with adobe floors and walls), make pottery, and are adept at weaving.

Circa AD 850 The Anasazi establish a settlement (now called **Pueblo Grande**), which by the year 1000 becomes Nevada's first ghost town. According to one of the most popular theories, the Anasazi were driven out of the area by a Southern Paiute tribe who called themselves Tudinu, or "Desert People."

1776 While blazing the Old Spanish Trail, Father Francisco Garces encounters the Tudinu.

1822 Previously under Spanish jurisdiction, the territory that will be Nevada becomes part of Mexico when that country gains its independence.

1826 Fur trader and frontiersman Jedediah Smith, en route from Salt Lake City to San Diego, becomes the first American to travel through southern Nevada. He misses **Las Vegas Valley** by about 40 miles.

1829 Rafael Rivera, a young scout with a Spanish trading party traveling west from Sante Fe, New Mexico, is the first white man to set foot in what will later become Las Vegas.

1840 The Old Spanish Trail, later called the Mormon Trail, becomes the primary path between Sante Fe and Southern California, Mexico's two main trade centers. The trail passes through Las Vegas, then called **Big Springs,** a popular watering stop.

1844 Pathfinder John C. Frémont, leading the party exploring the route to Oregon beyond the Mississippi River, passes through Big Springs and is the area's first famous visitor.

1848 Nevada becomes US territory after Mexico cedes what are now the western United States, following the Mexican-American War.

1855 Mormon missionaries, led by William Bringhurst, establish the first white settlement in Las Vegas. About 30 Mormons build a fort and begin teaching agriculture and religion to local Indians.

1858 Disputes between Mormon miners and farmers in the Las Vegas Mission prompt Mormon leader Brigham Young to dismantle the tiny settlement, leaving it to the Indians once again.

1861 Two days before leaving office, President James Buchanan signs the law that officially forms the Territory of Nevada.

1864 Near the end of the Civil War, President Abraham Lincoln declares Nevada the 36th state in the Union. "Battle Born" later becomes the state motto.

1865 Gold miner Octavius Decatur Gass rebuilds the former Mormon settlement and renames it **Las Vegas Ranch,** an oasis for weary desert travelers.

1880 Gass's creditor Archibald Stewart forecloses on **Las Vegas Ranch.** Four years later, Stewart is shot and killed, putting his wife, Helen, in charge of the 640-acre spread and some 400 head of cattle.

1902 Helen Stewart sells portions of her ranch to Montana senator William Clark, owner of the **San Pedro, Los Angeles, and Salt Lake Railroad,** for $55,000.

1904 A squatters' settlement springs up less than a mile west of **Las Vegas Ranch.**

1905 The final spike in the rail route connecting Salt Lake City to Los Angeles is hammered into the ground near **Jean,** Nevada, about 23 miles south of Las Vegas. The railroad auctions off land near the tracks on 15 May, and the town of Las Vegas is officially born; the *Las Vegas Age,* a weekly newspaper, is founded by editor Charles "Pop" Squires. The new town also gets its first real hotel, a 30-room canvas-topped structure called the **Hotel Las Vegas.**

1906 **Block 16**—the parcel of land bounded by **Second Street** (now called **Casino Center Boulevard**), **First Street,** and **Ogden** and **Stewart Avenues**—is the only section of town where liquor can be sold legally. This area becomes the town's red-light district, and travelers flock to its saloons, brothels, and gambling halls.

1907 A single-cylinder engine powers the first electric lights on **Fremont Street.** Meanwhile, the Las Vegas Land and Water Company drills the town's first well and discovers that the valley rests on a ready supply of underground water.

1910 A state law prohibiting all forms of gambling takes effect on 1 October.

1911 With a population of 1,500, Las Vegas is incorporated as the first city in Nevada. Locals elect four city commissioners and a mayor, Peter Buol. President William Howard Taft waves from his railcar as he passes through town.

1912 **Las Vegas Ranch** owner Helen Stewart, known as the "First Lady of Las Vegas," deeds 10 acres of her property to the local Paiute; Edward W. Griffith opens the **Majestic Theater,** featuring motion pictures and vaudeville acts.

1915 Las Vegans enjoy 24-hour electrical service for the first time; Hollywood discovers Las Vegas when the Kalem Motion Picture Company films four episodes of *The Hazards of Helen* series in various locations around town.

1919 The Prohibition Enforcement Act (the 18th amendment to the Constitution, banning the production, distribution, and possession of alcohol) becomes law but is ignored around Las Vegas.

1920 The first airplane lands in Las Vegas.

1925 Fremont Street is paved from **Main Street** to **Fifth Street** (what is now **Las Vegas Boulevard**).

1926 **Western Airlines** provides the first commercial flight service to Las Vegas.

1928 Congress passes the Boulder Canyon Project Act and appropriates $165 million to build the world's largest arch-gravity dam in **Black Canyon,** about 30 miles southeast of Las Vegas along the **Colorado River.**

1929 The *Las Vegas Review,* which started as the *Clark County Review* in 1909, becomes the town's first daily newspaper (in 1949 it takes the name *Las Vegas Review-Journal*); signmaker Thomas Young, of Ogden, Utah, installs a neon sign in the window of the **Oasis Club** Downtown, setting a Las Vegas trend.

**1931** The Six Companies, Inc., of San Francisco begins construction on **Hoover Dam** in April; the state government sparks an economic boom when it lowers the residency requirement for those seeking a divorce from three months to six weeks, then legalizes wide-open gambling, which, despite state and federal laws, had never disappeared entirely; Mayme V. Stocker is awarded **Clark County**'s first gaming license for her **Northern Club,** at 15 Fremont Street.

**1932** The **Apache Hotel,** boasting three floors, a hundred rooms, and the town's first elevator, opens on the northwest corner of Fremont and Second Streets. (**Binion's Horseshoe Hotel and Casino** occupies that site today.)

**1935** Hoover Dam is dedicated by President Franklin D. Roosevelt. However, President Hoover is so unpopular stemming from his perceived responsibility for the Depression, that the dam is known as **Boulder Dam** for more than a decade; the local Elks Club founds Helldorado Days, an annual event celebrating the town's heritage; some 5,000 Shriners meet in Las Vegas at what is the town's first full-scale convention.

**1938** The construction of Hoover Dam on the Colorado River creates **Lake Mead,** the largest artificial lake in the US, stretching 110 miles upstream.

**1941** Considered the first resort on the **Strip,** the 65-room **El Rancho Vegas** opens on 3 April at what is today the intersection of **Las Vegas Boulevard South** and **West Sahara Avenue** (now a vacant lot). Meanwhile, the $250,000 **El Cortez Hotel** opens Downtown at Fremont and Sixth Streets.

**1942** Production begins at the Basic Magnesium Plant, about 15 miles southeast of Las Vegas. The town of **Henderson** springs up around the plant, which eventually employs 10,000 wartime workers to produce magnesium used in bombs, airplanes, and engine parts; the **Last Frontier** (later renamed the **New Frontier**) is the second resort to open on Las Vegas Boulevard South (not yet called the Strip); under pressure from the federal government, local authorities shut down the infamous Block 16 red-light district.

**1945** **Bonanza Airlines** (later to become **Hughes Air West** after Howard Hughes purchases it in 1968) institutes flights between Reno and Las Vegas; the Nevada legislature orders the State Tax Commission to issue licenses to casino operators and to regulate their conduct.

**1946** Flashy New York mobster Benjamin "Bugsy" Siegel opens the **Flamingo Hotel** on Las Vegas Boulevard South.

**1947** Singer Lena Horne debuts at the **Flamingo,** but can't stay there, because African-Americans are not allowed to eat or sleep in local hotels; **Golden Nugget** founder Guy McAfee coins the term "the Strip."

**1948** The **Thunderbird Hotel & Casino** (later the **Silverbird** and the **El Rancho**) is the fourth resort to open on the Strip; **McCarran Field,** named after Nevada senator Pat McCarran, becomes the county airport.

**1950** The 300-room **Desert Inn** goes into business on the Strip. The Committee to Investigate Organized Crime, led by Tennessee senator Estes Kefauver, comes to town and questions **Desert Inn** owners Wilbur Clark and Moe Dalitz, and Lieutenant Governor Cliff Jones, co-owner of the **Thunderbird;** the *Las Vegas Free Press* (later the *Las Vegas Sun*) is founded under publisher Hank Greenspun; Clark County's population is listed as 48,289.

**1951** The Atomic Energy Commission detonates the first of many atom bombs above ground at the Nevada Test Site, about 100 miles from Las Vegas; Texan Benny Binion remodels the **Eldorado Club,** turning it into the **Horseshoe Club,** the first carpeted Downtown casino.

**1952** The **Sands** and the **Sahara** hotels debut on the Strip.

**1954** The **Desert Showboat Motor-Hotel,** later the **Showboat Hotel,** opens to become the first big casino on **Boulder Highway.**

**1955** The Gaming Control Board is created to act as the enforcement and investigative arm of the State Tax Commission; the first high-rise on the Strip, the nine-story **Riviera Hotel,** is christened, followed a month later by the **Dunes Hotel.**

**1956** Guests begin staying at Nevada's tallest building, the 15-story **Fremont Hotel** in **Glitter Gulch;** Elvis Presley bombs in his Las Vegas debut at the **New Frontier.**

**1957** The first permanent building on the campus of the University of Nevada, Las Vegas (then known as **Nevada Southern**) is erected; the **Tropicana Hotel** opens at a cost of $15 million.

**1958** After four years of construction, the thousand-room **Stardust** (considered the world's largest resort complex at the time), goes into business on the Strip.

**1959** State lawmakers create the five-member Gaming Commission, which has the power to set policy and grant or deny licenses to casinos; the **Las Vegas Convention Center** opens for business.

**1960** **El Rancho Vegas** is destroyed in a mysterious fire, never to be rebuilt.

**1964** The **Las Vegas Convention Center** hosts two concerts by the Beatles.

**1965** The 26-story **Mint Hotel,** later part of **Binion's Horseshoe,** opens its doors at 100 Fremont Street; heavyweight champion Muhammad Ali successfully defends his title for the first time by beating Floyd Patterson at the **Convention Center.**

**1966** The opening of the **Aladdin** on the Strip ends a nine-year drought for new hotel-casinos; Howard Hughes moves into the **Desert Inn** on Thanksgiving Day, taking over the ninth floor and embarking on a $300-million Las Vegas real estate shopping spree; **Caesars Palace** opens decadently with a $1-million, three-day party.

**1967** Lawmakers pass the Corporate Gaming Act, which allows publicly traded corporations to acquire gambling licenses without requiring every stockholder to be individually licensed; Elvis Presley marries Priscilla Beaulieu at the **Aladdin;** in March, Howard Hughes pays Moe Dalitz $13.2 million for the **Desert Inn,** in part because the reclusive millionaire doesn't want to leave the ninth floor. (Hughes eventually buys the **Sands, Castaways, Frontier, Landmark,** and **Silver Slipper** hotels.)

**1968** **Circus Circus,** later to become the first family-oriented casino, opens on the Strip, across the street from the **Riviera.**

**1969** Eight years after breaking ground on **Paradise Road,** the Hughes-owned **Landmark Hotel** is open for business. The following day financier Kirk Kerkorian opens his huge **International** (now the **Las Vegas Hilton**) next door to the **Las Vegas Convention Center;** Elvis returns triumphantly to town, playing the **Hilton** 13 years after his disappointing debut.

**1970** Four years to the day after he arrived, Howard Hughes moves out of the **Desert Inn** and leaves Las Vegas; the Hilton Corporation buys the **Flamingo,** marking the first time a major hotel chain has bought a Las Vegas property.

**1973** The now-famous "Four Corners," at the intersection of **Flamingo Road** and the Strip, is complete when the **MGM Grand Hotel** (now **Bally's**) opens. With 2,100 rooms, the newcomer gains the title "world's largest resort hotel," until the **Las Vegas Hilton** adds 1,500 rooms to overtake it by more than a thousand.

**1976** Singer Neil Diamond is the first star to perform in the $10-million **Aladdin Theater for the Performing Arts.**

**1977** Clark County gaming revenues surpass $1 billion, an all-time high.

**1978** The ABC-TV series *Vega$,* starring Robert Urich, premieres, revealing the town's touristy side.

**1980** In November, a fire at the **MGM Grand Hotel** kills 84 people and injures nearly 700. That, coupled with another deadly fire at the **Las Vegas Hilton** a few months later, leads to stricter fire code regulations for Clark County's high-rise hotels.

**1983** **Cashman Field,** a Downtown stadium and convention facility that is the home field for the **Las Vegas Stars** minor-league baseball team, opens with an exhibition game between the **San Diego Padres** and the **Seattle Mariners;** the city hosts its first Panasonic Las Vegas Invitational golf tournament.

**1984** Las Vegas celebrates the 50th Helldorado Days and the accompanying Helldorado Rodeo.

**1985** The National Finals Rodeo, which brings thousands of tourists to Las Vegas each December, is held here for the first time.

**1989** **Golden Nugget** boss Steve Wynn opens **The Mirage,** a 3,049-room hotel-casino that cost an estimated $630 million to build. Its man-made volcano, which explodes on schedule throughout the evening, is instituted as one of the city's most popular photo opportunities.

**1990** The owners of **Circus Circus** complete the 4,032-room **Excalibur Hotel and Casino** at half the construction cost of **The Mirage;** local sports fans rejoice when the **University of Nevada, Las Vegas**'s **Runnin' Rebels** win their first **NCAA** college basketball title, beating **Duke University** on 2 April.

**1993** Steve Wynn builds the 3,000-room **Treasure Island** resort next to **The Mirage,** while the Circus Circus corporation is creating the equally massive, pyramid-shaped **Luxor** resort. The biggest project of all takes shape on the northeast corner of **Tropicana Avenue** and the Strip, the new 5,009-room **MGM Grand Hotel and Theme Park.**

**1994** The city's expansion continues with the openings of **Boomtown** (now **Silverton**) in May, **Boulder Station Hotel and Casino** in August, and **The Fiesta** in December.

**1995** **Hard Rock Hotel and Casino** becomes an instant hit when it opens in March.

**1996** The much anticipated **Stratosphere** opens in April with the **Monte Carlo** opening its doors two months later.

**1997** The Big Apple takes a bite out of Las Vegas when **New York–New York Hotel & Casino** makes its debut. This newest extravaganza is quickly dubbed "The Greatest City in Vegas."

**1998** The $1.7-billion **Bellagio**—a full destination resort inspired by the Italian village on Lake Como—opens, as does the $750-million **Paris–Las Vegas Casino Resort,** complete with the sights and sounds of the romantic city on the Seine.

**1999** March marks the opening of the lavish billion-dollar resort housing both the **Mandalay Bay Resort & Casino** and **Four Seasons Hotel;** April's hotel entry is the $2-billion **Venetian Resort Hotel Casino,** built on the site of the **Sands Hotel.**

**2000** The new century ushers in another new face on the Strip—the $1.2-billion **Aladdin Las Vegas,** replacing its namesake on the same site.

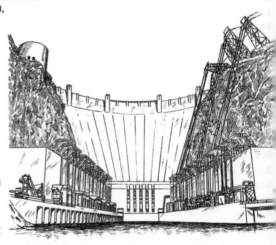

*Hoover Dam*

# Index

# Restaurants

Only restaurants with star ratings are listed below. All restaurants are listed alphabetically in the main (preceding) index. Always call in advance to ensure a restaurant has not closed, changed its hours, or booked its tables for a private party. The restaurant price ratings are based on the average cost of an entrée for one person, excluding tax and tip.

★★★★ An Extraordinary Experience
★★★ Excellent
★★ Very Good
★ Good

$$$$ Big Bucks ($40 and up)
$$$ Expensive ($22-$40)
$$ Reasonable ($15-$22)
$ The Price Is Right (less than $15)

## Hotels

The hotels listed below are grouped according to their price ratings; they are also listed in the main index. The hotel price ratings reflect the base price of a standard room for two people for one night during the peak season.

$$$$     Big Bucks ($125 and up)
$$$     Expensive ($85-$125)
$$     Reasonable ($50-$85)
$     The Price Is Right (less than $50)

# Features

# Bests

# Maps

**Page**     **Entry#**     **Notes**

| Page | Entry# | Notes |
|------|--------|-------|